adventures in
POMPOM
LAND

adventures in POMPOM LAND

25 Cute Projects Made from Handmade Pompoms

MYKO DIann BOCEK

LARK CRAFTS
Asheville

LARK CRAFTS

An Imprint of Sterling Publishing
387 Park Avenue South
New York, NY 10016

If you have questions or comments about
this book, please visit: larkcrafts.com

Editor: **Beth Sweet**
Art Director: **Kristi Pfeffer**
Layout: **Michelle Owen**
Photographer: **Jen Altman**
Cover Designer: **Kristi Pfeffer**

Library of Congress Cataloging-in-Publication Data

Bocek, Myko Diann.
  Adventures in pompom land : 25 cute projects made from handmade pompoms /
Myko Diann Bocek. -- First edition.
      pages cm
 Includes bibliographical references and index.
 ISBN 978-1-4547-0386-0
1. Soft toys. 2. Soft toy making. I. Title.
 TT174.3.B63 2013
 745.592'4--dc23
                                        2012021395
10 9 8 7 6 5 4 3 2 1

First Edition

Published by Lark Crafts
An Imprint of Sterling Publishing Co., Inc.
387 Park Avenue South, New York, NY 10016

Text © 2013, Myko Diann Bocek
Photography © 2013, Lark Crafts, an Imprint of Sterling Publishing Co., Inc.
Illustrations © 2013, Lark Crafts, an Imprint of Sterling Publishing Co., Inc.

Distributed in Canada by Sterling Publishing,
c/o Canadian Manda Group, 165 Dufferin Street
Toronto, Ontario, Canada M6K 3H6

Distributed in the United Kingdom by GMC Distribution Services,
Castle Place, 166 High Street, Lewes, East Sussex, England BN7 1XU

Distributed in Australia by Capricorn Link (Australia) Pty Ltd.,
P.O. Box 704, Windsor, NSW 2756 Australia

Manufactured in China

ISBN 13: 978-1-4547-0386-0

For information about custom editions, special sales, and premium and corporate
purchases, please contact Sterling Special Sales Department at 800-805-5489 or
specialsales@sterlingpub.com.

Requests for information about desk and examination copies available to college and
university professors must be submitted to academic@larkbooks.com. Our complete
policy can be found at www.larkcrafts.com.

Dedication

This book is in loving memory of my late father,
who always encouraged me to pursue my love of art.

Contents

THE PROJECTS

Yellow Chick
32

Bunny
35

Mouse
38

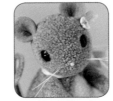
Kitten
42

Bluebird
48

Elephant
51

Lop-Eared Bunny
54

Ladybug
57

Teddy Bear
60

Lamb
63

Puppy
67

Swan
71

Seal
74

Piglet
77

Squirrel
80

Raccoon
84

Hedgehog
88

Fox
92

Pony
96

Snowy Owl
100

Halloween
Imp
103

Halloween
Bat
106

Halloween
Black Cat
109

Thanksgiving
Turkey
113

Snowman and
Snowgirl
116

Introduction

Back in 2000 I fell in love with an article in *Martha Stewart Living* magazine about making pompom animals from handmade pompoms. My children were much younger at the time; we created a few, had immense fun, and took great pleasure in making them. Then in 2007 I was watching Martha Stewart's television show and was inspired once more after a segment that featured Jennifer Murphy making little pompom bunnies. Again, I made some. Over the next couple years my work evolved, and I began to create my own pompom animal designs. As I started creating again, I was filled with joy in rediscovering my artistic passion! Friends and family loved my little woolen creatures, and they encouraged me to continue in my pursuits, which I gratefully did. That creative path has led me to my own online shop and the authorship of this book.

In *Adventures in Pompom Land*, you'll learn all about making pompoms by hand, and you'll find yourself in the company of creatures of all kinds: from a mischievous masked Raccoon and a softly-spiked Hedgehog to a gentle-eyed Lamb and an elegant Swan. Say hello to springtime with a sweet Yellow Chick, have years of good luck with a Halloween Black Cat, and celebrate winter with the charming Snowman and Snowgirl duo. Pompom creatures make perfect heartfelt gifts for loved ones and friends as holiday presents and ornaments, wedding cake toppers, home décor, heirloom treasures, pincushions—the list goes on and on.

The 25 projects in this book all reference basic techniques explained in the Pompom-Making Essentials, which walks you step-by-step through the process of winding, tying, cutting, fluffing, and shaping a pompom by hand. You'll learn how to make multi-colored pompoms, how to shape a pompom into smaller head shapes and larger body shapes, how to add armatures, and how to create a cute expression for your creature with the easy placement of facial details. You'll also learn the basics of needle felting, which is a technique used to form some of the projects' tails, legs, and feet.

Once you get the hang of making a pompom, you'll realize how versatile this craft can be—let these projects inspire your imagination and discover how your creativity unfolds into personalized, beloved pompom creatures for all occasions.

Myko Diann Bocek

Pompom-Making Essentials

Welcome to Pompom Land! The sweet and expressive projects in this book are all created with a few basic supplies and a few easy-to-learn techniques. Once you get into the groove of making pompoms, the sky's the limit when it comes to dreaming up cute critters and scenes for your very own Pompom Land.

Pompom Materials and Tools

There are a few materials you'll need on hand to form the elements of your pompom creatures, and they can all be sourced from craft supply stores. In fact, many of them are probably already among your crafting supplies at home!

100% Wool Yarn and 100% Wool Roving Yarn

All of the projects in this book use 100% wool yarn, wool felt, and wool roving. I can find basic wool yarn colors at my craft store, but if you want to use other custom shades be sure to visit a local yarn shop because they usually have a larger selection. I have also tried my hand at dyeing my own wool with powdered clothing dye you can mix in a tub or your washing machine. (Wool roving and felt can also be dyed to match, if necessary. Simply follow the directions on the package to make custom colors.) If you choose to dye your yarn, synthetic or synthetic-blend yarn will not take dye well, if at all. Using 100% wool gives your handcrafted animals that rich heirloom-like vintage quality.

Several projects call for the use of wool roving yarn. This yarn is not twisted like traditional yarn. It is much fluffier and chunkier. It is wonderful for use in certain projects to add dimension, and it also adds to the illusion in creating fluffy feathers, manes, and tails.

✽ **NOTE**: *Roving yarn is different from wool roving, which is described in the Needle Felting Supplies section on page 16.*

100% Wool Felt

Wool felt can be purchased in different millimeter thicknesses. I like to use the 2 to 3 mm thickness for the ears, but regular 1 mm wool felt works just as well. Using synthetic felt will not give you the same results. Synthetic felt does not hold up well over time; it will pill and stretch out and generally does not look as nice as pure wool felt.

Cardboard Sleeve

You will need a strong, flat, smooth piece of cardboard approximately 5 x 3 inches (12.7 x 7.6 cm) to wrap the bundle of yarn around to create the pompoms. If you are feeling really industrious, I suggest you cut out a thin piece of plywood commonly used for making dollhouses, which will hold up better over time. Lightly sand the edges so the yarn will not catch on any rough spots when you slide it off the board, which can ruin your pompom. It's also helpful to wrap packing tape around the edges of the sleeve, which will help the yarn slide off easier.

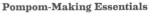

Pompom-Making Essentials

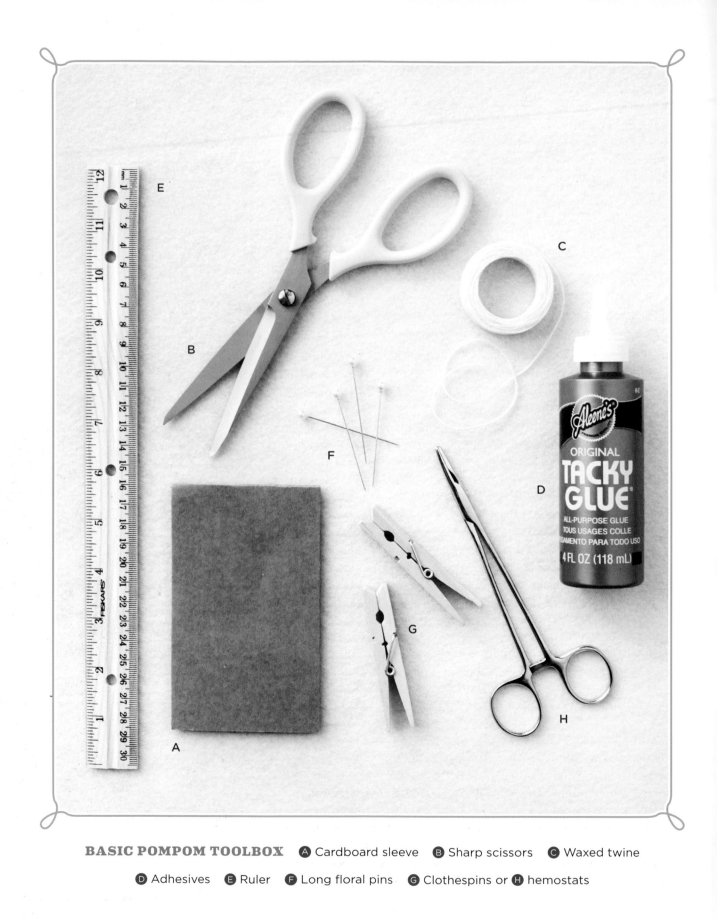

BASIC POMPOM TOOLBOX Ⓐ Cardboard sleeve Ⓑ Sharp scissors Ⓒ Waxed twine

Ⓓ Adhesives Ⓔ Ruler Ⓕ Long floral pins Ⓖ Clothespins or Ⓗ hemostats

Sharp Scissors

Trimming and sculpting the pompoms takes a lot of cutting, and it is necessary to have good-quality scissors. A pair of nice, strong, *sharp* scissors helps immensely in cutting and trimming pompoms. Weak, flimsy scissors will not consistently cut smoothly through the wool yarn. Also, your wrist and hand will tire quickly. Cheap, dull scissors will "chew" and pull the yarn out of your knotted pompom, which results in sloppy, uneven work. Cutting wool is essentially cutting hair, which can dull your scissors over time, so you may need to sharpen them occasionally.

Waxed Twine

To tie off the pompoms I use white waxed twine, which is found in the jewelry section of craft stores. Using the waxed twine keeps your knots from slipping loose while tightening the knot to secure the yarn bundle. It is essential to tie a knot as tightly as possible to create a good, fluffy pompom.

Adhesives

I prefer to use white craft glue for creating my little animals, and I've found tacky glue works the best. Don't be tempted to use hot glue when attaching pompoms, no matter how easy it may seem. Hot glue hardens very quickly after it's applied, and it seeps through the fibers of a pompom to create hard, stringy strands that you won't be able to cut away. It will also create a thick, hard disc of glue within your pompoms, which will permanently mat the yarn's fibers together. Also, since you'll be arranging and attaching pompoms by hand, hot glue can burn your fingers. Craft glue is your friend!

Long Floral Pins

Long floral pins help temporarily hold pompoms in place when you glue them together. These are the same pins used for wearing corsages or boutonnieres, and they can be found in the floral supply section of craft stores. When the glue holding pompoms together has dried completely, gently twist and pull the floral pin to remove it.

Clothespins or Hemostats

Clothespins are handy tools for securely holding glued felt together while the glue dries. This will be most helpful when you're pinching the bottom edge of a felt ear ❶ or creating a folded felt beak. If you'd like to try another option, hemostats are clamping instruments commonly used in the medical field. They can be found in some craft stores or sporting goods stores (fishermen often use them to remove hooks from fish), and they'll also do a good job of securely pressing felt to hold it in shape while the glue dries.

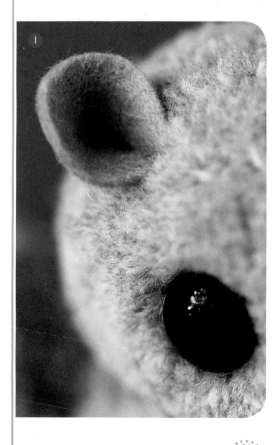

✳ **NOTE**: *As with any craft including small, hard elements, glass eyes may pose a choking hazard to young children.*

Glass Eyes

The projects in this book were made with glass eyes commonly used in teddy bear and doll assembly Ⓐ. These eyes come in pairs: some are securely attached to a wire stem with one eye on each end, and others are attached to wire loops. For the eyes on wire stems, simply use wire cutters to snip the wire to about ½ inch (1.3 cm) below the glass eye. Squeeze glue into the pompom where you'd like to place an eye, and insert the wire into the pompom fibers and glue.

Glass eyes come in a variety of colors, shapes, and sizes: I prefer to use the all-black glass eyes ranging between 10mm an 14mm in diameter. Not all craft stores carry glass eyes, so see the Resource section (page 125) for a few suggestions of retailers that sell them.

Don't want to use glass eyes for your pompom creatures? No problem. Instead, use black glass or onyx beads from your local craft store or bead shop.

Wire Cutters

Wire cutters are handy for a multitude of reasons when creating your projects! You can get a few different sizes for different uses. Larger ones are needed for more heavy-duty cutting (of wooden dowels, for example) and smaller ones for cutting pipe cleaners and thin floral wire.

Embroidery Floss

Embroidery floss serves several uses. To make the wrapped wire feet on the birds and chicks, I use the heavier floss (perle cotton), which has a slight sheen. You can also use the floss to hang little signs or gift tags from your animals. They come in a wide variety of beautiful colors.

Ribbons

Choosing the right ribbon also makes a big difference. It cannot be too stiff or heavy, and it should be scaled to the size of your woolen pompom animal. I prefer silk ribbon because it is very light, pliable, and beautiful. I also use 12 mm seam-binding ribbon for the perfect vintage-inspired finishing touch. I also like 4 mm velvet and delicate lace ribbons.

Floral Supplies

I like to use vintage millinery supplies that I scavenge at thrift stores and yard sales. Many can be found online as well. I find the paper forget-me-not flowers are the perfect size and scale for the pompom animals. Velvet leaves are also a staple and can be found easily online. For a dainty feminine touch, you can glue a tiny millinery forget-me-not flower and/or a leaf at your pompom animal's ear.

Floral wire and tape are also valuable in creating certain projects. I use the floral wire to create feet for the birds and arches on bases. The tape I use for wrapping the stems of millinery flowers when making a tiny bouquet.

Making Clothes for Your Pompom Creatures

You can certainly sew some adorable little clothes for your animals. I like to make simple outfits that do not require a lot of sewing. I have created little top hats and scarves out of wool felt, such as on the Snowman and Snowgirl (page 116) and little bonnets out of velvet millinery flowers and leaves, such as on the Bluebird (page 48). You can cut simple vests out of wool felt and make little skirts out of a wide piece of lace. The ideas are endless!

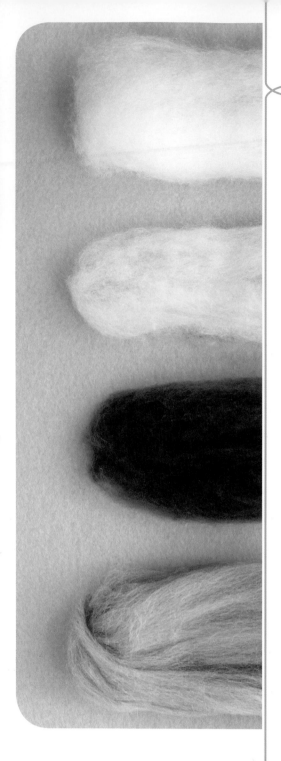

Needle Felting Supplies

Many of the pompom creatures in this book have needle-felted appendages such as little arms, legs, paws, and tails. The needle felting technique is quite simple: use a felting needle to repeatedly pierce layers of wool roving; the barbs on the felting needle catch hold of the fibers in the wool and enmesh them together to create a firm, dense shape. The supplies described below can be found at your local craft store and online. There are many varieties and brands of tools; feel free to experiment with different types of needles and work surfaces to see what suits your preference.

100% Wool Roving

Wool roving is wool that has been carded, or combed, so the fibers are all oriented in the same direction, and then it is gently twisted into a soft, springy bundle (it's not yet twisted into yarn). I use 100% wool roving in my work, and it can be found in craft stores and online in many colors. Measuring and working with roving isn't extremely precise, and the density of your needle-felted appendages depends on the amount of roving you use and how much you needle felt it. But once you begin adding roving to an armature or rolling it together, you'll realize how easy it is to simply add more layers of roving to your work until it reaches the desired density.

✺ **NOTE**: *When you use wool roving in your projects, gently pull a strip of it from the bundle; don't cut it with scissors.*

Felting Needles

Felting needles are barbed steel needles used to interlock the fibers of wool. As you move the felting needle up and down, the barbs on the needle catch the fibers of wool roving and blend them together, compressing them into felt. These needles have incredibly sharp points, so be sure to keep them away from children and use caution as you work with them. They're usually about 3 1/2 to 4 inches (8.9 to 10.2 cm) long and come in a variety of sizes and gauges. The gauge is indicated by number; the higher the number, the finer the needle.

I like using a pen-style felting needle tool, which allows you to use one, two, three, and sometimes even four needles at once to needle felt areas of varying measurements. The needle sizes and lengths can be adjusted in a pen-style tool, and I find that they're quite easy to hold and control, especially when the needles are set close together.

Work Surface for Needle Felting

You'll need a work surface specifically for needle felting that will allow your needle to go through the fiber (and beyond it) without puncturing the work surface or breaking the needle. I use a large brush felting mat to work on my projects, and I find it's especially helpful in making small ears, feet, and tails. There are also dense foam surfaces created especially for needle felting, and some people like to use upholstery foam to support their work.

Pipe Cleaners

I like to use pipe cleaners rather than floral wire for the armature frames of appendages. The chenille on the pipe cleaner grabs the roving and keeps it from spinning as you needle felt. I order 100% cotton chenille pipe cleaners online, but you can use any coordinating-color pipe cleaners easily found at the craft store. You'll want to use like colors in your projects, as dark colors can show through light-colored roving, and vice versa. If you need to tint the color of your pipe cleaner, simply rub a piece of chalk into its fibers for a quick fix.

Also, for some pompom animals (such as the Mouse, page 38, and the Halloween Imp, page 103), you do not need to needle felt the tail. You can just simply use the pipe cleaner and trim one end to a point. Be sure to trim any sharp metal wire edges of the pipe cleaner with your wire cutters.

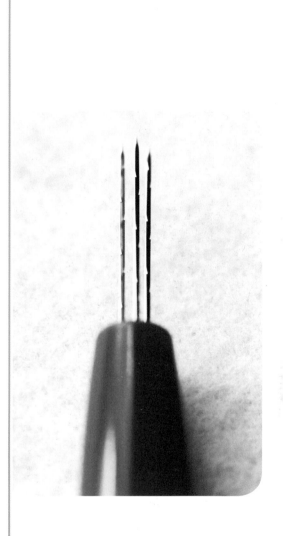

Making Pompoms by Hand

1. Choosing Your Yarn

There are many types of wool yarn on the market. I like to use a cream color yarn made by Patons for the majority of my projects. It's springy, it takes dye for custom colors nicely, it's not too thin, and it's readily available at many craft stores at reasonable prices. For other projects I use wool roving yarn. This yarn is not twisted like traditional yarn; instead, it is loosely spun. It creates a chunkier and fluffier effect. This yarn works nicely for creating feathers for birds such as the Snowy Owl (page 100) and Swan (page 71). It also comes in handy for the tails of the Squirrel (page 80) and Hedgehog (page 88). Experiment with different yarns to find just the look you want for your animal.

I have made all of the projects in this book with either Patons Classic Wool yarn or Patons Classic Wool Roving yarn, though the approximate yarn measurements I reference in the project instructions are meant to apply to any brand of yarn or roving yarn. The wool yarn I've used is medium weight and comes in 3 1/2-ounce (100 g) skeins measuring 210 yards (192 m). The wool roving yarn I've used is bulky weight and comes in 3 1/2-ounce (100 g) skeins measuring 120 yards (109 m).

In my project instructions, I've provided the yardage needed and referenced fractions of skeins based on the amount and type of yarn I've used. You should feel free to experiment with different brands and types of yarn, so here's an approximate comparison you can apply to any brand of yarn:

100% Wool Yarn

1 skein of Patons 100% wool yarn, *Classic Wool*	IS EQUIVALENT TO	210 yards (192 m)
1/8 skein of Patons 100% wool yarn		26 yards (24 m)
1/4 skein of Patons 100% wool yarn		53 yards (48 m)
1/3 skein of Patons 100% wool yarn		69 yards (63 m)
1/2 skein of Patons 100% wool yarn		105 yards (96 m)
2/3 skein of Patons 100% wool yarn		139 yards (127 m)
3/4 skein of Patons 100% wool yarn		158 yards (144 m)

100% Wool Roving Yarn

	IS EQUIVALENT TO	
1 skein of Patons 100% wool roving yarn, *Classic Wool Roving*		120 yards (109 m)
¼ skein of Patons 100% wool roving yarn		30 yards (27 m)
⅓ skein of Patons 100% wool roving yarn		40 yards (36 m)
½ skein of Patons 100% wool roving yarn		60 yards (55 m)
⅔ skein of Patons 100% wool roving yarn		79 yards (72 m)
¾ skein of Patons 100% wool roving yarn		90 yards (82 m)

2. Wrap Yarn around the Cardboard Sleeve

Beginning in the center of the cardboard sleeve, wrap the yarn around and around with consistent and gentle tension. Gradually alternate the yarn from left to right, keeping it centered and evenly distributed. Try not to wrap the yarn too tightly, because it will be difficult to slide it off of the cardboard sleeve in the next step.

For pompoms made of more than one color, wrap the first color uniformly as you would a regular pompom, and then wrap the second color directly next to—but not overlapping—the first color. (See Making Multicolor Pompoms, page 30, for some tips.)

It's okay if you run out of yarn while you're wrapping: simply continue wrapping (in the same direction) with a new strand of yarn until you've reached the thickness and density you need for your pompom.

3. Slide Yarn off the Cardboard Sleeve

After you've wrapped the yarn around the cardboard sleeve, gently slide the bundle off one end of the sleeve. The yarn should retain its dense bundled shape; keep it intact.

4. Tie the Yarn Bundle with Waxed Twine

I use waxed twine to tie off my yarn bundles when making pompoms. The wax on the twine prevents the knot from slipping loose; you need to tie it as tightly as possible to make your

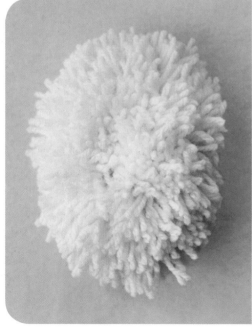

pompom fluffy and to prevent the yarn from pulling loose after you snip the looped ends. Before wrapping the yarn around the cardboard sleeve, I usually cut the twine in 12- to 14-inch (30.5 to 35.6 cm) lengths so that when I slide the bundle off, I can lay the bundle down on it. Then tie a simple knot and tighten it as much as possible. Next, flip the bundle over to its other side and, using the excess twine from the first knot, tie another knot. Again tighten it as much as possible. Then make a double knot to secure it. Trim the twine.

5. Cut the Pompom's Loops

Once you've tied your wrapped bundle of yarn tightly, slide the blade of your scissors into the loops at one end of the bundle. Gently tug the loops taut so they're all roughly the same length, and then snip through them. Repeat this step on the loops of the bundle's other end. Now, instead of a tied bundle of loops, you'll have the fluffy beginnings of a pompom.

6. Shape the Pompom

The main point to keep in mind when shaping a pompom is to work *gradually*. It's kind of like trimming a bonsai tree or pruning shrubs—make small cuts as you go. To sculpt and shape a pompom into a smooth ball, one of my techniques is to constantly flip and turn the ball while cutting. I also constantly rake the yarn ends with the blade of my scissors as I trim to fluff up any stray strands of yarn that need to be trimmed down. As you trim and cut, picture the shape in your mind that you want to create.

The most common shape I use for the pompom animal's head is a small egg shape. It lends itself well to practically almost every animal design. As you become more experienced you can make slight variations to create other head or body shapes for different animals.

I often shape the body into a pear shape, meaning the bottom half is thicker and heavier (like the bottom of a pear) and the top tapers off to a more narrow shape, half of which will be the neck and shoulders of your animal. The larger pompoms already resemble a large hourglass shape after cutting the looped ends, so by simply trimming away the excess yarn you can begin to see the body shape in rough form. Just continue trimming down, pausing to stop and look periodically as you sculpt.

For many of the animals, you can create the illusion of its haunches, knees, and tummy as it sits by cutting a V shape from the front center bottom of the belly area. At the base of the pompom, the V shape should measure approximately 1 inch (2.5 cm) wide, 1½ inches (3.8 cm) long, and ¼ inch (6 mm) deep; these measurements are very rough and will depend on the size of the pompoms you make and sculpt. There really is no right or wrong here. Sculpt and trim the yarn to shape the front of the body pompom; the sides of the V can curve a bit to form the belly and haunches.

TIPS ON SHAPING THE NOSE AND MUZZLE

For many of the creatures, after making and roughly forming the head pompom into the appropriate size and shape (usually an egg shape), you can trim and cut out a pointed nose in the lower center half of the head pompom.

Determine the top and the bottom of the head, and position the nose a bit lower than the center of the pompom. Begin to trim and shape the pointed area where the nose will be. Depending on the animal, the nose may be very pointy, like the Fox (page 92), or a little more rounded, like the Mouse (page 38).

For some animals, such as the Puppy (page 67), Piglet (page 77), and Teddy Bear (page 60), trim the yarn a bit deeper on the top half of the head just above the snout or muzzle area, as shown below. This creates a more realistic shape for the nose.

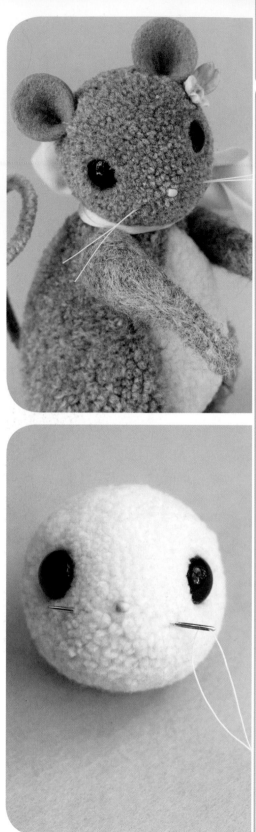

Adding Facial Features

Positioning the Nose and Eyes

After you have trimmed the head into the desired shape, use an upside-down triangle pattern to determine where you want the nose and eyes to be (the nose will be at the bottom of the inverted triangle). Squeeze a small drop of glue into the pompom fibers for the nose and gently insert the nose bead. If you're using glass eyes on a wire stem, use wire cutters to trim the wire to about ½ inch (1.3 cm) below the glass eye. If you're using glass eyes with a wire loop in the back, keep the loop in its original shape. Carefully squeeze a pea-size drop of glue for each eye into the fibers of the pompom and gently nestle the wire end of the eye into the pompom. If you're using glass beads for your creature's eyes, position them so the holes of the beads are not exposed or visible. Let the glue dry completely.

Creating and Attaching Whiskers

Purchase upholstery thread at a craft or fabric store. It is thicker and stronger than regular thread. Sometimes, the thread curls when you take it off the spool, so I like to thread my needle with a double strand and then take my flat iron (or household iron) to straighten the thread before use. Make a knot in the center of the double strand and place a smidge of glue on the knot. I usually insert the threaded needle through the cheeks and just under the nose; the glued knot will catch somewhere near the middle of the head. Then I simply cut the threads evenly to the desired length on each side of the head.

Creating and Attaching Wool Felt Ears

Wool felt comes in different thicknesses. The thinner wool felt is easier to use and manipulate, though I prefer thicker felt for my pompom creatures. I'll often pinch and glue the bottom edges of felt ears together before inserting them into the pompom, which gives the ears expressive dimension. When using the thicker wool, clothespins or hemostats are needed to hold the pinched, glued edges together until dry. After determining the exact location where I want the ears to be, I use the sharp, pointy end of my scissors to make a deep part into the wool "fur." I then squeeze the glue into the part before permanently securing the ears by pinching the wool fibers around them.

❋ **NOTE:** *Use pink chalk to add a little color to some projects' ears.*

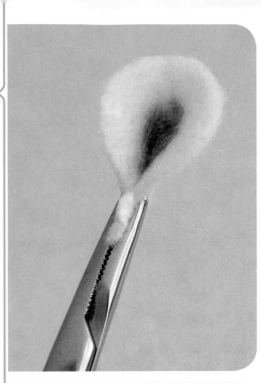

Using Templates

In the back of the book, you'll find the templates you need to make ears and other small shapes for the pompom creatures. Copy the templates onto paper and cut them out. Place the paper shape(s) onto the felt and either trace them with an air-soluble fabric-marking pen (the ink disappears after exposure to air for a length of time), or hold or pin them in place and cut around them. Try to cut the shapes in one fluid motion, which will prevent ragged or uneven edges in the details.

Attaching Pompoms

Attaching pompoms to one another is quite simple, especially since you need only a few tools: pompoms, glue, a long floral pin, and patience. You'll essentially be gluing the pompoms together and giving the glue plenty of time to set up.

To attach a pompom head to a pompom body, make a part in the yarn at the top of the body pompom and squeeze a nickel-size dollop of glue into the part. (If your critter features arms made from pipe-cleaner armatures, attach the pipe cleaners *before* gluing on the head. You can needle felt the wool roving on the arms after you've attached the head.) Align and position the head pompom to your liking, and press it onto the glue. To keep the head and body from detaching before the glue sets up, use a long floral pin to hold them in place. Remove the pin after the glue has set up.

NOTE: ***You'll add the appendage armature(s) before attaching the head and body pompoms together, but you'll needle felt the armature(s) after you've attached the head and body together.***

Creating Appendages

Most of the creatures in this book have appendages made by needle felting wool roving to pipe cleaner armatures like the Mouse's arms (page 38). Other creatures have appendages made by needle felting wool roving to thin wooden dowels like the Lamb's legs (page 63). Some of the smaller appendages, like the Puppy's back paws (page 67), are made without armatures of any kind.

Adding an Armature

This step is actually easier than you may think. All you need are a pipe cleaner and glue! I simply make a deep part in the top of the neck and shoulder area, squeeze some glue into the part, and then wedge the pipe cleaner down into the glue. I then pinch the wool fibers around the pipe cleaner to secure and let it dry. Just remember to glue the pipe cleaner armatures in *first* before the head or you will have to start over! Also, it is natural to want to finish your creature *before* letting the glue dry. Be patient. Let the glue dry, because disturbing it before it sets up will ruin the pompom.

Wrapping an Armature in Roving

NOTE: ***When your pompom critter is made of multiple pompoms, attach the head and body pompoms to one another (and let the glue dry fully!) before you needle felt the pipe cleaner armatures for appendages.***

To needle felt over a pipe cleaner armature after the glue has set up, pull off a piece of roving the size of a thick strip of bacon and wrap it tightly around the pipe cleaner arms Ⓐ Ⓑ. Use more roving near the upper arm and shoulder area and taper it off at the end to form a paw. As you needle felt the roving with your needle tool, the fibers will compress, and you will wrap and needle felt more layers of roving around your armature until it is the right size.

Needle Felting Appendages

The needle felting technique is quite simple and favors repetition. Simply insert your felting needle straight down into the layers of wool roving and then extract it through the same hole, working straight up and down Ⓒ. As the needle moves in and out of the roving, the barbs grasp and push the fibers in the wool and enmesh them together to create a firm, dense, compact shape.

When you're creating appendages for the pompom creatures, make sure you needle felt the roving tightly and compactly around any armature so the roving will not unravel. Flip the pompom creature over and around on the felting mat so you can access every angle of the appendage Ⓓ. (This is why you need to wait until any glue on the creature is completely dry—all that flipping

and rotating might detach an unsecured head or other detail!) Simply keep adding layers of wool roving to the appendage until you have formed your desired shape and size. Tuck any stray, loose ends of roving into the fibers of the pompom and gently needle felt them in place.

Creating Needle-Felted Tails

To make a thick, long tail, take a pipe cleaner and wrap roving around it, with more roving at the base where it will attach to the body and becoming thinner at the tail's tip. Place it on the needle felting mat and begin needle felting. Needle felt it until it is nice and compact; trim off any excess or stray roving fibers with a pair of sharp scissors. To make a smaller, more rounded tail like the Bunny's (page 35), roll a piece of roving into a marble-size ball and needle felt it, adding layers of roving as necessary.

Attaching Feet and Small Appendages

Inserting the bottom feet is easy enough. Needle felt a piece of roving into a tight, compact cigar shape and cut it in half. Make two parts into the bottom of the pompom where you want the feet to go, each about 1/2 inch (1.3 cm) deep. Place a line of glue in each and then gently push in the feet, leaving the rounded toe end sticking out at the front of the body. Set the animal upright to get the right angle so that it stands, and let the glue dry. Be sure not to place the animal directly on a table that can be ruined by glue adhering to it while the animal is drying.

✻ **NOTE**: *Use this simple gluing technique to adhere other small appendages to pompoms, such as the Bunny's tail.*

Making Bases

You can create a variety of unique and wonderful little bases for your animals with relative ease. Small bases can showcase a special pompom creation and can be quite charming. A larger base can house two or more animals, and you can create little vignettes or perhaps even a wedding cake topper. For some pompom creations, like the Squirrel (page 80), the base provides stability for an otherwise asymmetrical creature.

You can find small, unfinished wooden disks at your local craft store in different diameters and thicknesses. I like to use pieces 3 to 4 inches (7.6 to 10.2 cm) in diameter. Paint them in any color you desire. You can also decoupage them with vintage paper found in old books, or coat them with glue and add glass glitter (see the Halloween Black Cat, page 109). To add more dimension and soften the wooden disk's look, rather than leaving the painted wood bare, I prefer to cut out, with scalloped-edge or zigzag pinking scissors, a round piece of 3 mm wool felt that is slightly larger than the wooden disk and glue it to the wood (see the Snowman and Snowgirl, page 116).

Polystyrene foam floral disks are also a staple of mine when creating bases. They, too, are found in a wide variety of sizes and shapes. Let your imagination run wild! You can cover the flat foam disk with wool felt. Use vintage trim, rickrack, or ribbon to embellish the edge. After attaching your animal to the base, you can add millinery flowers and leaves.

I have also found cute papier-mâché boxes at my local craft store to paint and embellish. Topped with a little woolen pompom creature, these make special gifts as well as keepsake boxes. Again, paint these and add bits of ribbon, lace, trim, glitter, and/or millinery flowers.

When I am out hunting in my local thrift and antique shops I like to look for old-fashioned bun-shaped pincushions. These make great vintage-inspired bases for your pompom animals, and they're a wonderful gift for that friend who likes to sew. Simply glue your animal to the top, and you have a sweet and useful pincushion. Glue a little spool of thread in your animal's paws for an added touch of cuteness!

If you are comfortable with needle felting (see page 24), needle felt a base for your critter, like I did for the Mouse paddling in a Leaf Boat on page 38. I have created wonderful red-and-white polka-dotted mushrooms for my little mice to sit upon, or a mossy little cushion for a bunny to enjoy. Again, the sky's the limit!

Tips and Troubleshooting Guide

Using Enough Yarn

One of the easiest mistakes to make while creating pompoms is not using enough yarn. It is very important that the pompoms be *extremely* dense and full in order to sculpt them and so they're able to support some of the added features such as the Elephant's trunk and the Fox's tail. Most of the animals in this book are between 5 and 6 ½ inches (12.7 and 16.5 cm) tall, and it will take about one-third of the yarn skein to make the head and almost half of the skein to create the body of most of the creatures included in these pages. If there is not enough yarn used, the pompom will be limp and skimpy, and will not give you the desired results.

Tying Knots

It can be a bit tricky to tie the knot as tightly as possible for your pompoms. As described on page 13, using waxed twine will help you immensely. There have been times when I was tying a knot as tightly as I could, and the twine broke. You can still salvage the pompom: keep the pompom intact and simply retie it again with another piece of waxed twine. It might be a good idea to cut a couple of 12- to 14-inch (30.5 to 35.6 cm) lengths of waxed twine before you start winding the pompom. The twine can cut your fingers similar to paper, so use care when tightly pulling and tying.

Shaping Pompoms

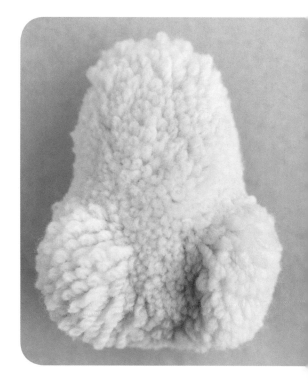

To sculpt and shape a pompom into a smooth ball, one of my techniques is to constantly flip and turn the ball while cutting. I also constantly "rake" the yarn ends with the blade of my scissors as I trim to fluff up any stray strands of yarn that need to be trimmed down. This is a very gradual process, and the most reliable way to achieve a symmetrical, controlled shape is to trim the pompom with small snips. Think of this like a haircut—once you've cut something, you can't get it back!

To create the illusion of the animal's haunches, you will trim a V shape of yarn from the front bottom center of the body's (usually)

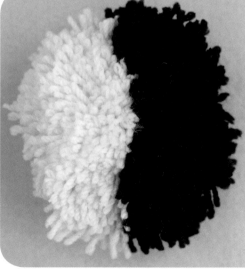

pear shape to create the illusion of a tummy and to sculpt the haunches and knees of the sitting animal on each side. The width at the very base of the V is approximately 1 inch (2.5 cm), which is trimmed about $1/4$ inch (6 mm) lower than the surrounding yarn or "fur." The height of the V shape is about $1\frac{1}{2}$ inches (3.8 cm), and the sides can curve a bit to form the rounded belly area. Start smaller and trim more yarn, if desired, as you sculpt this body pompom. It might take a little practice to perfect this technique, but hang in there—you'll soon be shaping pompom haunches like a pro!

Making Multicolor Pompoms

One of the most complex techniques to master is combining multiple yarn colors in a pompom, but once you can see how the wrapped multicolor yarn bundle slides off the cardboard sleeve and translates into a tied pompom, you'll be able to manipulate and shape a multicolor pompom with ease.

With most multicolor pompoms, you should wrap the different colors side by side, not overlapping each other. After you become a bit experienced making pompoms, you will notice how the yarn in the pompom bundle unfolds and opens when the looped ends are cut. Shape the pompom so that the colors stay separate

within the pompom: a great example is the Hedgehog (page 88), which has dark brown and cream yarn in its head. I kept the dark brown yarn a bit longer than the cream yarn as I trimmed the pompom: the result is a "smooth" cream face, while the back of its dark brown head looks "spiky." Another good example is the Fox (page 92), which has an orange and cream head. For projects like these, you can gently tweak and tug the different colors of yarn into place before you begin shaping the pompom. This might take some practice, but don't feel discouraged if your first attempts aren't exactly what you have in mind. Part of the beauty of making pompoms by hand is the satisfaction you'll feel when you transform plain old yarn into a dense, dimensional shape. Be patient with your efforts and have fun—you're creating some seriously cute creatures!

Yellow Chick

Little chicks are so adorable: they're perfect to make for spring and celebrating new life. Make a few to adorn your home, tuck in an Easter basket, or give as special gifts this year. Use these same directions to also create ducklings by rounding the beak and wrapping the embroidery floss or perle cotton around the wire feet to create a webbed appearance.

1. Following steps 2–6 of Making Pompoms by Hand on pages 19–21, make a 2½-inch (6.4 cm) round ball-shaped pompom from yellow yarn for the head. I used approximately ¼ skein of Patons medium-weight Classic Wool, which is approximately 53 yards (48 m).

2. Using the template on page 121, cut out a beak from orange wool felt.

3. Locate where you want the beak to be on the ball-shaped pompom. Make a small part into the pile of the yarn and place a small drop of glue there. Insert the wool felt beak. Pinch the fibers around the glue and wool felt beak to secure it.

4. Using the inverted triangle layout (see Positioning the Nose and Eyes on page 22), decide where you want the eyes to be. Make a part in the yarn, carefully squeeze in a pea-size drop of glue for each eye, and gently insert the wire end of each glass eye into the pompom. Let the glue dry.

YOU WILL NEED

Basic Pompom Toolbox (page 12)

100% wool yarn: yellow

100% wool felt: orange

Template: beak (page 121)

2 black glass eyes, 10 or 12 mm

Wire cutters

32 inches (81.3 cm) of 18-gauge floral wire

Embroidery floss or perle cotton: yellow or orange

Ribbon

Millinery flowers

FINISHED MEASUREMENTS
4 ¾ inches (12 cm) tall

Yellow Chick

5. Make another slightly larger pompom from yellow yarn and trim it into an egg shape for the body, about 3½ inches (8.9 cm) long. I used approximately ⅓ skein of Patons medium-weight Classic Wool, which is approximately 69 yards (63 m). Sculpt and trim the tail end into a soft point.

6. Glue the finished head onto the body. To create a cute, inquisitive expression, tilt the head to one side. Squeeze a nickel-size dollop of glue at the top of the body pompom and position the head as desired. You will need to let the glue set up and dry, which can take a few hours. To keep the head from falling off before the glue sets up, use a long floral pin to hold it in place. Remove the pin after the glue has set up.

7. Using wire cutters, cut eight 4-inch (10.2 cm) pieces of floral wire.

8. To create the legs, take four pieces of wire, hold them together, and lightly coat the bundle with glue. Working from top to bottom, wind the embroidery floss or perle cotton tightly and uniformly around the wires. Stop approximately 1½ inches (3.8 cm) from the bottom. Bend each of the four wires out at a 90° angle to make individual toes. Three will face forward; one will face backward to provide the support needed for the chick to stand. Continue wrapping each "toe" wire individually with embroidery floss to cover the floral wire. Repeat with the remaining four pieces of floral wire to create the other leg. Use wire cutters to snip off any excess wire length. Tuck any ends of embroidery floss underneath and let the glue dry.

9. At the bottom of the Chick's body, make two separate parts into the wool plush for the legs and squeeze a dollop of glue into each. Insert the wire legs into the body. Pinch the wool fibers around the wrapped wires to secure them. Set the Chick upright and make any adjustments necessary so that it can dry standing upright.

10. Embellish your Chick with a ribbon and millinery flowers.

✽ **NOTE:** *The top hat described on page 115 can also be used for your little Chick.*

Bunny

Baby bunnies are adorable and hard to resist. They're also my favorite animals to make and a favorite for gift giving during spring and Easter time.

Basic Pompom Toolbox
(page 12)

100% wool yarn: cream

100% wool felt: cream

100% wool roving: cream

Pink seed bead

2 black glass eyes,
10 or 12 mm

Template: ears
(page 122)

Pink chalk

Sewing needle

White upholstery thread

6-inch (15.2 cm)
white pipe cleaner

Needle felting supplies
(page 16)

Ribbon

Millinery flowers

Tiny basket

FINISHED MEASUREMENTS
5 3/4 inches (14.6 cm) tall at
the top of the head, 7 1/2 inches
(19 cm) tall at the tip of
the longest ear

1. Following steps 2–6 of Making Pompoms by Hand on pages 19–21, make a 2 1/2-inch (6.4 cm) egg-shaped pompom from cream yarn for the head. I used approximately 1/3 skein of medium-weight Patons Classic Wool, which is approximately 69 yards (63 m).

2. On the narrow end of the egg shape, locate where you want the nose to be. Make a small part into the "fur," place a small drop of glue in the part, and insert a pink seed bead. Pinch the fibers around the glue and bead to secure it. Let dry.

3. Using the inverted triangle layout (see Positioning the Nose and Eyes on page 22), decide where you want the eyes to be. Make a part in the yarn, carefully squeeze in a pea-size drop of glue for each eye, and gently insert the wire end of each glass eye into the pompom. Let the glue dry.

4. Using the template on page 122, cut two ears out of the wool felt. Rub the inside of each ear with pink chalk and blend it in with your finger. Squeeze a bit of glue onto the bottom flat part of each ear shape and pinch the lower edge together to give it dimension. Repeat this for the second ear. Use clothespins or hemostats to hold the ear bases together as they dry.

5. After the ears have dried, make a small part on top of the head over each eye, squeeze a bit of glue into the pile, and insert the ears. Pinch the fibers around the ears to secure them, and let dry.

6. Following the instructions for Creating and Attaching Whiskers (page 22), thread a sewing needle with a 5-inch (12.7 cm) double strand of white upholstery thread. Tie a knot in the middle, place a tiny smidge of glue on the knot, and "sew" in the whiskers. Snip off any excess so the whiskers are even on both sides.

7. Make another slightly larger pompom from cream yarn and trim it into a pear-shaped pompom for the body, about 3 3/4 inches (9.5 cm) tall. I used approximately 1/2 skein of medium-weight Patons Classic Wool, which is approximately 105 yards (96 m). The narrow top will be the Bunny's neck, and the heavier, rounded end will be the bottom of the Bunny as it sits upright. To create the illusion of the seated Bunny's haunches and tummy, trim out a V shape from the front center bottom of the belly area.

8. Glue the pipe cleaner into the top half of the pompom body. Simply make a horizontal part deep into the wool at the top, squeeze in a dime-size dollop of glue, and place the pipe cleaner snugly down into it; pinch the fibers of the wool yarn to secure it. This will become the frame for the arms of the Bunny, which you will needle felt. (See Creating Appendages on page 24.)

9. Glue the finished head onto the body. To create a cute, inquisitive expression, tilt the head to one side. Squeeze a nickel-size dollop of glue at the top of the body pompom and position the head as desired. To keep the head from falling off before the glue sets up, use a long floral pin to hold it in place until dry. Remove the pin after the glue has set up.

10. After the glue has fully dried, bend the pipe cleaners into the desired position and trim each arm to approximately 2½ inches (6.4 cm). Bend down and tightly crimp the sharp cut ends of the pipe cleaners because they can poke through the needle-felted ends.

11. Needle felt the Bunny's feet by rolling a golf ball–size bit of roving into a cigarlike shape and start needle felting to compact it down (see Attaching Feet and Small Appendages on page 26). Once it is a tight, dense 3-inch (7.6 cm) cigar shape, cut it evenly in half to make the two feet.

12. At the bottom of the pear shape make two separate slits into the wool "fur" and glue the hind feet into the body. Let dry.

13. After the pipe cleaner and glue have set up, take a thick bacon-size strip of roving and wrap it tightly around the pipe cleaner arms. Use more roving near the upper arm and shoulder area and taper off at the end to form a tiny paw. Needle felt the roving tightly to make it compact around the pipe cleaner so it will not unravel (see Needle Felting Appendages on page 24).

14. For the tail, take a bit of roving and needle felt a marble-size ball. On the backside bottom of the Bunny, insert the glue bottle tip and squeeze in a bit of glue. Place the Bunny tail in the glue and pinch the wool fibers around to secure it. Let dry.

15. Embellish your Bunny with a ribbon, millinery flowers, and a little basket.

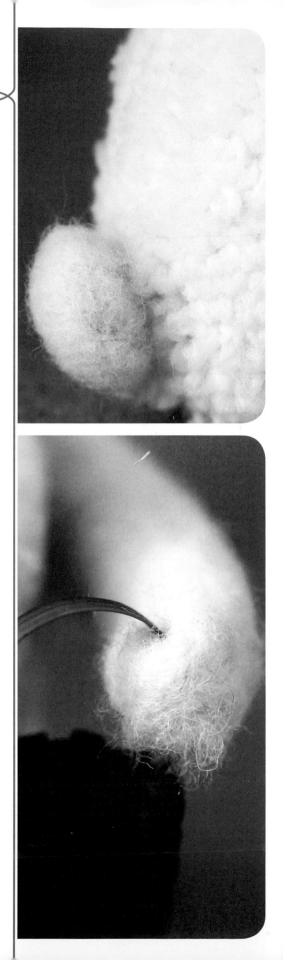

Mouse

This little Mouse is three parts charming, one part mischievous, and entirely filled with adventure: she's ready to journey down the river in her needle-felted leaf boat!

1. Following steps 2–6 of Making Pompoms by Hand on pages 19–21, make a 2½-inch (6.4 cm) egg-shaped pompom from gray yarn for the head. I used approximately ⅓ skein of Patons medium-weight Classic Wool, which is approximately 69 yards (63 m).

2. On the narrow end of the egg-shaped pompom, locate where you want the nose to be. Make a small part in the "fur," place a small drop of glue in the part, and insert the pink seed bead. Pinch the fibers around the glue and the bead to secure it. Let dry.

3. Using the inverted triangle layout (see Positioning the Nose and Eyes on page 22), decide where you want the eyes to be. Make a part in the yarn, carefully squeeze in a pea-size drop of glue for each eye, and gently insert the wire end of each glass eye into the pompom. Let the glue dry.

4. Using the template on page 121, cut two ears out of the wool felt. Rub the inside of each ear with pink chalk and blend it in with your finger. Squeeze a dollop of glue onto the bottom flat part of each ear shape and pinch the lower edge together, with the pink area inside, to give it dimension. Repeat this for the second ear. You can use clothespins or hemostats to hold the ear bases together as they dry.

5. After the ears have dried, make a small part on top of the head over each eye, squeeze a bit of glue into the pile, and insert the ears. Pinch the fibers around each ear to secure them and let dry.

6. Following the instructions for Creating and Attaching Whiskers (page 22), thread a sewing needle with a 5-inch (12.7 cm) double strand of white upholstery thread. Tie a knot in the center, place a tiny smidge of glue on the knot, and "sew" in the whiskers. Snip off any excess so the whiskers are even on both sides.

7. Make another slightly larger pompom by mixing gray yarn and cream yarn and trim it into a slightly pear-shaped pompom for the body, about 3¾ inches (9.5 cm) tall. I used approximately ⅓ skein of gray Patons medium-weight Classic Wool, which is approximately 69 yards (63 m), and approximately ¼ skein of cream Patons medium weight Classic Wool, which is approximately 53 yds (48 m). The cream yarn will be the Mouse's tummy and the gray will be his

back and haunches. Using the heavier, fuller end of the pompom as the bottom, start shaping and trimming the pompom into a rounded pear shape. To create the definition of the Mouse's tummy and haunches, carefully trim out a V shape from the cream yarn on the center bottom of the belly area (see Shaping Pompoms page 29). Continue to trim the cream yarn down as necessary.

8. Glue the 6-inch (15.2 cm) pipe cleaner into the top half of the pompom body. Simply make a horizontal part deep into the wool at the top, squeeze in a dime-size dollop of glue, and place the pipe cleaner snugly down into it. Pinch the fibers of the wool yarn around the pipe cleaner to secure it. This will become the frame for the arms of the Mouse, which you will needle felt. (See Creating Appendages on page 24.)

9. Glue the finished head onto the body. To create a cute inquisitive expression, tilt the head to one side. Squeeze a nickel-size dollop of glue at the top of the body pompom and position the head as desired. To keep the head from falling off before the glue sets up, use a long floral pin to hold it in place. Remove the pin after the glue has set up.

10. After the glue has fully dried, bend the pipe cleaners into the desired position and trim each arm to approximately 2½ inches (6.4 cm). Bend down and tightly crimp the sharp cut ends of the pipe cleaners because they will poke through the needle-felted paws.

11. Needle felt the Mouse's feet by rolling a golf ball–size bit of gray roving into a cigarlike shape and start needle felting to compact it down. Once it is a tight, dense 3-inch (7.6 cm) cigar shape, cut it evenly in half to make the two feet.

12. At the bottom of the pear shape, make two separate parts into the wool "fur" and glue the feet into the body. Let it dry sitting upright.

13. After the pipe cleaner and glue have set up, take a thick bacon-size strip of roving and wrap it tightly around the pipe cleaner arms. Use more roving near the upper arm and shoulder area and taper off at the end to form a tiny paw. Needle felt the roving tightly to make it compact around the pipe cleaner so it will not unravel (see Needle Felting Appendages on page 24).

14. For the tail, trim the fuzzy fibers on one end of the 10-inch (25.4 cm) pipe cleaner with scissors to form a point. Shape the tail into a curled design. Squeeze a dollop of glue into the back bottom of your Mouse and insert the pipe cleaner. Squeeze the wool fibers around the tail to secure it. Let dry.

15. Embellish your Mouse with a ribbon and millinery flowers as desired.

16. To make the Leaf Boat, needle felt the green roving into a flat leaf shape. Add more roving as necessary and continue needle felting to bind the fibers together. Keep turning the leaf over and needle felt both sides until it becomes firm and dense and measures approximately 4 inches (10.2 cm) wide and 5¼ inches (13.3 cm) long. Mold the leaf into a shallow concave leaf shape that the Mouse can sit inside. Cut a 4-inch (10.2 cm) length of fabric-covered floral wire, coat one end with glue, and wedge it into the leaf to create a stem. Let the glue dry.

17. Cut a 7-inch (17.8 cm) length of fabric-covered floral wire and glue a velvet millinery leaf to one end to create a paddle for your Mouse to hold.

Kitten

Little kitties are sure to bring a smile to anyone's face! These instructions are for the Kitten sitting upright, but you can easily create a playful Kitten lying down by attaching the head toward the back of the shoulders, trimming the haunches more to the sides, and arranging the arms so they support the Kitten's body.

1. Following steps 2–6 of Making Pompoms by Hand on pages 19–21, make a 3-inch (7.6 cm) smooth, fat, egg-shaped pompom from white or cream yarn for the head. I used approximately ⅓ skein of Patons medium-weight Classic Wool, which is approximately 69 yards (63 m).

2. On the narrow end of the egg shape, locate where you want the nose to be. Make a small part into the "fur" of the yarn, squeeze in a small drop of glue, and insert a pink seed bead. Pinch the fibers around the glue and bead to secure it. Let dry.

3. Using the inverted triangle layout (see Positioning the Nose and Eyes on page 22), decide where you want the eyes to be. Make a part in the yarn, carefully squeeze in a pea-size drop of glue for each eye, and gently insert the wire end of each glass eye into the pompom. Let the glue dry.

4. Using the template on page 123, cut two ears out of the wool felt. Rub pink chalk inside each ear and blend it in with your finger.

5. Make a small part on top of the head over each eye and squeeze in a bit of glue. Insert the ears and pinch the fibers around the base of the ears to secure them; let dry.

6. Following the instructions for Creating and Attaching Whiskers (page 22), thread a sewing needle with a 5-inch (12.7 cm) double strand of white upholstery thread. Tie a knot in the middle, place a tiny smidge of glue on the knot, and "sew" in the whiskers. The knot should be approximately in the center front of the head. Snip off any excess so the whiskers are even on both sides.

7. Make another slightly larger pompom from white or cream yarn and trim it into a pear shape for the body, about 3¾ inches (9.5 cm) tall. I used approximately ½ skein of Patons medium-weight Classic Wool, which is approximately 105 yards (96 m). The narrow top will be the Kitten's neck and the heavier, rounded end will become the bottom of the Kitten as it sits upright. To create the illusion of the Kitten's haunches and tummy, trim out a V shape from the front center bottom of the belly area.

Kitten

8. Glue the 6-inch (15.2 cm) pipe cleaner into the top half of the pompom body. Simply make a horizontal part deep into the wool at the top, squeeze in a dime-size dollop of glue, and place the pipe cleaner snugly down into it. Pinch the fibers of the wool yarn to secure it. This will become the frame for the arms of the Kitten, which you will needle felt. (See Creating Appendages on page 24.)

9. Glue the finished head onto the body. To create a cute, inquisitive expression, tilt the head to one side. Squeeze a nickel-size dollop of glue at the top of the body pompom and position the head as desired. You will need to let the glue set up and dry, which can take a while. To keep the head from falling off before the glue sets up, use a long floral pin to hold it in place. Remove the pin after the glue has set up.

10. After the pipe cleaner and glue have fully dried, bend the pipe cleaner into the desired position and trim each arm to approximately 3 inches (7.6 cm). Bend down and tightly crimp the sharp cut ends of the pipe cleaners because they can poke through and show out the end of the needle-felted paws.

11. Needle felt the Kitten's hind feet by rolling a golf ball–size bit of roving into a cigarlike shape and start needle felting to compact it down (see Attaching Feet and Small Appendages on page 26). Once it is a tight, dense 3-inch (7.6 cm) cigar shape, cut it evenly in half to make the two back paws.

12. At the bottom of the pear shape make two separate long slits into the wool "fur" and glue the feet into the body. Let it dry sitting upright.

13. After the pipe cleaner and glue have set up, take a thick bacon-size strip of roving and wrap it tightly from top to bottom around the pipe cleaner arms. Use more roving near the upper arm and shoulder area and taper off at the end to form a tiny paw. Needle felt the roving tightly to make it compact around the pipe cleaner so it will not unravel. Shave off excess "fuzzies" with scissors for a neater appearance, if desired (see Needle Felting Appendages on page 24).

14. For the tail, wrap wool roving tightly around the 8-inch (20.3 cm) pipe cleaner. Place a bit more roving toward one end, which will attach to the body, and let it taper off at the other end, which becomes the tip of the tail. Needle felt the entire tail evenly so the roving does not unravel. When finished, make a part at the bottom backside of the body pompom, squeeze in a small dollop of glue, and insert the tail. Gently pinch the wool fibers around it to secure the tail. Let dry. Curl the tail as desired.

15. Embellish your Kitten with little ribbons, tiny bells, and millinery flowers, if desired.

❋ **NOTE**: *There are other cute ideas for embellishments, too. Needle felt a little ball of yarn to place at the Kitten's feet or needle felt a tiny fish!*

❋ **VARIATION**: *To make a version of the Kitten lying down: attach the head pompom more toward the back of the body pompom; trim the haunches more to the sides of the body; and needle felt all four feet instead of using an armature for the front two.*

Bluebird

Bluebirds symbolize happiness and well-being: just take a look at this little gal's bright-eyed expression and you'll feel happy, too!

1. Following steps 2–6 of Making Pompoms by Hand on pages 19–21, make a 2½-inch (6.4 cm) round ball-shaped pompom from aqua yarn for the head. I used approximately ¼ skein of Patons medium-weight Classic Wool, which is approximately 53 yards (48 m).

2. Using the template on page 121 cut out a beak shape from orange or yellow wool felt.

3. Locate where you want the beak to be on the ball-shaped pompom. Make a small part into the pile of the yarn, place a drop of glue, and insert the wool felt beak. Pinch the fibers around the glue and wool felt beak to secure it. Let dry.

4. Using the inverted triangle layout (see Positioning the Nose and Eyes on page 22), decide where you want the eyes to be. Make a part in the yarn, carefully squeeze in a pea-size drop of glue for each eye, and gently insert the wire end of each glass eye into the pompom. Let the glue dry.

YOU WILL NEED

Basic Pompom Toolbox
(page 12)

100% wool yarn:
aqua blue

100% wool felt:
orange or yellow

Template: beak
(page 121)

2 black glass eyes,
10 or 12 mm

Wire cutters

32 inches (81.3 cm) of
18-gauge floral wire

Embroidery floss or
perle cotton: yellow or orange

Ribbon

Millinery flowers

FINISHED MEASUREMENTS
4 ¾ inches (12 cm) tall

Bluebird

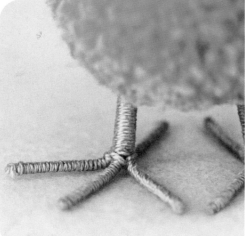

5. Make another slightly larger pompom from aqua blue yarn and trim it into an egg shape for the body, about 3½ inches (8.9 cm) from front to back and about 4 inches (10.2 cm) from top to bottom. Keep the yarn longer at the tail end and shape the back slightly. I used approximately ⅓ skein of Patons medium-weight Classic Wool, which is approximately 69 yards (63 m).

6. Glue the finished head onto the body. To create a cute, inquisitive expression, tilt the head to one side. Squeeze a nickel-size dollop of glue at the top of the body pompom and position the head as desired. You will need to let the glue set up and dry, which can take a few hours. To keep the head from falling off before the glue sets, use a long floral pin to hold it in place. Remove the pin after the glue has set up.

7. Using wire cutters, cut eight 4-inch (10.2 cm) pieces of floral wire.

8. To create each foot, take four pieces of wire, hold them together, and lightly coat the bundle with glue. Working from top to bottom, wind the embroidery floss or perle cotton tightly and uniformly around the wires. Stop approximately 1½ inches (3.8 cm) from reaching the bottom. Next, bend each wire out at a 90° angle to make individual toes. Three will face forward; one will face backward to provide the support needed for the Bluebird to stand. Continue wrapping each "toe" wire individually with embroidery floss to cover the floral wire. Repeat with the remaining four pieces of floral wire to create the other leg. Use wire cutters to snip off any excess wire length. Tuck any ends of embroidery floss underneath and let the glue dry.

9. At the bottom of the Bluebird's body, make two separate parts into the wool plush for the legs and squeeze a dollop of glue into each. Insert the wire legs and feet into the body. Pinch the wool fibers around the wrapped wire to secure. Set the Bluebird upright and make adjustments so that it can dry standing upright.

10. Embellish your Bluebird with a ribbon and millinery flowers.

✳ **NOTE:** *As another option in fashioning your Bluebird, purchase chicken feathers (different varieties are available) at your local craft store and use them, dyed to match the yarn, as the bird's tail instead. Simply make a part in the yarn, squeeze in a bit of glue, and insert the feathers.*

Elephant

They say Elephants have incredible memories—this little fellow's bright eyes
and friendly expression make him a creature you'll never forget.

Basic Pompom Toolbox
(page 12)

100% wool yarn:
gray

100% wool felt: gray, and
two colors of your choice

100% wool roving:
gray

4-inch (10.2 cm)
gray pipe cleaner

Needle felting supplies
(page 16)

2 black glass eyes,
10 or 12 mm

Template:
ears (page 122)

Wire cutters

12-inch (30.5 cm) length of
wooden dowel, 5 mm in diameter

Scallop-edge scissors or zigzag
pinking shears (optional)

Micro hole punch (optional)

Ribbon

FINISHED MEASUREMENTS
**5 ¾ inches (14.6 cm) tall
at the top of the head**

1. Following steps 2–6 of Making Pompoms by Hand on pages 19–21, make a 3-inch (7.6 cm) smooth, fat, egg-shaped pompom from gray yarn for the head. I used approximately ⅓ skein of Patons medium-weight Classic Wool, which is approximately 69 yards (63 m).

2. On the narrow end of the egg shape, locate where you want the nose to be and make a small part into the wool plush. Add glue and insert the pipe cleaner for the Elephant's trunk, curving it slightly. Pinch the fibers of the wool yarn around the pipe cleaner to secure it. Let dry.

3. Take a strip of gray wool roving, wrap it around the pipe cleaner tightly, and begin to needle felt the roving to the desired thickness for the Elephant's trunk (see Creating Appendages on page 24).

4. Using the inverted triangle layout (see Positioning the Nose and Eyes on page 22), decide where you want the eyes to be. Make a part in the yarn, carefully squeeze in a pea-size drop of glue for each eye, and gently insert the wire end of each glass eye into the pompom. Let the glue dry.

5. Using the template on page 122, cut two ears from the wool felt.

6. Make a small part in the wool on each side of the head and squeeze a bit of glue into the part; insert the ears. Pinch the fibers around the base of the ears to secure them, and let the glue dry.

7. Make another slightly larger pompom from the gray yarn and trim it into a fat bun-shaped pompom for the body measuring approximately 4 inches (10.2 cm) in length and diameter. I used approximately ½ skein of medium-weight Patons Classic Wool, which is approximately 105 yards (96 m).

8. To create the Elephant's legs, use your wire cutters and cut four equal pieces from the wooden dowel to create legs approximately 3 inches (7.6 cm) long.

9. Wrap each leg thickly with strips of wool roving and begin to needle felt around the dowel (see Needle Felting Appendages on page 24). Needle felt the roving tightly and evenly around the legs. Be sure to needle felt over the bottom of the dowel so it is not exposed. Shave off any excess "fuzzies" with your scissors for a neater appearance, if desired.

10. Make four deep parts on the bottom of the Elephant's body where you want to position the legs. Add glue in each part and insert the legs, firmly pinching the wool fibers around the legs to secure them. Adjust the legs as necessary so the Elephant can stand. Let it dry standing upright.

11. Glue the finished head onto the body. To create a cute, inquisitive expression, tilt the head to one side. Squeeze a nickel-size dollop of glue at the top of the body pompom and position the head as desired. You will need to let the glue set up and dry, which can take a while. To keep the head from falling off before the glue sets up, use a long floral pin to hold it in place. Remove the pin after the glue has set up and dried.

12. For the tail, cut nine pieces of gray yarn into 6-inch (15.2 cm) lengths and tightly knot them together at one end. Divide the yarn into three sections, each with three pieces of yarn, and braid the three sections together. Knot the end and even it off with scissors. Make a part in the pompom body where you want to insert the tail, squeeze in a small dollop of glue, and insert the tail. Gently pinch the wool fibers around to secure the tail. Let dry.

13. Using the scallop-edge scissors or pinking shears if possible, cut an oval from each color of felt, one measuring 3 inches (7.6 cm) long and the other 2 1/2 inches (6.4 cm) long. Decorate the edges of the ovals with a micro hole punch, if desired. Glue the smaller oval onto the larger one, then glue both onto the back of the Elephant, using a pipe cleaner or ribbon to hold them in place while the glue dries.

14. Embellish your Elephant with a ribbon.

✻ **NOTE:** *Other ideas for embellishments include tiny bells, millinery flowers, and/or the top hat described on page 115.*

Lop-Eared Bunny

With bashful lop ears and an armful of springtime flowers,
this sweet bunny is ready to hippity-hop into your heart.

1. Following steps 2–6 of Making Pompoms by Hand on pages 19–21, make a 2½- to 3-inch (6.4 to 7.6 cm) egg-shaped pompom from white or cream yarn for the head. I used approximately ⅓ skein of Patons medium-weight Classic Wool, which is approximately 69 yards (63 m).

2. On the narrow end of the egg-shaped pompom, locate where you want the nose to be. Make a small part into the "fur," place a small drop of glue in the part, and insert the pink seed bead. Pinch the fibers around the glue and the bead to secure it. Let dry.

3. Using the inverted triangle layout (see Positioning the Nose and Eyes on page 22), decide where you want the eyes to be. Make a part in the yarn, carefully squeeze in a pea-size drop of glue for each eye, and gently insert the wire end of each glass eye into the pompom. Let the glue dry.

4. Using the template on page 124, cut two ears from the black wool felt. Using the template as a guide, use a flat iron or a regular household iron to create a folded edge at the base of the Bunny's ears so they will flop over.

5. Make a small part on top of the head over each eye, squeeze a bit of glue into the parted pile, and insert the ears. Pinch the fibers around the ears to secure them and let the glue dry.

6. Following the instructions for Creating and Attaching Whiskers (page 22), thread a sewing needle with a 5-inch (12.7 cm) double strand of white upholstery thread. Tie a knot in the center, place a tiny smidge of glue on the knot, and "sew" in the whiskers. Snip off any excess so the whiskers are even on both sides.

7. Make another slightly larger pompom from white or cream yarn and trim it into a pear-shaped pompom for the body, about 4 inches (10.2 cm) tall. I used approximately ½ skein of Patons medium-weight Classic Wool, which is approximately 105 yards (96 m). The narrow top will be the Bunny's neck, and the heavier, rounded end will be the bottom of the Bunny as it sits upright. To create the illusion of the Bunny's haunches and tummy, trim out a V shape from the front center bottom of the belly area.

8. Glue the pipe cleaner into the top half of the pompom body. Simply make a horizontal part deep into the wool at the top, squeeze in a dime-size dollop of glue, and place the pipe cleaner snugly down into it. Pinch the fibers of the wool yarn to secure the pipe cleaner. This will become the frame for the arms of the Bunny, which you will needle felt. (See Creating Appendages on page 24.)

9. Glue the finished head onto the body. Squeeze a nickel-size dollop of glue at the top of the body pompom and position the head as desired. To keep the head from falling off before the glue sets up, use a long floral pin to hold it in place. Remove the pin after the glue has set up and dried.

10. After the glue has fully dried, bend the pipe cleaners into the desired position and trim each arm to approximately 2½ inches (6.4 cm). Bend down and tightly crimp the sharp cut ends of the pipe cleaners because they will poke through the needle-felted ends.

11. Needle felt the Bunny's feet by rolling a golf ball–size bit of white or cream roving into a cigarlike shape and start needle felting to compact it down (see Attaching Feet and Small Appendages on page 26). Once it is a tight, dense 3-inch (7.6 cm) cigar shape, cut it evenly in half to make the two feet.

12. At the bottom of the pear shape make two separate slits into the wool "fur" and glue the hind feet into the body. Let it dry sitting upright.

13. After the pipe cleaner and glue have set up, take a thick bacon-size strip of roving and wrap it tightly around the pipe cleaner arms. Use more roving near the upper arm and shoulder area and taper off at the end to form a tiny paw. Needle felt the roving tightly to compact it around the pipe cleaner so it will not unravel (see Needle Felting Appendages on page 24).

14. For the tail, take a bit of black roving and needle felt a marble-size ball. On the backside bottom of the Bunny, insert the glue bottle and squeeze in a bit of glue. Place the Bunny tail in and pinch the wool fibers around to secure it. Let dry.

15. Embellish your Bunny with a ribbon and millinery flowers.

Lop-Eared Bunny

Ladybug

Ladybugs are said to bring good luck. With her sweetly curled antennae and clever felt feet, the recipient of this project will be lucky, indeed. The Ladybug's red and black body pompom is made by layering the two colors of yarn: three sections of wrapped black yarn become six black spots on this pretty lady's back.

YOU WILL NEED

Basic Pompom Toolbox
(page 12)

100% wool yarn:
black, red

100% wool felt:
black

2 black glass eyes,
10 or 12 mm

8-inch (20.3 cm)
black pipe cleaner

Template:
feet (page 123)

Ribbon

Millinery flowers

FINISHED MEASUREMENTS
5 inches (12.7 cm) long from
front to back;
2½ inches (6.4 cm) tall at
the top of the back

1. Following steps 2–6 of Making Pompoms by Hand on pages 19–21, make a 1¾-inch (4.4 cm) round, ball-shaped pompom from black yarn for the head. I used approximately ¼ skein of Patons medium-weight Classic Wool, which is approximately 53 yards (48 m).

2. Using the inverted triangle layout (see Positioning the Nose and Eyes on page 22), decide where you want the eyes to be. Make a part in the yarn, carefully squeeze in a pea-size drop of glue for each eye, and gently insert the wire end of each glass eye into the pompom. Let the glue dry.

3. Cut two 3-inch (7.6 cm) lengths of the black pipe cleaner to create the Ladybug's antennae. On one end of each pipe cleaner curl the ends into a spiral. You can do this by hand or by winding the pipe cleaner around a pencil. Make a tiny part on the top of the head above each eye. Insert the tip of the glue bottle and squeeze in a tiny dollop of glue. Insert the uncurled end of each pipe cleaner into the head at this spot and pinch the fibers around it to secure the antennae. Let dry.

4. The Ladybug's body pompom is made a bit differently than other multicolor pompoms in this book. Instead of only winding different colors of yarn side-by-side, this black and red pompom is made by winding multicolor layers of yarn on top of each other. Overall, I used a total of approximately ¼ skein of red Patons medium-weight Classic Wool, which is approximately 53 yards (48 m), and a total of approximately ⅛ skein of black Classic Wool for the spots, which is approximately 26 yards (24 m).

5. Your goal will be to make the black spots roughly the same size, which means you'll want to use about the same amount of black yarn each time you wind it on the cardboard sleeve. When I want to keep relatively small amounts of yarn equal in size, I find it helpful to count my number of wraps. You can also pre-cut the shorter lengths of yarn used in the second and third layers.

✳ **NOTE:** *Think of this pompom as being made from four layers of yarn. The three sections of wrapped black yarn will eventually become the Ladybug's six black spots.*

LAYER 1 Wrap approximately one third of the red yarn around the cardboard sleeve, about 18 yards (16 m).

Ladybug

LAYER 2 On top of the first all-red layer, wrap a sequence of black-red-black yarn: wrap about 9 yards (8 m) of black on the left; about 6 yards (5 m) of red in the center; and about 9 yards (8 m) of black on the right.

LAYER 3 On top of the first and second layers, wrap a reverse sequence of red-black-red yarn: wrap about 6 yards (5 m) of red on the left; about 9 yards (8 m) of black in the center; and about 6 yards (5 m) of red on the right.

LAYER 4 On top of the first, second, and third layers, wrap another all-red layer of yarn, about 18 yards (16 m).

6. Slide the four-layer bundle of yarn off the cardboard sleeve, tie it with waxed twine, and cut the pompom's loops as described in Steps 3-5 of Making Pompoms by Hand (pages 19–21).

7. The flat bottom of the Ladybug's body pompom is created by pressing all the yarn fibers upward by hand so a flattened side naturally forms—don't cut the fibers. Once you cut the loops of the pompom, you'll see six areas of black yarn that will form the Ladybug's spots. Comb and gently tug the yarn fibers with your fingers to arrange the black sections of yarn into evenly-spaced spots surrounded by red yarn.

8. When you've arranged the black and red yarn, trim and sculpt the pompom into a hemisphere or dome measuring approximately 4½ inches (11.4 cm) in length. The flattened side of the pompom will become the Ladybug's underbelly.

9. Glue the finished head onto the body by squeezing a dollop of glue at the top of the body pompom and positioning the head as desired. To keep the head from falling off before the glue sets up, use a long floral pin to hold it in place. Remove the pin after the glue has dried.

10. Using the template on page 123, cut out six feet from black wool felt.

11. Glue the feet onto the bottom of the body pompom as shown, with three feet on each side.

12. Add ribbon and floral embellishments, as desired, to your little Ladybug.

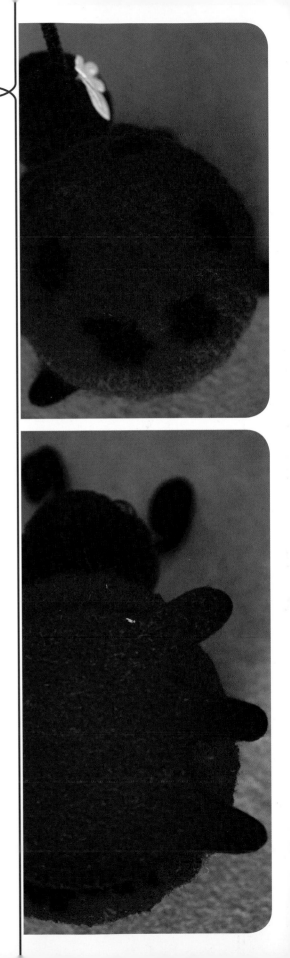

Teddy Bear

Teddy bears embody the classic toy and youthful companion throughout the ages. Create your own heirloom bear using the techniques described here, or use a few simple adjustments to transform your bear into a Panda.

1. Following steps 2–6 of Making Pompoms by Hand on pages 19–21, make a 3-inch (7.6 cm) smooth, fat, egg-shaped pompom from gray yarn for the head. I used approximately ⅓ skein of Patons medium-weight Classic Wool, which is approximately 69 yards (63 m). Sculpt a muzzle for the Teddy Bear's face (see Tips on Shaping the Nose and Muzzle, page 21).

2. On the muzzle, locate where you want the nose to be. Make a small part into the "fur," place a small drop of glue in the part, and insert the black seed bead. Pinch the fibers around the glue and the bead to secure it. Let the glue dry.

3. Using the inverted triangle layout (see Positioning the Nose and Eyes on page 22), decide where you want the eyes to be. Make a part in the yarn, carefully squeeze in a pea-size drop of glue for each eye, and gently insert the wire end of each glass eye into the pompom. Let the glue dry.

4. Using the template on page 123, cut two ears out of the wool felt. Place glue on the bottom flat part of the ear shape and pinch the lower edge together to create dimension. Repeat this for the second ear. Use clothespins or hemostats to hold the ear bases together as they dry.

5. Make a small part on the top of the head above each eye, squeeze a bit of glue into the part, and insert the ears. Pinch the fibers around the base of the ears to secure them and let the glue dry.

Teddy Bear

6. Make another slightly larger pompom from the gray yarn and trim it into a pear-shaped pompom for the body, about 4 inches (10.2 cm) in length and diameter. I used approximately ½ skein of Patons medium-weight Classic Wool, which is approximately 105 yards (96 m). Using your scissors, sculpt a fat little belly for the Teddy Bear.

7. To create the gray Teddy Bear's arms and legs, make a deep part at the top of the pear shape of the body and glue in a pipe cleaner approximately 7 inches (17.8 cm) in length, with even parts sticking out on each side for the arms. Repeat with another pipe cleaner in the pompom's heavier bottom end for the legs. Pinch the fibers around the glue and pipe cleaners to secure them. These will become the frames for the legs, which you will needle felt. (See Creating Appendages on page 24.) Let the glue dry.

8. Trim the pipe cleaners to approximately 3½ inches (8.9 cm) long for each of the arms and legs. Fold down and crimp any sharp edges of the pipe cleaners because they can poke out of the needle-felted paws.

9. Bend the bottom pipe cleaners so the Teddy Bear is sitting with his bottom legs sticking out in front.

10. Wrap each pipe cleaner appendage thickly and firmly in wool roving and needle felt around each of the pipe cleaners. Needle felt the roving tightly, making the top ends slightly thicker than the bottoms of the leg (see Needle Felting Appendages on page 24). Add more roving to the Teddy Bear's feet to create and shape toes.

11. Glue the finished head onto the body. To create a cute, inquisitive expression, tilt the head to one side. Squeeze a nickel-size dollop of glue at the top of the body pompom and position the head as desired. You will need to let the glue set up and dry, which can take a while. To keep the head from falling off before the glue sets up, use a long floral pin to hold it in place. Remove the pin after the glue has set up.

12. For the tail, needle felt a bit of roving into a flattened, pea-size oval. Make a part at the bottom backside, squeeze in a small dollop of glue, and insert the tail. Gently pinch the wool fibers around the tail to secure it. Let dry.

13. Tie a ribbon around your Teddy Bear's neck.

Lamb

Little lambs are a sweet sign of spring and new life, making this project a
wonderful gift to give when the days grow warmer and spring is in the air.

Basic Pompom Toolbox
(page 12)

100% wool yarn:
white or cream

100% wool felt:
white or cream

100% wool roving yarn:
white or cream

100% wool roving:
white or cream

2 black glass eyes,
10 or 12 mm

Template:
ears (page 121)

Pink chalk

Wire cutters

12-inch (30.5 cm)
length of wooden dowel,
5 mm in diameter

Needle felting supplies
(see page 16)

Ribbon

Tiny bells

Millinery flowers

FINISHED MEASUREMENTS
6 inches (15.2 cm) tall

1. Following steps 2–6 of Making Pompoms by Hand on pages 19–21, make a 3-inch (7.6 cm) smooth, fat, egg-shaped pompom from white yarn for the head. I used approximately ⅓ skein of Patons medium-weight Classic Wool, which is approximately 69 yards (63 m).

2. Using the inverted triangle layout (see Positioning the Nose and Eyes on page 22), decide where you want the eyes to be. Make a part in the yarn, carefully squeeze in a pea-size drop of glue for each eye, and gently insert the wire end of each glass eye into the pompom. Let the glue dry. The Lamb has no nose.

3. Using the template on page 121, cut two ears out of the wool felt. Rub pink chalk inside each ear and blend it in with your finger. Squeeze a dollop of glue onto the bottom flat part of each ear shape and pinch the lower edge together, with the pink area inside, to give it dimension. Repeat this for the second ear. You can use clothespins or hemostats to hold the ear bases together as they dry.

4. Make a small part on each side of the head, squeeze a bit of glue into the part, and insert the ears. Pinch the fibers around the base of the ears to secure them and let the glue dry.

5. Make another slightly larger pompom from white roving yarn and trim it into a fat bun-shaped pompom for the body, measuring about 4 inches (10.2 cm) in length and diameter. I used approximately ⅓ skein of Patons bulky-weight Classic Wool Roving yarn, which is approximately 40 yards (36 m).

6. To create the Lamb's legs, use your wire cutters to cut four equal pieces of the wooden dowel to create legs approximately 3 inches (7.6 cm) long.

7. Wrap each leg thickly in wool roving and needle felt around the dowel (see Needle Felting Appendages on page 24). Needle felt the roving tightly, making the top of the leg near the body slightly thicker than the bottom. Be sure to needle felt over the bottom of the dowel so it is not exposed. Shave off any excess "fuzzies" with scissors for a neater appearance, if desired.

8. Make four deep parts on the bottom of the Lamb's body where you want to position the legs. Add glue in each part and insert the legs, firmly pinching the wool fibers around the legs to secure them. Adjust the legs as necessary so the Lamb can stand. Let it dry standing upright.

9. Glue the finished head onto the body. To create a cute, inquisitive expression, tilt the head to one side. Squeeze a nickel-size dollop of glue at the top of the body pompom and position the head as desired. You will need to let the glue set up and dry, which can take a while. To keep the head from falling off before the glue sets up, use a long floral pin to hold it in place. Remove the pin after the glue has set up and dried.

10. For the tail, take a bit of roving and needle felt a flattened marble-size oval shape. Make a part at the bottom backside, squeeze in a small dollop of glue, and gently insert the tail. Pinch the wool fibers around the tail to secure it. Let dry.

11. Embellish your Lamb with ribbons, tiny bells, and millinery flowers, as desired.

Puppy

Say hello to a crafter's best friend: this wiggly, waggy, playful pompom pup.

Basic Pompom Toolbox
(page 12)

100% wool yarn:
gray

100% wool felt:
gray

100% wool roving:
gray

Black seed bead

2 black glass eyes,
10 or 12 mm

Template:
ears (page 121)

Hair-straightening flat iron
or household iron

Sewing needle

Black upholstery thread

Two 6-inch (15.2 cm)
pipe cleaners

Needle felting supplies
(page 16)

Narrow ribbon

Tiny bell

FINISHED MEASUREMENTS
6 ¼ inches (15.9 cm) tall

1. Following steps 2–6 for Making Pompoms by Hand on pages 19–21, make a 3-inch (7.6 cm) smooth, fat, egg-shaped pompom from gray yarn for the head. I used approximately ⅓ skein of Patons medium-weight Classic Wool, which is approximately 69 yards (63 m). Scupt a muzzle for the Puppy's face (see Tips on Shaping the Nose and Muzzle, page 21).

2. On the muzzle, locate where you want the nose to be. Make a small part into the "fur," place a small drop of glue, and insert the black seed bead. Pinch the fibers around the glue and the bead to secure it.

3. Using the inverted triangle layout (see Positioning the Nose and Eyes on page 22), decide where you want the eyes to be. Make a part in the yarn, carefully squeeze in a pea-size drop of glue for each eye, and gently insert the wire end of each glass eye into the pompom. Let the glue dry.

4. Using the template on page 121, cut two ears out of the wool felt. With the template as a guide, use a flat iron or household iron to create a crease in the Puppy's ears so they will flop over.

5. Make a small part on top of the head over each eye and squeeze a bit of glue into the part in the wool fibers; insert the ears. Pinch the fibers around the base of the ears to secure them and let the glue dry.

6. Following the instructions for Creating and Attaching Whiskers (page 22), thread a sewing needle with a 5-inch (12.7 cm) double strand of black upholstery thread. Tie a knot in the middle, place a tiny smidge of glue on the knot, and "sew" in the whiskers; the knot should be in the approximate center front of the head. Snip off any excess so the whiskers are even on both sides.

7. Make another slightly larger pompom from gray yarn and trim it into a pear-shaped pompom for the body, about 4 inches (10.2 cm) tall. I used approximately 1/2 skein of Patons medium-weight Classic Wool, which is approximately 105 yards (96 m). The narrow top will be the Puppy's neck, and the heavier, rounded end will become the bottom of the Puppy as it sits upright. To create the illusion of the Puppy's haunches and tummy, trim out a V shape from the front center bottom of the belly area.

8. Glue a 6-inch (15.2 cm) pipe cleaner into the top half of the pompom body. Simply make a horizontal part deep into the wool at the top, squeeze in a dime-size dollop of glue, and place the pipe cleaner snugly down into it. Pinch the fibers of the wool yarn around the pipe cleaner to secure it. This will become the frame for the arms of the Puppy, which you will needle felt. (See Creating Appendages on page 24.)

9. Glue the finished head onto the body. To create a cute, inquisitive expression, tilt the head to one side. Squeeze a nickel-size dollop of glue at the top of the body pompom and position the head as desired. You will need to let the glue set up and dry, which can take a while. To keep the head from falling off before the glue sets up, use a long floral pin to hold it in place. Remove the pin after the glue has set up.

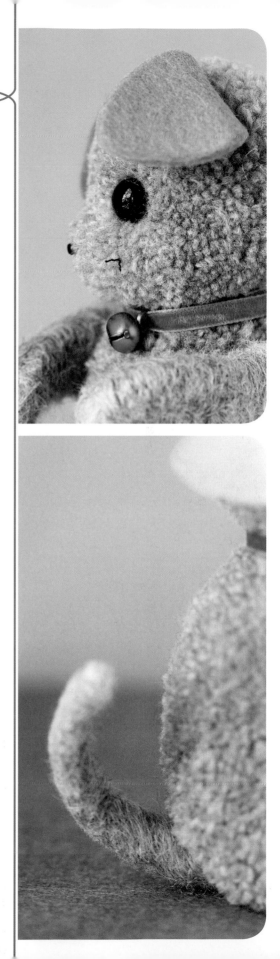

10. After the glue has fully dried, bend the pipe cleaner into the desired position and trim the arms to approximately 3 inches (7.6 cm). Bend down and tightly crimp the sharp cut ends of the pipe cleaners because they can poke through and show out the end of the needle-felted paws.

11. Needle felt the Puppy's hind feet by rolling a golf ball–size bit of roving into a cigarlike shape and start needle felting to compact it down (see Attaching Feet and Small Appendages on page 26). Once it is a tight, dense 3-inch (7.6 cm) cigar shape, cut it evenly in half to make the two back paws.

12. At the bottom of the pear shape make two separate long slits into the wool "fur" and glue the feet into the body. Let it dry sitting upright.

13. After the pipe cleaner and glue have set up, take a thick bacon-size strip of roving and wrap it tightly from top to bottom around the pipe cleaner arms. Use more roving near the upper arm and shoulder area and taper off at the end to form a paw. Needle felt the roving tightly to compact it around the pipe cleaner so it will not unravel. Shave off any excess "fuzzies" with your scissors for a neater appearance, if desired.

14. For the tail, cut a pipe cleaner approximately 5 1/4 inches (13.3 cm) long and wrap roving tightly around it from top to bottom. Place a bit more roving toward the end that will attach to the body and taper it off at the tip of the tail. Needle felt the entire tail evenly so the roving does not unravel. When finished, make a part at the bottom backside of the Puppy, squeeze in a small dollop of glue, and gently insert the tail. Gently pinch the wool fibers around the tail to secure it. Let dry.

15. Embellish your Puppy with a narrow ribbon "collar" strung with a tiny bell.

❋ **NOTE:** *For other cute accessories for your Puppy, needle felt a bone or a dog dish.*

Swan

No other bird is as graceful or as beautiful as a swan. These make great gifts as love tokens—swans (like many birds) symbolize eternal love because they mate for life.

1. Following steps 2–6 of Making Pompoms by Hand on pages 19–21, make a 4 x 5-inch (10.2 x 12.7 cm) tear-shaped oval pompom from white roving yarn for the body. I used approximately 1/3 skein of Patons bulky-weight Classic Wool Roving, which is approximately 40 yards (36 m). Wool roving yarn is much fluffier than regular wool yarn and will create beautiful feathers on the Swan. The pointed end of the pompom will be the Swan's tail. Flatten the bottom so the pompom sits level and flush.

2. Using your wire cutters, cut a 6- to 7-inch length of 18-gauge floral wire and fold it in half. Bend the doubled wire into a graceful S-curve that will be the frame of the needle-felted head and neck. Use wire cutters to trim the neck length accordingly.

3. Thickly wrap the neck armature with white wool roving, concentrating more roving on the folded end, which will become the Swan's head. Begin needle felting to keep the roving from unraveling (see Creating Appendages, page 24).

4. Continue needle felting, adding more roving as necessary, building up and making a slightly rounded end over the folded wire. Needle felt this into a marble-size head, about 1 inch (2.5 cm) long, compacting the roving around the head and neck tightly and evenly.

5. Make the beak by shaping and needle felting a bit of orange roving into a slim, pointy triangle about ½ inch (1.3 cm) long. Remember to needle felt the beak from multiple angles, creating a dense shape. Attach the beak by needle felting it directly onto the white roving of the head.

6. Decide where to place the eyes on each side of the Swan's head. Use a pencil to poke a hole into the roving on each side of the head to create an indentation, insert the tip of the glue bottle, and squeeze in a tiny bit of glue. Place a glass eye into each drop of glue and gently push it in. Let the glue dry.

7. Needle felt a bit of black roving around the beak and each eye to create detail for the Swan's face.

8. Make a part in the rounded end of the pompom body and squeeze in a large dollop of glue. Insert the needle-felted neck and head. Pinch the wool fibers around the neck to secure it. Let dry.

Seal

Seals are known for their playfulness: now, instead of only getting to see them play at the zoo or circus, you can create one to look at all year long! Try your hand at a white or spotted seal as a friend for this gray fellow.

1. Following steps 2–6 of Making Pompoms by Hand on pages 19–21, make a 2½-inch (6.4 cm) egg-shaped pompom from gray yarn for the head. I used approximately ⅓ skein of Patons medium-weight Classic Wool, which is approximately 69 yards (63 m).

2. On the narrow end of the egg shape, locate where you want the nose to be. Make a small part into the "fur," place a small drop of glue, and insert a black seed bead. Pinch the fibers around the glue and the bead to secure it.

3. Using the inverted triangle layout (see Positioning the Nose and Eyes on page 22), decide where you want the eyes to be. Make a part in the yarn, carefully squeeze in a pea-size drop of glue for each eye, and gently insert the wire end of each glass eye into the pompom. Let the glue dry.

4. Following the instructions for Creating and Attaching Whiskers (page 22), thread a sewing needle with a 5-inch (12.7 cm) double strand of black upholstery thread. Tie a knot in the center, place a tiny smidge of glue on the knot, and "sew" in the whiskers. Snip off any excess so the whiskers are even on both sides.

YOU WILL NEED

Basic Pompom Toolbox
(page 12)

100% wool yarn:
gray

100% wool felt:
gray

100% wool roving:
color of your choice for the ball

Black seed bead

2 black glass eyes,
10 or 12 mm

Sewing needle

Black upholstery thread

Templates:
flippers, tail
(page 124)

Needle felting supplies
(page 16)

Pipe cleaner

Ribbon

FINISHED MEASUREMENTS
**4½ inches (11.4 cm) tall
at the tip of the nose,
4¼ inches (10.8 cm) long
without the felt tail**

Seal

5. Make another slightly large pompom from gray yarn and trim it into an oblong, tear-shaped pompom for the body, about 4 inches (10.2 cm) long. I used approximately ½ skein of Patons medium-weight Classic Wool, which is approximately 105 yards (96 m). The heavier, rounded end will be the Seal's upper chest and neck. The narrow end will taper off to the Seal's tail. Trim the bottom of the pompom flat so the Seal can lie on its belly.

6. Using the template on page 124, cut two flippers from the wool felt. Make a part in the wool yarn fur on each side of the front end of the body pompom at a slight diagonal, squeeze glue into the part, and insert a flipper on each side. Pinch the fibers around each flipper to secure them and let dry.

7. Using the template on page 124, cut out the tail flipper from the wool felt. Make a horizontal part at the end of the tail, squeeze some glue into the part, and insert the tail flipper. Pinch the fibers around the tail to secure it and let dry.

8. Glue the finished head onto the body with the Seal's nose pointing straight up. Squeeze a nickel-size dollop of glue at the top of the body pompom and position the head as desired. To keep the head from falling off before the glue sets up, use a long floral pin to hold it in place. Remove the pin after the glue has set up and dried.

9. Using a roving color of your choice, needle felt a ball for the Seal to balance on its nose. Roll a small bit of roving into a ball and needle felt into a dense, smooth, round shape about ¾ inch (1.9 cm) in diameter. Don't make the ball too large or it will be too heavy for the Seal to "balance" on its nose. Trim any loose "fuzzies" to make the ball neater.

10. Make a tiny snip in the needle-felted ball. Cut a ¾-inch (1.9 cm) length of pipe cleaner, dip one end into the glue, and insert it into the ball halfway. Let dry.

11. Make a tiny part as close to the Seal's nose as you can and squeeze in a bit of glue. Insert the pipe cleaner from the needle-felted ball into the part and pinch the yarn fibers around the pipe cleaner to secure it. Allow the glue to dry completely. Now your Seal is balancing a ball on the end of his nose!

12. Tie a ribbon around your Seal's neck.

Piglet

That little piggy went to market, and this little piggy stayed home to be with you!

Basic Pompom Toolbox
(page 12)

100% wool yarn:
pink

100% wool felt:
pink

100% wool roving:
pink

Embroidery needle

Embroidery floss:
pink

2 black glass eyes,
10 or 12 mm

Template:
ears (page 121)

Hair-straightening flat iron
or household iron

Two 6-inch (15.2 cm)
pink pipe cleaners

Needle felting supplies
(page 16)

Ribbon

FINISHED MEASUREMENTS
5½ inches (14 cm) tall

1. Following steps 2–6 of Making Pompoms by Hand on pages 19–21, make a 3-inch (7.6 cm) smooth, fat, egg-shaped pompom from pink yarn for the head. I used approximately ⅓ skein of Patons medium-weight Classic Wool, which is approximately 69 yards (63 m).

2. Because the narrower end of the pompom head will become the Piglet's nose, after shaping the head and snout (see Tips on Shaping the Nose and Muzzle, page 21), trim the snout's end flat.

3. Take a bit of pink wool felt and cut an oval about ¾ x ½ inch (1.9 x 1.3 cm). Embroider two little nostrils using French knots or simple straight stitches with the pink embroidery floss. Glue the little oval onto the end of the nose to make the Piglet's snout.

4. Using the inverted triangle layout (see Positioning the Nose and Eyes on page 22), decide where you want the eyes to be. Make a part in the yarn, carefully squeeze in a pea-size drop of glue for each eye, and gently insert the wire end of each glass eye into the pompom. Let the glue dry.

5. Using the template on page 121, cut two ears from the pink wool felt. With the template as a guide, use a flat iron or household iron to create a crease at the base of the Piglet's ears so they will flop over.

6. Make a small part on each side of the head, squeeze a bit of glue into each part in the wool fibers, and insert the ears. Pinch the fibers around the base of the ears to secure them and let the glue dry.

7. Make another slightly larger pompom from pink yarn and trim it into a pear-shaped pompom for the body, measuring approximately 4 inches (10.2 cm) in length and diameter. I used

approximately ½ skein of Patons medium-weight Classic Wool, which is approximately 105 yards (96 m). To create the illusion of the Piglet's tummy and haunches as it sits, trim out a V shape from the front center bottom of the belly area.

8. Glue a pipe cleaner into the top half of the pompom body. Simply make a horizontal part deep into the wool at the top, squeeze in a dime-size dollop of glue, and place the pipe cleaner snugly down into it. Pinch the fibers of the wool yarn around the pipe cleaner to secure it. This will become the frame for the arms of the Piglet, which you will needle felt. (See Creating Appendages on page 24.)

9. After the pipe cleaner and glue have set up, take a thick bacon-size strip of pink roving and wrap it tightly around each pipe cleaner arm. Use more roving near the upper arm and shoulder area and taper off at the end to form a tiny hoof. Needle felt the roving tightly to compact it around the pipe cleaner so it will not unravel (see Needle Felting Appendages on page 24).

10. Needle felt the Piglet's feet by rolling a golf ball–size bit of pink roving into a cigarlike shape and continue needle felting to compact it down. Once it is a tight, dense 3-inch (7.6 cm) cigar shape, cut it evenly in half to make the two feet.

11. Take your scissors and vertically snip the ends of all four appendages to create the cloven hooves on the Piglet. Continue to needle felt the loose roving ends and shape them into hooves.

12. Glue the finished head onto the body. To create a cute, inquisitive expression, tilt the head to one side. Squeeze a nickel-size dollop of glue at the top of the body pompom and position the head as desired. You will need to let the glue set up and dry, which can take a while. To keep the head from falling off before the glue sets up, use a long floral pin to hold it in place. Remove the pin after the glue has set up and dried.

13. For the tail, cut a 4-inch (10.2 cm) length of pink pipe cleaner and twist it around a pencil to make a corkscrew. Make a part at the bottom backside of the Piglet, squeeze in a small dollop of glue, and insert the tail. Gently pinch the wool fibers around the tail to secure it. Let dry.

14. Embellish your little Piglet with a ribbon.

Squirrel

Squirrels pair curiosity and cuteness to perfection: this chap's bushy tail and inquisitive look complete his lively expression. Give him a pal or two to keep him company up in the trees by making the Bluebird or Raccoon.

1. Following steps 2–6 for Making Pompoms by Hand on pages 19–21, make a 2½-inch (6.4 cm) fat, egg-shaped pompom from gray yarn for the head. I used approximately ⅓ skein of Patons medium-weight Classic Wool, which is approximately 69 yards (63 m).

2. On the narrow end of the egg shape, locate where you want the nose to be. Make a small part into the pile of the yarn, place a small drop of glue in the part, and insert the pink seed bead. Gently pinch the fibers around the glue and the bead to secure it. Let dry.

3. Using the inverted triangle layout (see Positioning the Nose and Eyes on page 22), decide where you want the eyes to be. Make a part in the yarn, carefully squeeze in a pea-size drop of glue for each eye, and gently insert the wire end of each glass eye into the pompom. Let the glue dry.

4. Using the template on page 121, cut two ears out of the wool felt, rub the inside of each ear with a bit of pink chalk, and blend it in with your finger. Squeeze a dollop of glue onto the bottom flat part of each ear shape and pinch the lower edge together, with pink inside, to give it dimension. Repeat this for the second ear. Use clothespins or hemostats to hold the ear bases together as they dry.

5. After the ears have dried, make a small part on top of the head over each eye, squeeze a bit of glue into the pile, and insert the ears. Pinch the fibers around the ears to secure them and let dry.

6. Make another slightly larger pompom from gray yarn and trim it into a pear-shaped pompom for the body, about 4 inches (10.2 cm) tall. I used approximately ½ skein of medium-weight Patons Classic Wool, which is approximately 105 yards (96 m). The narrow top will be the Squirrel's neck, and the heavier, rounded end will be the bottom of the Squirrel sitting upright. To create the illusion of the Squirrel's haunches and tummy, trim out a V shape from the front center bottom of the belly area.

7. Glue the pipe cleaner into the top half of the pompom body. Simply make a horizontal part deep into the wool at the top, squeeze in a dime-size dollop of glue, and place the pipe cleaner snugly down into it; pinch the fibers of the wool yarn around the pipe cleaner to secure it. This will become the frame for the arms of the Squirrel, which you will needle felt. (See Creating Appendages on page 24.) Let the glue dry.

YOU WILL NEED

Basic Pompom Toolbox
(page 12)

100% wool yarn: gray

100% wool felt: gray

100% wool roving: gray

100% wool roving yarn: gray

Pink seed bead

2 black glass eyes,
10 or 12 mm

Template:
ears (page 121)

Pink chalk

6-inch (15.2 cm)
gray pipe cleaner

Needle felting supplies
(page 16)

Ribbons

Piece of a tree branch, limb,
or trunk, 3 inches (7.6 cm)
in diameter, for the base

FINISHED MEASUREMENTS
**5½ inches (14 cm) tall
(without the wooden base)**

Squirrel

81

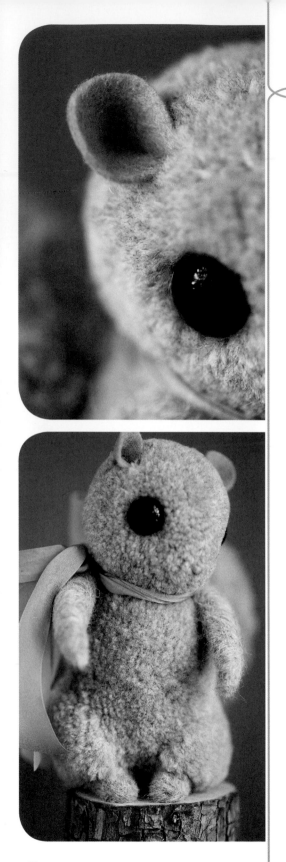

8. Glue the finished head onto the body. To create a cute, inquisitive expression, tilt the head to one side. Squeeze a nickel-size dollop of glue at the top of the body pompom and position the head as desired. You will need to let the glue set up and dry, which can take a few hours. To keep the head from falling off before the glue sets up, use a long floral pin to hold it in place. Remove the pin after the glue has set up.

9. After the glue has fully dried, bend the pipe cleaner into the desired position and trim each arm to approximately 2 ½ inches (6.4 cm). Bend down and crimp the sharp ends of the pipe cleaners because they will poke through the needle-felted paws.

10. Needle felt the Squirrel's feet by rolling a golf ball–size bit of wool roving into a cigarlike shape and needle felting to compact it down. Once it is a tight, dense 3-inch (7.6 cm) cigar shape, cut it evenly in half to make the two little feet.

11. At the bottom of the pear shape make two separate parts into the wool "fur" and glue and insert the feet into the body. Let it dry standing upright.

12. After the pipe cleaner and glue have set up, wrap a thick bacon-size strip of roving tightly around the pipe cleaner armatures from top to bottom. Use more roving near the upper arm and shoulder area and taper it toward the end to form a tiny paw. Needle felt the roving tightly to compact it around the pipe cleaner so it will not unravel. Bend down at the wrist to create the illusion of paws.

13. For the tail, make another pompom from wool roving yarn. I used approximately ⅓ skein of Patons bulky-weight Classic Wool Roving yarn, which is approximately 40 yards (36 m). The Squirrel's tail looks like a rounded arc with longer, fluffier roving yarn at the end, and shorter, denser roving yarn at the base. The knotted waxed twine will be located in the center of the tail's curved arc. Begin shaping the pompom by trimming the fibers on one side of the waxed twine shorter than the other side, as the shorter, denser part of the tail will be attached to the Squirrel's body. On the other side of the twine, trim the roving yarn fibers so they're slightly longer and fluffier. The longer fibers will naturally tend to droop a bit, which will create the curve of the tail. Comb the fibers with your fingers as you gradually sculpt the curved tail to approximately 6 to 7 inches (15.2 to 17.8 cm) long.

14. Make a large part in the back of the Squirrel's body and squeeze in a big dollop of glue both in the part and on the lower portion of one side of the tail; snugly insert the glued pompom tail into the part. To hold the tail in place as the glue sets up, tie a ribbon or a pipe cleaner around the tail and the body; remove it when the glue is dry. Please note that the tail often makes the Squirrel heavy in the back, so your Squirrel may tip. Gluing the Squirrel onto a simple base (like the tree section shown) will keep this from happening.

15. Tie a ribbon or two around your Squirrel's neck.

❋ **NOTE**: *Want to make additional embellishments for your Squirrel? Needle felt an acorn, which the Squirrel can hold in its front paws. Tiny woven baskets found in miniature shops and filled with millinery flowers, berries, or pinecones are another cute object for your Squirrel to hold.*

Raccoon

Don't be fooled by his endearing black mask and beguiling gaze, this Raccoon is a little woodland bandit: he might very well steal your heart.

1. Following steps 2–6 of Making Pompoms by Hand on pages 19–21, make a 2½- to 3-inch (6.4 to 7.6 cm) egg-shaped pompom from gray, cream, and black yarn for the head. Wind the yarns side by side (see Making Multicolor Pompoms on page 30) in the following order: gray, cream, black, cream. I used approximately ¼ skein of gray Patons medium-weight Classic Wool, which is approximately 53 yards (48 m); ⅛ skein, or 26 yards (24 m), of cream; ¼ skein, or 53 yards (48 m), of black; and ¼ skein, or 53 yards (48 m), of cream.

2. The gray will be at the top of the Raccoon's head. The next cream patch will be part of its face, the black will be the "mask" around the eyes, and the remaining cream patch at the edge of the pompom will be sculpted and trimmed into the Raccoon's pointed, narrow nose (see Tips on Shaping the Nose and Muzzle, page 21).

3. On the pointed snout, locate where you want the nose to be. Make a small part into the "fur," place a small drop of glue in the part, and insert the black seed bead. Pinch the fibers around the glue and the bead to secure it.

4. Using the inverted triangle layout (see Positioning the Nose and Eyes on page 22), decide where you want the eyes to be. Make a part in the yarn, carefully squeeze in a pea-size drop of glue for each eye, and gently insert the wire end of each glass eye into the pompom. Let the glue dry.

5. Using the template on page 123, cut two ears out of the gray wool felt. Make a small part on top of the head over each eye, squeeze a bit of glue into the pile, and insert the ears. Pinch the fibers around each ear to secure it and let the glue dry.

6. Following the instructions for Creating and Attaching Whiskers (page 22), thread a sewing needle with a 5-inch (12.7 cm) double strand of black upholstery thread. Tie a knot in the center, place a tiny smidge of glue on the knot, and "sew" in the whiskers. Snip off any excess so the whiskers are even on both sides.

7. Make another slightly larger pompom from gray yarn and trim it to a pear shape for the body, about 4¼ inches (10.8 cm) tall. I used approximately ½ skein of Patons medium-weight Classic Wool, which is approximately 105 yards (96 m). The narrow top

YOU WILL NEED

Basic Pompom Toolbox
(page 12)

100% wool yarn:
gray, cream, black

100% wool felt: gray

100% wool roving:
gray, black

Black seed bead

2 black glass eyes,
10 or 12 mm

Template:
ears (page 123)

Sewing needle

Black upholstery thread

6-inch (15.2 cm)
gray pipe cleaner

Needle felting supplies
(page 16)

Ribbon

FINISHED MEASUREMENTS
6½ inches (16.5 cm) tall

will be the Raccoon's neck and the heavier, rounded end will be the bottom of the Raccoon as it sits upright. To create the illusion of the seated Raccoon's haunches and tummy, trim out a V shape from the front center bottom of the belly area.

8. Glue the pipe cleaner into the top half of the pompom body. Simply make a horizontal part deep into the wool at the top, squeeze in a dime-size dollop of glue, and place the pipe cleaner snugly down into it. Pinch the fibers of the wool yarn around the pipe cleaner to secure it. This will become the frame for the arms of the Raccoon, which you will needle felt. (See Creating Appendages on page 24.)

9. Glue the finished head onto the body. Squeeze a nickel-size dollop of glue at the top of the body pompom and position the head as desired. To keep the head from shifting or falling off before the glue sets up, use a long floral pin to hold it in place. Remove the pin after the glue has set up and dried.

10. After the glue has fully dried, bend the pipe cleaners into the desired position and trim each arm to approximately 2½ inches (6.4 cm). Bend down and tightly crimp the sharp cut ends of the pipe cleaners because they will poke through the needle-felted paws.

11. Take a thick bacon-size strip of gray roving and wrap it tightly around the pipe cleaner arms. Use more roving near the upper arm and shoulder area and taper off at the end to form a tiny paw. Needle felt the roving tightly to make it compact around the pipe cleaner so it will not unravel (see Needle Felting Appendages on page 24). Needle felt black roving to the front paws as well, so the Raccoon has little black socks. Shave off excess "fuzzies" with scissors for a neater appearance, if desired.

12. Make the Raccoon's feet by rolling a golf ball–size bit of black roving into a cigarlike shape and start needle felting to compact it down. Once it is a tight, dense 3-inch (7.6 cm) cigar shape, cut it evenly in half to make the two feet.

13. At the bottom of the pear shape make two separate slits into the wool "fur" and glue the hind feet into the body, adjusting them as necessary so the Raccoon sits upright. Let dry.

14. For the tail, wind the gray and black yarns side by side (see Making Multicolor Pompoms on page 30) in the following order: gray, black, gray, black. I used approximately ⅓ skein of gray Patons medium-weight Classic Wool, which is approximately 69 yards (63 m); ⅛ skein, or 26 yards (24 m) of black; ⅛ skein, or 26 yards (24 m) of gray; and ⅛ skein, or 26 yards (24 m) of black. Instead of trimming the pompom into a ball shape, however, trim it into a straighter torpedo shape approximately 6 inches (15.2 cm) in length with the black end yarn at the tip of the Raccoon's tail.

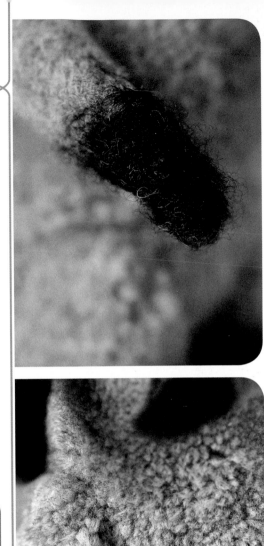

15. For added structural security when attaching the tail, snip a piece of pipe cleaner approximately 1 to 2 inches (2.5 to 5.1 cm) and glue it into the end of the tail that will be attached to the body. Let dry. Make a part at the bottom backside, squeeze a dollop of glue into the part, and gently but snugly insert the end of the tail with the attached pipe cleaner. Gently pinch the wool fibers to secure the tail. To hold the tail in place on the body as the glue sets up, tie a ribbon or a pipe cleaner around the tail and the body, then remove it when the glue is dry.

16. Embellish your Raccoon with a ribbon.

Raccoon

Hedgehog

You won't have to avoid prickly spikes on this little guy—his soft, fluffy backside is made with wool roving yarn, and his sweet expression is just meant for company. Perhaps he's waiting for his woodland friends, Raccoon and Fox, to come for tea.

1. Following steps 2–6 of Making Pompoms by Hand on pages 19–21, make a 3-inch (7.6 cm) pompom from both brown roving yarn and cream wool yarn for the head. Wind the yarns side by side (see Making Multicolor Pompoms on page 30); I used approximately ¼ skein of Patons bulky-weight Classic Wool Roving yarn, which is approximately 30 yards (27 m), in brown, and approximately ¼ skein of Patons Classic Wool, which is approximately 53 yards (48 m), in cream.

2. The cream yarn will become the Hedgehog's face; move all the cream yarn to one side of the pompom. Sculpt and trim the cream yarn into a more pointed and narrower shape for the Hedgehog's snout and nose (see Tips on Shaping the Nose and Muzzle, page 21). Continue to carefully trim and shave down the cream yarn only, cutting it approximately ¼ inch (6 mm) lower than the fluffier brown roving yarn. The longer brown roving yarn forms the Hedgehog's spiky hair on its head.

3. On the cream yarn at the narrow end of the egg shape, locate where you want the nose to be. Make a small part into the "fur" of the yarn, place a small drop of glue, and insert the black seed bead. Pinch the fibers around the glue and the bead to secure it. Let the glue dry.

4. Using the inverted triangle layout (see Positioning the Nose and Eyes on page 22), decide where you want the eyes to be. Make a part in the yarn, carefully squeeze in a pea-size drop of glue for each eye, and gently insert the wire end of each glass eye into the pompom. Let the glue dry.

5. Using the template on page 121, cut two ears out of the cream wool felt. Rub the inside of each ear with pink chalk and blend it in with your finger. Make a small part between the brown roving yarn and the cream face yarn over each eye, squeeze a bit of glue into the parts, and insert the ears. Pinch the fibers around the ears to secure them and let them dry.

6. Make another slightly larger pompom by mixing brown roving yarn and cream wool yarn and trim it into a slightly pear-shaped pompom for the body, about 3¾ inches (9.5 cm) tall. I used approximately ⅓ skein of brown Patons bulky-weight Classic Wool Roving yarn, which is approximately 40 yards (36 m), and ⅓ skein

YOU WILL NEED

Basic Pompom Toolbox
(page 12)

100% wool yarn:
cream

100% wool felt:
cream

100% wool roving yarn:
brown

100% wool roving:
brown

Black seed bead

2 black glass eyes,
10 or 12 mm

Template:
ears (page 121)

Pink chalk

6-inch (15.2 cm) pipe cleaner

Needle felting supplies
(page 16)

Ribbon

FINISHED MEASUREMENTS
6 ½ inches (16.5 cm) tall

of cream Patons medium-weight Classic Wool, which is approximately 69 yards (63 m). The cream yarn will be the Hedgehog's tummy. Using the heavier, fuller end of the pompom as the bottom, start shaping and trimming the pompom into a rounded shape. To create the definition of the Hedgehog's tummy and haunches, carefully trim cream yarn on the center bottom of the belly area (see Shaping Pompoms page 29). Allow the brown roving yarn to remain a bit longer like the spiky hair around the face.

7. Glue the pipe cleaner into the top half of the pompom body. Simply make a horizontal part deep into the wool at the top, squeeze a dime-size dollop of glue, and place the pipe cleaner snugly down into it; pinch the fibers of the wool yarn to secure it. This will become the frame for the arms of the Hedgehog, which you will needle felt. (See Creating Appendages on page 24.)

8. Glue the finished head onto the body. To create a cute, inquisitive expression, tilt the head to one side. Squeeze a nickel-size dollop of glue at the top of the body pompom and position the head as desired. To keep the head from shifting or falling off before the glue sets, use a long floral pin to hold it in place until dry. Remove the pin after the glue has set up and dried.

9. After the glue has fully dried, bend the pipe cleaners into the desired position and trim each arm to approximately 2 1/2 inches (6.4 cm). Bend down and tightly crimp the sharp ends of the pipe cleaners because they will poke through the needle-felted ends of the paws.

10. Needle felt the Hedgehog's feet by rolling a golf ball–size bit of brown roving into a cigarlike shape and start needle felting to compact it down (see Attaching Feet and Small Appendages on page 26). Once it is a tight, compact 3-inch (7.6 cm) cigar shape, cut it evenly in half to make the two feet.

11. At the bottom of the body pompom make two separate slits into the wool "fur" and glue the hind feet into the body. Let it dry sitting upright.

12. After the pipe cleaner and glue have set up, take a thick, bacon-size strip of roving and wrap it tightly around the pipe cleaner arms. Use more roving near the upper top of the arm and shoulder area and taper it off at the end to form a tiny paw. Needle felt the roving tightly to make it compact around the pipe cleaner so it will not unravel (see Needle Felting Appendages on page 24).

13. Tie a ribbon around your Hedgehog's neck.

Fox

Foxes are often referred to as the thieves of the animal kingdom, and this little fox is sure to steal your heart.

1. Following steps 2–5 of Making Pompoms by Hand on pages 19–21, make a round ball-shaped pompom from both orange and white yarns for the head. Wind the yarns side by side (see Making Multicolor Pompoms on page 30); I used approximately ⅓ skein of orange Patons medium-weight Classic Wool, which is approximately 69 yards (63 m), and ¼ skein, which is approximately 53 yards (48 m), of white.

2. The Fox's face is orange with a white chin. Assess your pompom and determine how you will begin trimming and sculpting the rough, uneven ball into a smooth, sculpted egg shape, 3 inches (7.6 cm) in diameter, with the top of the head in orange and the bottom in white. The Fox's nose should fall roughly where the orange and white yarns meet. With this in mind, trim the narrow end of the egg shape into the nose, sculpting it to be more tapered and pointy. (See Tips on Shaping the Nose and Muzzle, page 21.)

3. Locate where you want the nose to be between the orange and white yarn and make a small part into the "fur." Place a small drop of glue and insert a black seed bead for the nose. Pinch the fibers around the glue and bead to secure it. Let dry.

4. Using the inverted triangle layout (see Positioning the Nose and Eyes on page 22), decide where you want the eyes to be. Make a part in the yarn, carefully squeeze in a pea-size drop of glue for each eye, and gently insert the wire end of each glass eye into the pompom. Let the glue dry.

5. Using the template on page 123, cut two triangular ears from the orange wool felt. Rub some black chalk around the outer edge of the ears, if desired.

6. Make a small part on top of the head over each eye and squeeze a bit of glue into the part of the wool fibers; insert the ears. Pinch the fibers around the base of the ears to secure them, and let dry.

7. Following the instructions for Creating and Attaching Whiskers on page 22, thread a sewing needle with a 5-inch (12.7 cm) double strand of black upholstery thread. Tie a knot in the middle, place a tiny smidge of glue on the knot, and "sew" in the short whiskers. The knot should be positioned approximately in the center front of the head. Snip off any excess so the whiskers are even on both sides.

YOU WILL NEED

Basic Pompom Toolbox
(page 12)

100% wool yarn: orange,
white or cream, black

100% wool felt:
orange

100% wool roving:
orange, black (optional)

Black seed bead

2 black glass eyes,
10 or 12 mm

Template:
ears (page 123)

Black chalk (optional)

Sewing needle

Black upholstery thread

8-inch (20.3 cm)
orange pipe cleaner

2-inch (5.1 cm)
orange pipe cleaner

Needle felting supplies
(see page 16)

FINISHED MEASUREMENTS
6 inches (15.2 cm) tall

8. Make another slightly larger pompom and trim it into a 4¼-inch (10.7 cm) pear-shaped pompom for the body, again mixing orange and white yarns side by side. I used approximately ½ skein of orange Patons medium-weight Classic Wool, which is approximately 105 yards (96 m), and approximately ⅓ skein, or 69 yards (63 m), of white. The white yarn will become the Fox's tummy. The narrower top of the pompom will be the Fox's neck, and the heavier, rounded end will become the bottom of the Fox as it sits upright. To create the illusion of the Fox's haunches and tummy, carefully trim the white yarn into a V shape on the center bottom of the white belly area.

9. Glue the 8-inch (20.3 cm) pipe cleaner into the top half of the pompom body. Make a part in the top of the narrow end of the pompom body. Squeeze in a dime-size dollop of glue. Place the pipe cleaner snugly down into the part, and pinch the fibers of the wool yarn to secure it. This will become the frame for the arms of the Fox, which you will needle felt. (See Creating Appendages on page 24.)

10. Glue the finished head onto the body. Squeeze in a nickel-size dollop of glue at the top of the body pompom and position the head as desired. You will need to let the glue set up and dry, which can take a while. To keep the head from falling off before the glue sets up, use a long floral pin to hold it in place. Remove the pin after the glue has set up and dried.

11. After the glue has fully dried, bend the pipe cleaner into the desired position and trim each arm to approximately 3 inches (7.6 cm). Bend down and tightly crimp the sharp cut ends of the pipe cleaners because they can poke through and show at the ends of the needle-felted paws.

12. Needle felt the Fox's hind feet by rolling a golf ball–size bit of orange roving into a cigarlike shape and start needle felting to compact it (see Attaching Feet and Small Appendages on page 26). Once it is a tight, dense 3-inch (7.6 cm) cigar shape, cut it evenly in half to make the two back paws. If you wish, needle felt black roving onto the end of these paws.

13. At the bottom of the pear-shaped body, make two separate long slits into the wool "fur" and glue the feet into the body. Let it dry sitting upright.

14. After the glue has set up, take a thick bacon-size strip of roving and wrap it tightly, top to bottom, around the pipe cleaner arms. Use more roving near the upper arm and shoulder area and taper off at the end to form a paw. Needle felt the roving tightly to make it compact around the pipe cleaner so it will not unravel (see Needle Felting Appendages on page 24). Needle felt black roving to the front paws as well, so the Fox has little black socks. Shave off excess "fuzzies" with scissors for a neater appearance, if desired.

15. For the tail, make an additional 6-inch (15.2 cm) pompom, again winding the orange and white yarn side by side. I used approximately ⅓ skein of orange Patons medium-weight Classic Wool, which is approximately 69 yards (63 m), and ¼ skein, which is approximately 53 yards (48 m), of white. Instead of trimming the pompom into a ball shape, however, trim it into a straighter torpedo shape approximately 6 inches (15.2 cm) in length with the white yarn at the tip of the Fox's tail.

16. For added structural security when attaching the tail, snip a piece of pipe cleaner approximately 1 to 2 inches (2.5 to 5.1 cm) and glue it into the end of the tail that will be attached to the body. Let dry. Make a part at the bottom backside, squeeze a dollop of glue into the part, and gently but snugly insert the end of the tail with the attached pipe cleaner. Gently pinch the wool fibers to secure the tail. You can use a piece of ribbon or an extra pipe cleaner to temporarily tie the tail to the Fox's body pompom as it dries in place.

✽ **NOTE:** *If you cannot find matching orange wool felt and orange yarn, you can dye cream-colored yarn, roving, and wool felt using orange dye found in many craft and grocery stores. Simply follow the directions on the package to make custom colors.*

Pony

For all of us who wished we had a pony in our childhood, here's our chance!
Move over, Black Beauty: this pompom cutie is galloping onto the scene.

1. Following steps 2–6 of Making Pompoms by Hand on pages 19–21, make a 3-inch (7.6 cm) smooth, fat, egg-shaped pompom from white or cream yarn for the head. I used approximately ⅓ skein of Patons medium-weight Classic Wool, which is approximately 69 yards (63 m).

2. On the narrow end of the shaped pompom, locate where you want the nose to be. Make two small marks with pink chalk for the nostrils and blend them in with your finger.

3. Using the inverted triangle pattern (see Positioning the Nose and Eyes, page 22), decide where you want the eyes to be; ponies' eyes are typically spaced far apart, one on each side of the head. Make a part in the yarn, carefully squeeze in a pea-size drop of glue for each eye, and gently insert the wire end of each glass eye into the pompom. Let the glue dry.

4. Using the template on page 123, cut two ears out of the wool felt. Rub pink chalk inside each ear and blend it in with your finger. To create dimension, place a bit of glue along the straight bottom of each ear and pinch the edges together, with the pink inside. Use clothespins or hemostats to hold the ear bases in place while they dry.

5. After the ears have dried, make a tiny part in the wool on top of the head over each eye and squeeze a bit of glue into the wool fibers; insert the ears. Pinch the fibers around the base of the ears to secure them and let dry.

6. Make another slightly larger pompom from white yarn and trim it into a fat bun-shaped pompom for the body measuring approximately 4 inches (10.2) in length and diameter. I used approximately ½ skein of Patons medium-weight Classic Wool, which is approximately 105 yards (96 m).

7. To create the Pony's legs, use your wire cutters to cut four equal pieces from the wooden dowel to create legs approximately 3 inches (7.6 cm) long.

8. Wrap each leg thickly in wool roving and needle felt around the dowel (see Needle Felting Appendages on page 24). Needle felt the roving tightly; the upper end should be slightly thicker than the bottom of the leg and the back legs should be a bit thicker than

Pony

❋ **NOTE**: *You can turn this Pony into a magical Unicorn by needle felting a thin, white cone-shaped horn and gluing it into the forehead.*

the front legs. Be sure to needle felt over the bottom of the dowels so they are not exposed. Shave off any excess "fuzzies" with scissors for a neater appearance, if desired.

9. Make four deep parts on the bottom of the Pony's body where you want to position the legs. Add glue in each part and insert the legs, firmly pinching the wool fibers around the legs to secure them. Adjust the legs as necessary so the Pony can stand. Let it dry standing upright.

10. To make the Pony's neck, fold the pipe cleaner in half. Cut the two ends so it is approximately 2 ½ inches (6.4 cm) in length. Take a thick piece of wool roving and wrap it around the pipe cleaner to make a fat cylindrical shape about 1 ¾ inches (4.4 cm) in diameter at the base and 1 ¼ inches (3.2 cm) in diameter at the top. Needle felt and compact the fibers down tightly. Trim any excess "fuzzies," if desired.

11. With the pipe cleaners sticking out of each end of the neck, the thicker part of the neck will be glued to the body. Squeeze a nickel-size dollop of glue into the body pompom and insert the neck. Pinch the fibers around the neck to secure it. Let dry.

12. Glue the finished head onto the top of the neck. You will need to let the glue set up and dry, which can take a while. To keep the head from shifting or falling off before the glue sets up, lay the Pony on its side and use a long floral pin to hold the head in place until dry. Remove the pin after the glue has set up and dried.

13. For the tail, cut approximately twelve 4-inch (10.2 cm) pieces of wool roving yarn. Tie the ends together. Make a part at the bottom backside, squeeze in a small dollop of glue, and gently insert the knotted end of the tail. Gently pinch the wool fibers around the tail to secure it. Let dry.

14. To create the mane, tie wool roving yarn into approximately ten bundles of 2-inch long (5.1 cm) strands. Using the sharp, pointed ends of the scissors, puncture holes along the top of the neck and head and squeeze in a bit of glue. Stuff the knotted ends of the bundles into the holes and pinch the fibers around the yarn bundles to secure them. Let dry. Trim the mane so it is shorter by the ears and eyes and longer on the neck.

15. Embellish your Pony with a ribbon and millinery flowers, as desired.

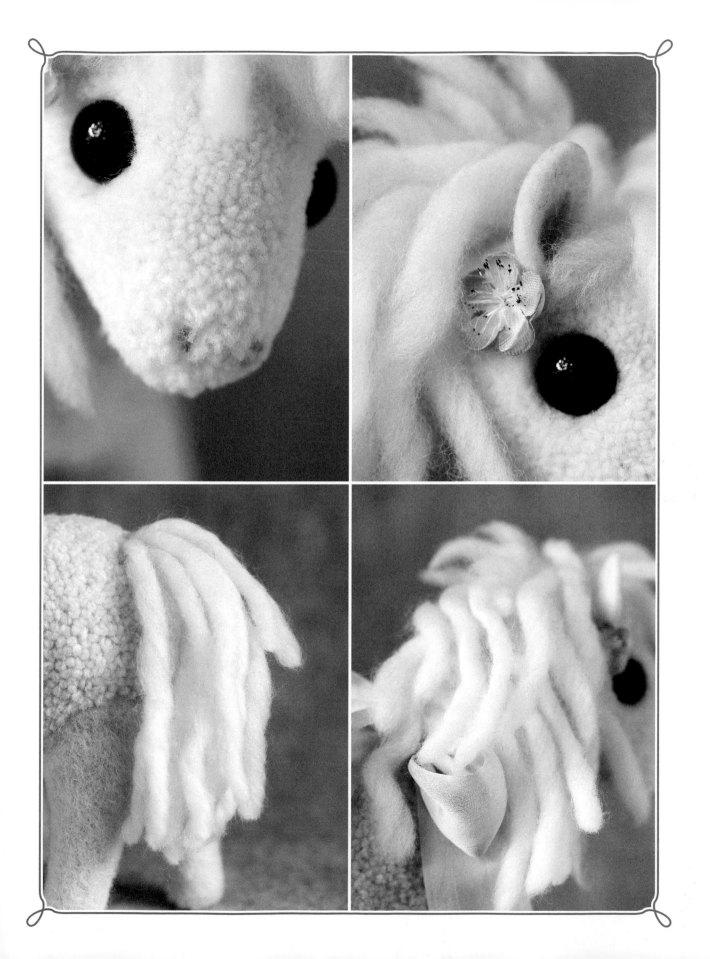

Snowy Owl

This fine-feathered friend is made with both yarn and roving yarn, which gives his tail feathers their longer, fluffier look. Try using larger glass eyes to give him an owlish gaze.

1. Following steps 2–6 of Making Pompoms by Hand on pages 19–21, make a 3-inch (7.6 cm) oval-shaped pompom from both bulky-weight white roving yarn and medium-weight cream yarn for the head. Wind the yarns side by side (see Making Multicolor Pompoms on page 30); I used approximately 1/3 skein of Patons Classic Wool Roving, which is approximately 40 yards (36 m), and approximately 1/8 skein of Patons Classic Wool, which is approximately 26 yards (24 m). The roving yarn is chunkier and thicker, which better lends itself to create the illusion of feathers; the other yarn will be sculpted to become the smooth part of the Owl's face.

2. Although both yarns are the same color, you will be able to see the difference between the textures of the roving yarn and the regular wool yarn. Push, pull, and gently manipulate the regular yarn to one side of the pompom, which will become the front of the Owl's head and face. Begin shaping and trimming the regular wool yarn into a heart shape, cutting it 1/4 inch (6 mm) lower than the fluffier roving yarn. This area defines the Owl's face.

3. Using the inverted triangle layout (see Positioning the Nose and Eyes on page 22), decide where you want the eyes to be. Make a part in the yarn, carefully squeeze in a pea-size drop of glue for each eye, and gently insert the wire end of each glass eye into the pompom. Let the glue dry.

4. Using the template on page 121, cut out the beak shape from beige wool felt.

5. Place the beak in the center of the face area. Make a small part into the pile of the yarn and place a small drop of glue. Attach the beak. Gently pinch the fibers around the glue and the felt beak to secure it. Let the glue dry.

6. Make another slightly larger pompom from the roving yarn and trim it into an oblong bun-shaped pompom for the body, about 4 1/2 inches (11.4 cm) tall and about 6 inches (15.2 cm) from the front of the chest to the tip of the tail feathers. I used approximately 1/2 skein of Patons bulky-weight Classic Wool Roving yarn, which is approximately 60 yards (55 m). Leave the roving yarn longer on one end to cut and shape the fluffy tail feathers.

YOU WILL NEED

Basic Pompom Toolbox
(page 12)

100% wool yarn:
cream

100% wool felt:
beige

100% wool roving yarn:
cream

2 black glass eyes,
14 mm

Template:
beak (page 121)

32 inches (81.3 cm) of
18-gauge floral wire

Embroidery floss or
perle cotton:
yellow or orange

Ribbon

FINISHED MEASUREMENTS
7 3/4 inches (19.7 cm) tall

7. Place the oval head on the body horizontally. To create a cute, inquisitive expression, tilt the head to one side. Squeeze a nickel-size dollop of glue at the top of the body pompom and position the head as desired. You will need to let the glue set up and dry, which can take a few hours. To keep the head from falling off before the glue sets up, use a long floral pin to hold it in place. Remove the pin after the glue has set up and dried.

8. Using wire cutters, cut eight 4-inch (10.2 cm) pieces of floral wire.

9. To create each foot, hold four pieces of wire together and lightly coat the bundle with glue. Working from top to bottom, wind the embroidery floss or perle cotton tightly and uniformly around the bundle of four wires. Stop approximately 1½ inches (3.8 cm) from the bottom. Bend each of the four wires out at 90° angles to make individual toes. Three will face forward; one will face backward to provide the support needed for the bird to stand. Continue wrapping each "toe" wire individually with embroidery floss to cover the floral wire. Repeat with the remaining four pieces of floral wire to create the other leg. Use wire cutters to snip off any excess wire length. Tuck any ends of embroidery floss underneath and let the glue dry.

10. At the bottom of the Owl's body, make two separate parts into the wool plush for the legs and squeeze a dollop of glue into each. Insert the wire legs snugly into the body. Pinch the wool fibers around the wrapped wires to secure them. Set the Snowy Owl upright and make any adjustments necessary so that it can stand. Let it dry in this position.

11. Tie a ribbon around your Snowy Owl's neck.

Halloween Imp

A roguish little imp can be a playful project for Halloween or perhaps a mischievous companion to a Valentine's Day cherub.

Basic Pompom Toolbox
(page 12)

100% wool yarn:
bright red

100% wool felt:
bright red, black

100% wool roving:
bright red

Pink seed bead

2 black glass eyes,
10 or 12 mm

Templates: ears, horns, tail,
pitchfork (page 122)

Two 6-inch (15.2 cm)
red pipe cleaners

Needle felting supplies
(page 16)

4-inch (10.2 cm) length
of wooden dowel,
2 mm in diameter

Wire cutters

Black craft paint

Paintbrush

Black ribbon (optional)

FINISHED MEASUREMENTS
Imp: 5 ¾ inches
(14.6 cm) tall
Pitchfork: 6 inches
(15.2 cm) tall

1. Following steps 2–6 of Making Pompoms by Hand on pages 19–21, make a 2½- to 3-inch (6.4 to 7.6 cm) smooth, round, ball-shaped pompom from bright red yarn for the head. I used approximately ⅓ skein of Patons medium-weight Classic Wool, which is approximately 69 yards (63 m).

2. Locate the center of the pompom where you want the nose to be and make a small part into the yarn. Squeeze in a small drop of glue and insert a pink seed bead. Pinch the fibers around the glue and bead to secure it. Let dry.

3. Using the inverted triangle layout (see Positioning the Nose and Eyes on page 22), decide where you want the eyes to be. Make a part in the yarn, carefully squeeze in a pea-size drop of glue for each eye, and gently insert the wire end of each glass eye into the pompom. Let the glue dry.

4. Using the templates on page 122, cut two ears and two horns out of the red wool felt.

5. Make a small part on top of the head over each eye and squeeze a bit of glue into each part; insert the horns. Pinch the fibers around each horn to secure it, and let dry.

6. On each side of the head make a small part and squeeze a drop or two of glue into the part; insert the ears. Pinch the fibers around each ear to secure it and let dry.

7. Make another slightly larger pompom from red yarn and trim it into a pear shape for the body, about 4 inches (10.2 cm) tall. I used approximately ½ skein of Patons medium-weight Classic Wool, which is approximately 105 yards (96 m). The narrow top will be the Imp's neck and the heavier, rounded end will be the bottom of the Imp as it sits upright. To create the illusion of the Imp's haunches and tummy, trim out a V shape from the front center bottom of the belly area.

8. Glue a pipe cleaner into the top half of the pompom body. Simply make a horizontal part deep into the wool at the top, squeeze in a dime-size dollop of glue, and place the pipe cleaner snugly down into the part; pinch the wool fibers around the pipe cleaner to secure it. This will become the frame for the arms of the Imp, which you will needle felt. (See Creating Appendages on page 24.)

9. Glue the finished head onto the body. Squeeze a nickel-size dollop of glue at the top of the body pompom and position the head as desired. To keep the head from falling off before the glue sets up, use a long floral pin to hold it in place until dry. Remove the pin after the glue has set up and dried.

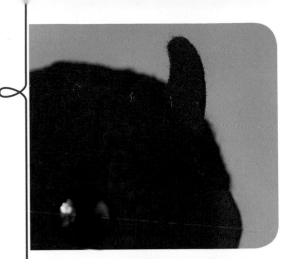

10. After the glue has fully dried, bend the pipe cleaner into the desired arm position and trim each arm to approximately 2½ inches (6.4 cm). Bend down and tightly crimp the sharp cut ends of the pipe cleaners because they will poke through the needle-felted ends.

11. Needle felt the Imp's feet by rolling a golf ball–size bit of red roving into a cigarlike shape and start needle felting to compact it down (see Attaching Feet and Small Appendages on page 26). Once it is a tight, dense 3-inch (7.6 cm) cigar shape, cut it evenly in half to make the two feet.

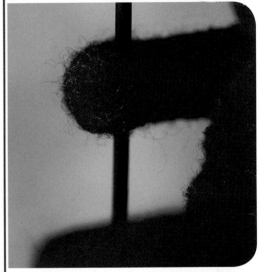

12. At the bottom of the pear shape make two separate slits into the wool "fur" and glue the hind feet into the body. Let it dry standing upright.

13. After the pipe cleaner and glue have set up, take a thick bacon-size strip of the red roving and wrap it tightly, top to bottom, around the pipe cleaner arms. Use more roving near the upper arm and shoulder area and taper off at the end to form a tiny hand. Needle felt the roving tightly to make it compact around the pipe cleaner so it will not unravel (see Needle Felting Appendages on page 24).

14. For the tail, cut a 5-inch (12.7 cm) piece of red pipe cleaner, and using the template on page 122, cut out a triangle from red felt and glue it securely to the end of the pipe cleaner. On the bottom backside of the devil make a part in the wool fiber, add some glue, and insert the tail. Pinch the wool fibers around to secure it. Let dry.

15. To create a tiny pitchfork for your little Imp to hold, cut off a 4-inch (10.2 cm) piece of the wooden dowel with wire cutters and paint it black. Let dry. Using the template on page 122, cut out the pitchfork's trident pattern from black felt and glue it onto the end of the dowel.

16. Place the pitchfork in the little Imp's hand and needle felt or glue it into place.

✿ **NOTE**: *You can also tie a black ribbon around the Imp's neck, if desired.*

Halloween Imp

Halloween Bat

Too cute to be scary, this little bat is sure to make someone smile on Halloween.

1. Following steps 2–6 of Making Pompoms by Hand on pages 19–21, make a 2½-inch (6.4 cm) round ball-shaped pompom from purple yarn for the head. I used approximately ⅓ skein of Patons medium-weight Classic Wool, which is approximately 69 yards (63 m).

2. Locate the center of the pompom where you want the nose to be and make a small part into the yarn, place a small drop of glue, and insert the pink seed bead. Pinch the fibers around the glue and bead to secure it. Let dry.

3. Using the inverted triangle layout (see Positioning the Nose and Eyes on page 22), decide where you want the eyes to be. Make a part in the yarn, carefully squeeze in a pea-size drop of glue for each eye, and gently insert the wire end of each glass eye into the pompom. Let the glue dry.

4. Using the template on page 121, cut two ears from the wool felt. Rub a little pink chalk inside each ear and blend it in with your finger. Place glue on the flat end of one ear and pinch the edge together, with the pink chalk inside, to create dimension. Repeat this for the second ear. Use clothespins or hemostats to hold the ear bases together until they are dry.

YOU WILL NEED

Basic Pompom Toolbox
(page 12)

100% wool yarn:
purple

100% wool felt:
purple

100% wool roving:
purple

Pink seed bead

2 black glass eyes,
10 or 12 mm

Templates:
ears, wings (page 121)

Pink chalk

Needle felting supplies
(page 16)

Black ribbon

FINISHED MEASUREMENTS
5½ inches (14 cm) tall

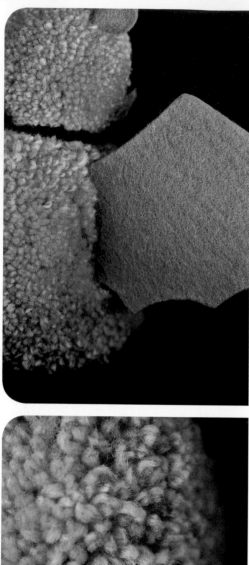

5. Make a small part on top of the head over each eye and squeeze in a bit of glue. Insert the ears and pinch the wool fibers around the ears to secure them. Let dry.

6. Make another slightly larger pompom from the purple yarn and trim it into a pear shape for the body, about 4 inches (10.2 cm) tall. I used approximately ½ skein of Patons medium-weight Classic Wool, which is approximately 105 yards (96 m). The narrower top will be the Bat's neck, and the heavier, rounded end will be the bottom of the Bat as it sits upright.

7. Using the template on page 121, cut two wings from the purple wool felt. Make a deep vertical part on the right side of the Bat's body. Squeeze a line of glue into the part and place the edge of a felt wing snugly into the part, pinching the fibers of the wool yarn to secure it. Repeat this process for the left wing and let the glue dry completely.

8. Glue the finished head onto the body. Squeeze a nickel-size dollop of glue at the top of the body pompom and position the head as desired. To keep the head from falling off before the glue sets up, use a long floral pin to hold it in place. Remove the pin after the glue has set up and dried.

9. Needle felt the Bat's feet by rolling a golf ball–size bit of roving into a cigarlike shape and start needle felting to compact it down (see Attaching Feet and Small Appendages on page 26). Once it is a tight, dense 3-inch (7.6 cm) cigar shape, cut it evenly in half to make the two feet.

10. At the bottom of the body make two separate slits into the wool "fur" and glue the hind feet into the body. Let it dry standing upright.

11. Tie a black ribbon around the Bat's neck, with the bow in back.

Halloween Bat

Halloween Black Cat

Black cats on Halloween are traditionally meant to be spooky,
but this little guy is nothing but sweet.

YOU WILL NEED

Basic Pompom Toolbox
(page 12)

100% wool yarn:
black

100% wool felt:
black

100% wool roving:
black

Pink seed bead

2 black glass eyes,
10 or 12 mm

Template:
ears (page 123)

Sewing needle

White upholstery thread

2 black pipe cleaners,
6 inches (15.2 cm) and
8 inches (20.3 cm) long

Needle felting supplies
(page 16)

Orange ribbon

Small drawstring jewelry or
muslin sachet bag (optional)

3-inch (7.6 cm) wooden disk,
decorated with paint, glitter,
and rickrack (optional)

FINISHED MEASUREMENTS
5 ¾ inches (14.6 cm) tall,
without base

1. Following steps 2–6 of Making Pompoms by Hand on pages 19–21, make a 2½-inch (6.4 cm) smooth, fat, egg-shaped pompom from black yarn for the head. I used approximately ⅓ skein of Patons medium-weight Classic Wool, which is approximately 69 yards (63 m).

2. On the narrow end of the egg shape, locate where you want the nose to be. Make a small part into the "fur," squeeze in a small drop of glue, and insert the pink seed bead. Pinch the fibers around the glue and the bead to secure it. Let the glue dry.

3. Using the inverted triangle layout (see Positioning the Nose and Eyes on page 22), decide where you want the eyes to be. Make a part in the yarn, carefully squeeze in a pea-size drop of glue for each eye, and gently insert the wire end of each glass eye into the pompom. Let the glue dry.

4. Using the template on page 123, cut two ears out of the wool felt.

5. Make a small part on the top of the head over each eye and squeeze a bit of glue into each part. Insert the ears and pinch the fibers around the base of the ears to secure them. Let dry.

6. Following the instructions for Creating and Attaching Whiskers (page 22), thread a sewing needle with a 5-inch (12.7 cm) double strand of upholstery thread. Tie a knot in the middle of the double strand, place a tiny smidge of glue on the knot, and "sew" in the whiskers. The knot should be approximately in the center front of the head. Snip off any excess so the whiskers are even on both sides.

7. Make another slightly larger pompom from the black yarn and trim it into a pear shape for the body, about 3¾ inches (9.5 cm) tall. I used approximately ½ skein of Patons medium-weight Classic Wool, which is approximately 105 yards (96 m). The narrow top will be the Cat's neck and the heavier, rounded end will become the bottom of the Cat as it sits upright. To create the illusion of the Cat's haunches and tummy, carefully trim out a V shape from the center bottom of the pear shape on the pompom's front side.

8. Glue the 6-inch (15.2 cm) pipe cleaner into the top half of the pompom body. Simply make a horizontal part deep into the wool at the top, squeeze in a dime-size dollop of glue, and place the pipe cleaner snugly down into it. Pinch the fibers of the wool yarn around it to secure the pipe cleaner. This will become the frame for the arms of the Cat, which you will needle felt. (See Creating Appendages on page 24.)

9. Glue the finished head onto the body. To create a cute, inquisitive expression, tilt the head to one side. Squeeze a nickel-size dollop of glue at the top of the body pompom and position the head as desired. You will need to let the glue set up and dry, which can take a while. To keep the head from falling off before the glue sets up, use a long floral pin to hold it in place. Remove the pin after the glue has set up and dried.

10. After the pipe cleaner and glue have fully dried, bend the pipe cleaners into the desired position and trim each arm to approximately 3 inches (7.6 cm). Bend down and tightly crimp the sharp cut ends of the pipe cleaners because they can poke through and show out the end of the needle-felted paws.

11. Needle felt the Cat's hind feet by rolling a golf ball–size bit of roving into a cigarlike shape and start needle felting to compact it down (see Attaching Feet and Small Appendages on page 26). Once it is a tight, dense 3-inch (7.6 cm) cigar shape, cut it evenly in half to make the two back paws.

12. At the bottom of the pear shape make two separate long slits into the wool "fur" and glue the feet into the body. Let it dry sitting upright.

13. After the pipe cleaner and glue have set up, take a thick bacon-size strip of roving and wrap it tightly, top to bottom, around the pipe cleaner arms. Use more roving near the upper arm and shoulder area and taper off at the end to form a tiny paw. Needle felt the roving tightly to make it compact around the pipe cleaner so it will not unravel (see Needle Felting Appendages on page 24). Trim off excess "fuzzies" with scissors for a neater appearance, if desired.

Halloween Black Cat

14. For the tail, wrap roving tightly around the 8-inch (20.3 cm) pipe cleaner. Place a bit more roving toward one end, which will attach to the body, and let it taper off at the other end, which becomes the tip of the tail. Needle felt the entire tail evenly so the roving does not unravel. When finished, make a part at the bottom backside of the body pompom, squeeze in a small dollop of glue, and gently insert the tail. Gently pinch the wool fibers around the tail to secure it. Let dry. Curl the tail to your preference.

15. To embellish your Cat for Halloween, tie an orange ribbon around its neck and use a little drawstring jewelry or muslin sachet bag as a trick-or-treat sack for the Cat to hold in its front paws. As another option, paint and embellish a smooth wooden disk to create a base for your pompom Cat.

❋ **NOTE:** *Additional embellishments for the Halloween Black Cat include a tiny papier-mâché pumpkin to hold in its paws or a pointed hat formed from a 3-inch (7.6 cm) circle of black felt that you cut in half: you can leave it like a clown's hat and attach little pompoms or fashion it into a witch's hat by adding a big circular brim. Purple and black ribbons are also nice to use for Halloween.*

Thanksgiving Turkey

Giving thanks never looked so cute! This dandy-looking Turkey makes a wonderful take-home gift for guests at Thanksgiving. Use multiple Toms to decorate your table; they can even serve as place-card holders for a holiday dinner.

Basic Pompom Toolbox
(page 12)

100% wool yarn:
red, brown

100% wool felt:
orange, brown, beige, cream,
dark brown

Templates:
beak (page 121), tail (page 122),
top hat (page 124)

2 black glass eyes,
10 or 12 mm

Wire cutters

32 inches (81.3 cm)
of 18-gauge floral wire

Embroidery floss or perle
cotton: orange or yellow

Ribbon

FINISHED MEASUREMENTS
5½ inches (14 cm) tall
Hat: 1¼ inches (3.2 cm) tall

1. Following steps 2–6 of Making Pompoms by Hand on pages 19–21, make a 2-inch (5.1 cm) round pompom from red yarn for the head. I used approximately ¼ skein of Patons medium-weight Classic Wool, which is approximately 53 yards (48 m).

2. Using the template on page 121, cut out a beak from orange wool felt.

3. Take the ball shape and locate where you want the beak to be. Make a small part into the pile of the yarn, squeeze in a small drop of glue, and insert the wool felt beak. Pinch the fibers around the glue and the beak to secure it. Let dry.

4. Using the inverted triangle layout (see Positioning the Nose and Eyes on page 22), decide where you want the eyes to be. Make a part in the yarn, carefully squeeze in a pea-size drop of glue for each eye, and gently insert the wire end of each glass eye into the pompom. Let the glue dry.

5. Make another slightly larger pompom from the brown yarn and trim it into an egg-shaped pompom for the body, about 3½ inches (8.9 cm) long. I used approximately ⅓ skein of Patons medium-weight Classic Wool, which is approximately 69 yards (63 m).

6. Glue the finished head onto the body. To create a cute, inquisitive expression, tilt the head to one side. Squeeze a nickel-size dollop of glue at the top of the body pompom and position the head as desired. You will need to let the glue set up and dry, which can take a while. To keep the head from falling off before the glue sets up, use a long floral pin to hold it in place. Remove the pin after the glue has set up and dried.

7. Using the template on page 122, cut out the tail pieces from the brown, beige, orange, and cream wool felts and glue them together with the smallest shape on top and the largest shape on the bottom.

8. At the tail end of the body make a part, squeeze in a bit of glue, and insert the tail. Pinch the wool fibers around the glue and the felt tail to secure them and let the glue dry.

9. Using wire cutters, cut eight 4-inch (10.2 cm) pieces of floral wire.

10. To create the legs, take four pieces of wire, hold them together, and lightly coat the bundle with glue. Working from top to bottom, wind the embroidery floss tightly and uniformly around the wires. Stop approximately 1½ inches (3.8 cm) from the bottom. Bend each of the four wires out at a 90° angle to make individual toes. Three will face forward; one will face backward to provide the support needed for the bird to stand. Continue wrapping each "toe" wire individually with embroidery floss to cover the floral wire. Repeat with the remaining four pieces of floral wire to create the other leg. Use wire cutters to snip off any excess wire length. Tuck any ends of embroidery thread underneath and let the glue dry.

11. At the bottom of the bird's body, make two separate parts into the wool plush for the legs and squeeze a dollop of glue into each. Insert the wire legs into the body. Pinch the wool fibers around the wrapped wires to secure them. Set the bird upright and make any necessary adjustments so that it can dry standing upright.

12. Create a little top hat for the Turkey: using the template on page 124, cut out the top hat shapes from dark brown felt. Apply a thin line of glue along one short end of the rectangle. Loop the rectangle to join both short ends together, creating a cylinder. Let the glue dry.

13. Apply a thin line of glue along one edge of the cylinder, and center the cylinder over the larger felt circle, gently pressing them together. Let the glue dry. Apply another thin line of glue along the remaining top edge of the cylinder. Place the smaller felt circle on top of the cylinder and allow the glue to dry.

14. Once the top hat's glue has dried, carefully trim an X in the bottom of the larger felt circle. Insert the tips of your scissors into the X and trim out the inside of the circle—this will allow the top hat to sit more fully upon the Turkey's head.

15. Tie a ribbon around the Turkey's neck.

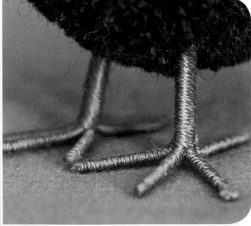

Snowman and Snowgirl

These cheerful snow people are sure to delight during the holiday season for generations to come. By changing a few little details, you can make either a snowgirl or a snowman, and if you're feeling ambitious, you could create an entire family of snow people.

1. Following steps 2–6 of Making Pompoms by Hand on pages 19–21, make three graduated sizes of pompoms using the white wool yarn. The top pompom should be about 2 inches (5.1 cm) in diameter; the middle pompom should be about 2½ inches (6.4 cm) in diameter; and the bottom pompom should be about 3 inches (7.6 cm). I used most of one skein of Patons medium-weight Classic Wool for the three pompoms: approximately ¼ skein, which is approximately 53 yards (48 m), for the head, and approximately ⅓ skein, or approximately 69 yards (63 m), for each of the two bottom pompoms.

2. Using a small marble-size bit of orange roving, needle felt a tiny carrot shape to use as the nose, about ½ inch (1.3 cm) long.

3. Locate where you want the nose to be on the smallest pompom and make a small part into the pile of the yarn. Place a small drop of glue in the part and insert the needle-felted carrot. Pinch the fibers around the carrot nose to secure it. Let dry.

4. Using the inverted triangle layout (see Positioning the Nose and Eyes on page 22), decide where you want the eyes to be. Make a part in the yarn, carefully squeeze in a pea-size drop of glue for each eye, and gently insert the wire end of each glass eye into the pompom. Let the glue dry.

5. To make the Snowgirl's felted arms, glue the pipe cleaner into the top half of the medium-size pompom. Simply make a horizontal part deep into the wool at the top, squeeze in a dime-size dollop of glue, and place the pipe cleaner snugly down into it; pinch the fibers of the wool yarn around the pipe cleaner to secure it. This will become the frame for the Snowgirl's arms, which you will needle felt. (See Creating Appendages on page 24.) Let the glue dry.

6. Trim and flatten the bottom of the smaller pompom head with your scissors. Trim and flatten the top and bottom of the middle-size pompom with your scissors. Repeat this step for the largest pompom as well. This creates the illusion that the snowballs have weight. Glue and stack all three pompoms together. Use floral pins to hold them together while they dry.

7. After the glue has fully dried, bend the Snowgirl's pipe cleaner into the desired position and trim each arm to approximately 3 inches (7.6 cm). Bend down and crimp the sharp ends of the pipe cleaners because they will poke through the needle-felted ends.

YOU WILL NEED

FOR BOTH THE SNOWMAN AND SNOWGIRL:
Basic Pompom Toolbox (page 12)

100% wool yarn: white

100% wool felt: white

100% wool roving: orange

2 black glass eyes, 10 or 12 mm (2 eyes for each)

3-inch (7.6 cm) flat wooden disk (1 disk for each)

Pale blue craft paint

Paintbrush

Clear glass glitter or mica

Scallop-edge scissors

FINISHED MEASUREMENTS
Snowman/Snowgirl:
5½ inches (14 cm) tall
(without pedestal or hat)

Snowman's hat:
1¼ inches (3.2 cm) tall

materials list continued on next page

Wrap a thick bacon-size strip of white roving tightly around the pipe cleaner armature from top to bottom. Needle felt the roving tightly to compact it around the pipe cleaner so it will not unravel (see Needle Felting Appendages on page 24).

8. Paint the 3-inch (7.6 cm) flat wooden disk with pale blue craft paint and let it dry. Coat the dry painted disk with glue and sprinkle clear glass glitter or mica over it; shake off the excess. Let the glue dry.

9. While the glue on the base dries, use the scallop-edge scissors to cut a circle of white felt measuring 3½ inches (8.9 cm) in diameter. Adhere this felt circle to the bottom of the dry, painted disk.

10. Glue the snow person onto the center of the painted and glittered wooden disk. Let the glue dry.

11. For the Snowman's twig arms, use the wire cutters to cut two tiny twigs approximately 2½ inches (6.4 cm) long. Make parts on each side in the middle pompom where you want the arms to be. Squeeze a bit of glue into each part and insert the twigs. Pinch the fibers around the twigs to secure them. Let dry.

12. Create a wool scarf by cutting a strip of wool felt approximately ½ x 7 inches (1.3 x 17.8 cm). Snip the ends to make the scarf's fringe. Wrap and tie it around your snow person's neck.

13. Embellish the Snowgirl with millinery flowers. To create her earmuffs, simply needle felt a 1-inch (2.5 cm) diameter ball of roving in any color of your choosing. Cut the ball in half. Cut a tiny strip of wool felt with the scallop-edge scissors for the earmuffs' headband. Glue the headband on the head and glue one ball half to each side of the head.

14. Using the template on page 124, cut out the Snowman's top hat shapes from felt. Apply a thin line of glue along one short end of the rectangle. Loop the rectangle to join both short ends together, creating a cylinder. Let the glue dry.

15. Apply a thin line of glue along one edge of the cylinder, and center the cylinder over the larger felt circle, gently pressing them together. Let the glue dry. Apply another thin line of glue along the remaining top edge of the cylinder. Place the smaller felt circle on top of the cylinder and allow the glue to dry.

16. Once the top hat's glue has dried, carefully trim an X in the bottom of the larger felt circle. Insert the tips of your scissors into the X and trim out the inside of the circle—this will allow the top hat to sit more fully upon the Snowman's head.

17. Cut a strip of velvet ribbon and glue it around the hat, just on top of the brim. Glue the small black beads (as the coal buttons) down the front of the Snowman.

❋ **NOTE:** *Add a nice wintry effect by lightly coating flowers and/ or berries with glue, dusting them with glass glitter or mica, and placing them as embellishments on the painted wooden disks or in the Snowman's or Snowgirl's hands.*

TEMPLATES

All templates are provided at 100%.

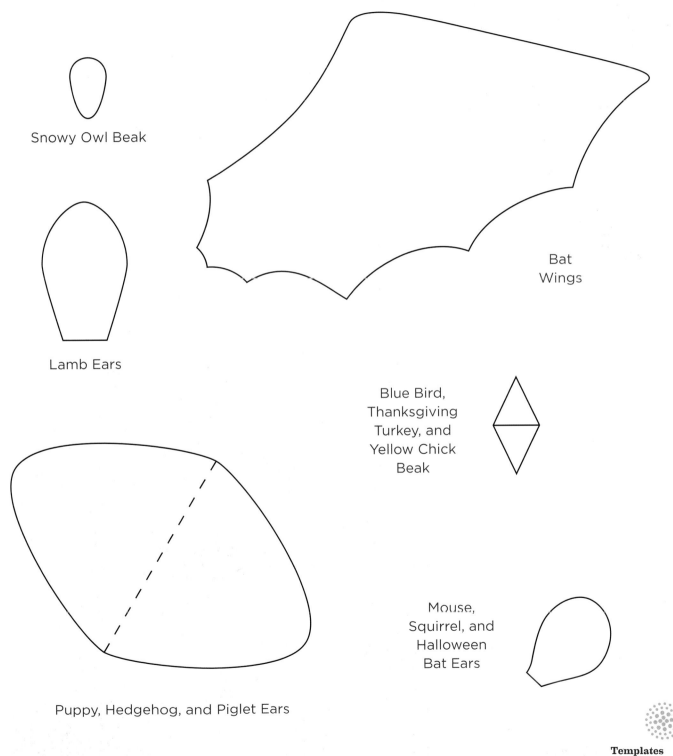

Snowy Owl Beak

Bat Wings

Lamb Ears

Blue Bird, Thanksgiving Turkey, and Yellow Chick Beak

Mouse, Squirrel, and Halloween Bat Ears

Puppy, Hedgehog, and Piglet Ears

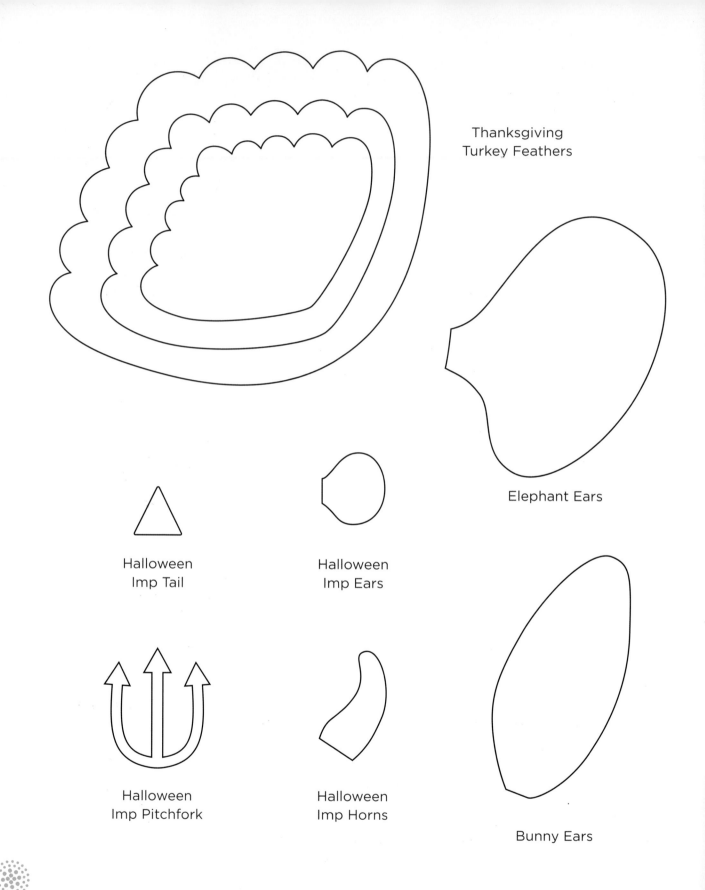

Thanksgiving
Turkey Feathers

Elephant Ears

Halloween
Imp Tail

Halloween
Imp Ears

Halloween
Imp Pitchfork

Halloween
Imp Horns

Bunny Ears

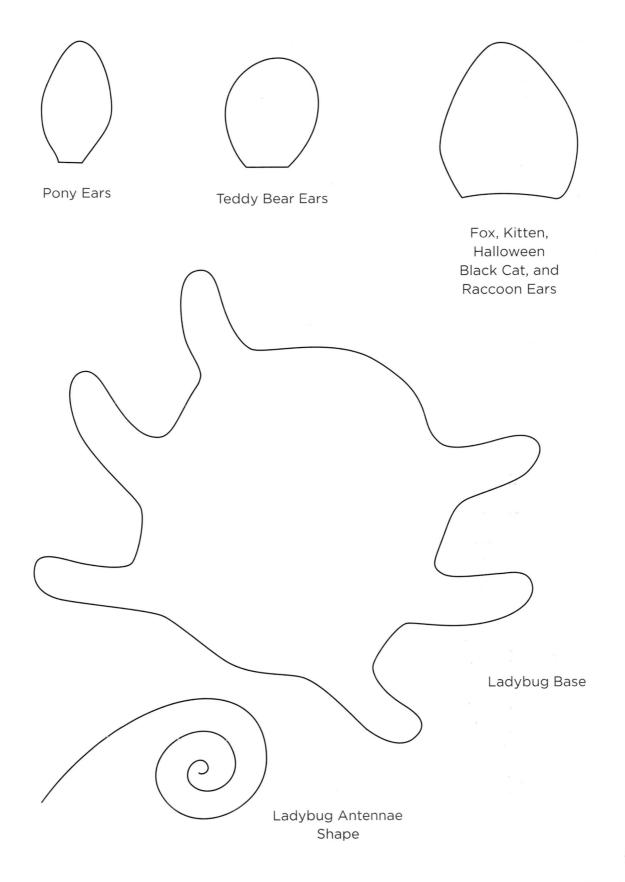

Pony Ears

Teddy Bear Ears

Fox, Kitten,
Halloween
Black Cat, and
Raccoon Ears

Ladybug Base

Ladybug Antennae
Shape

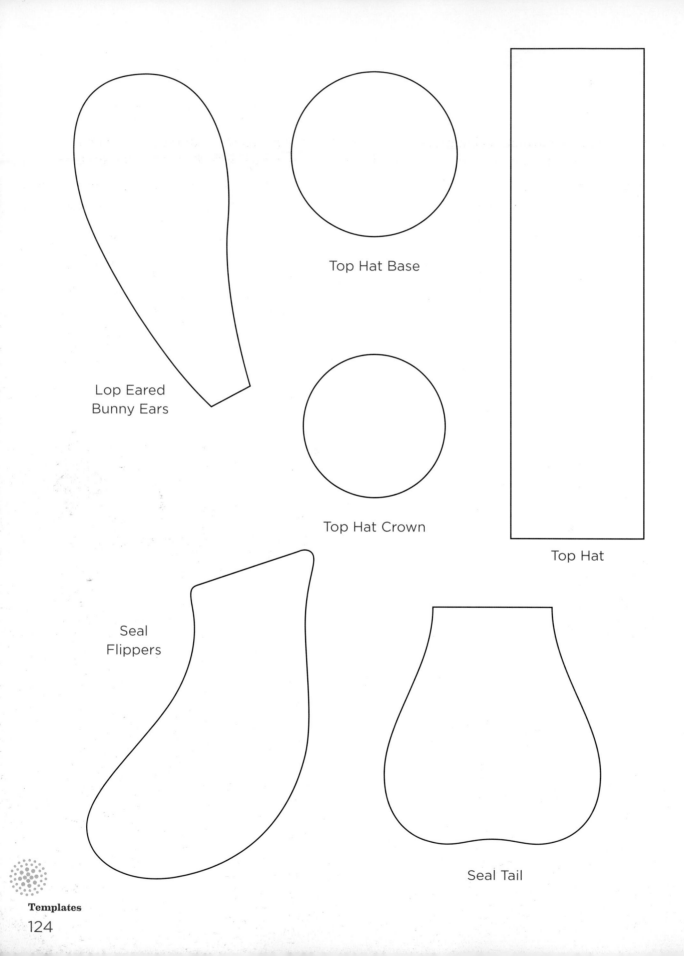

Lop Eared
Bunny Ears

Top Hat Base

Top Hat Crown

Top Hat

Seal
Flippers

Seal Tail

Resource List

Most of the tools and materials you'll need to make pompom creatures can be found in your local craft store, so here's a list of basic resource suggestions to get you started.

Yarn Supply and Needle Felting Supply

Patons
www.patonsyarns.com

Michaels
www.michaels.com

Jo-Ann Fabric and Craft Stores
www.joann.com

A.C. Moore Arts and Crafts
www.acmoore.com

Lion Brand Yarn
www.lionbrand.com

Red Heart Yarn
www.redheart.com

Additional Needle Felting Materials and Tools

Living Felt
www.livingfelt.com

The Felted Ewe
www.thefeltedewe.com

Clover
www.clover-usa.com

Paradise Fibers
www.paradisefibers.com

Millinery Supplies

Manny's Millinery Supply Company
www.shop.mannys-millinery.com

Judith M. Hats & Millinery Supplies
www.judithm.com

Glass Eyes

Glass Eyes Online
www.glasseyesonline.com

Hand Glass Craft
www.handglasscraft.com

G. Schoepfer Inc.
www.schoepferseyes.com

Shamrock Rose Teddy Bear Supplies
www.teddybearsupplies.flyingcart.com

About the Author

Myko Diann Bocek (pronounced Mike-o) is a designer, antique collector, mother, and student. Her half-Japanese heritage and her childhood experience growing up on a rural farm in Delaware both inform her love of vintage creations and all things cute.

Inspired by a television episode by fellow artist Jennifer Murphy on the *Martha Stewart Show* back in 2007, coupled with her love for vintage Steiff animals, Myko began making pompom animals during the evenings at home after work. She has since sold many of her original designs from her Etsy shop and she blogs at www.mykobocek.blogspot.com. She has been a featured craft artist in *Better Homes and Gardens' Holiday Crafts* magazine, as well as *Celebrate 365*. She currently lives in Arizona with her spouse and two youngest children (of four) and continues to create, collect, love, and learn. See more of Myko's work in her Etsy shop: www.etsy.com/shop/MykoBocekStudios.

Acknowledgments

I would like to thank my editor Beth Sweet for all of her help, guidance, and patience. Many thanks to Kristi Pfeffer for her wonderful design, to Michelle Owen for her artful layout, and to Jen Altman for capturing the expressive personality of each pompom creature in her photographs. Great applause goes to Kathy Brock for her copyediting wizardry. Thank you to Lark for giving me this opportunity. I am forever grateful.

Thank you to my childhood hero Beatrix Potter and artist Jennifer Murphy for giving me such inspiration and hope. Thank you to my husband, Brett, and to my dear friend Bill for your help and support. And last but not least, a huge thank you to my four amazing children, Shawn, Marina, Sierra, and Ian, who gave me the inspiration, willpower, and determination to create once again.

Index

I find that missions are consistently the best and the worst progra¬ The potential for transformation and kingdom impact is palpably ¬ lums of self-actualization, pity and judgment, and tourism too often ¬ and good into a narcissistic mush. How wonderful to have a research-based guide to avoiding the worst of what short-term missions can be, and leaning into the best.

Mark Oestreicher, Partner, the Youth Cartel

Short-term trips have massive potential to make long-term impact, especially when combined with thoughtful planning and preparation. *Sticky Faith Service Guide* offers the most practical and thorough advice on equipping teams for effective service that I've ever seen. Team leaders and participants, you don't want to miss out on the many ways that this outstanding book can help make your next trip a life-changing experience.

Peter Greer, president & CEO of HOPE International and coauthor of *Mission Drift*

Sticky Faith Service Guide creates an engaging, accessible guide to maximize the transformative impact of youths' journey on short-term mission trips. Based on years of experience coaching youth leaders, solid theology, cross-cultural sensitivity, and rich insights into spiritual forma-tion—this resource will deliver for groups what it promises: short-term service trips being translated into long-term change. Mission trips can be integral to the spiritual growth and discipleship of young adults, shaping their vision and vocation for life. Not to invest the time required for this before, during, and after the trip risks squandering that opportunity. I warmly recommend this resource as a ready-made guide for leaders and youth to make the most for the kingdom of their short-term service.

Tim Dearborn, Fuller Theological Seminary; author, *Short-Term Missions Workbook: From Mission Tourists to Global Citizens*

As an urban youth ministry practitioner, I have used mission trips to fortify my students in middle and high school. The challenge of maintaining a long-term lesson from a short-term trip is multifaceted. Like superglue, we must apply intentional pressure in multiple forms if we expect the faith of our students to bond to their lives. This book and student journal provide multiple ways for youth leaders to facilitate this process before, during, and after the trip. Youth leaders will embrace this material as another gift of information from the Sticky Faith family.

Virginia Ward, Director of Leadership and Mentored Ministry Initiatives, Gordon-Conwell Theological Seminary

This book is the definitive guide to leading service projects and mission trips in youth groups. With proven practical ideas built from the best research, Dr. Kara Powell and Brad Griffin provide youth workers with the understanding and tools necessary for helping spiritual growth "stick" in the lives of young people. This is my new recommended guide for youth workers who want to lead mission trips that make a difference in their students' lives.

Terry Linhart, professor of Christian Ministries, Bethel College–Indiana

What an incredible resource for churches and families. When I think about things I need to help students see and understand their unique abilities to change cycles of injustice in the world, I think about tools I can use to affirm their discoveries. This book affirms and guides the influence of the families and ministries while giving leaders practical help to move beyond thinking "service projects" to practicing justice in compassionate and sustainable ways. Every youth ministry and family would benefit from this read. Love it!

Brooklyn Lindsey, youth minister; Justice Advocate, The Justice Movement

Research findings on the long-term impact of short-term missions work is incredibly disheartening. Kara Powell and Brad Griffin have given the short-term missions world a thoughtful, practical, creative, and engaging toolbox of resources to help leaders and participants more effectively serve real world needs and address underlying causes, while being personally transformed in the process. This will be my number one go-to resource for equipping youth *and* adult workers tasked with the privilege and responsibility of leading short-term mission trips and local outreaches.

Rich Van Pelt, Senior Director, Ministry Relationships
& Partner Development, Compassion International

stickyfaith
service guide

moving students from mission trips to missional living

Kara Powell
& Brad M. Griffin

ZONDERVAN®   youth specialties

ZONDERVAN

Sticky Faith Service Guide
Copyright © 2009, 2016 by Kara E. Powell and Brad M. Griffin

Previously published as *Deep Justice Journeys Leader's Guide.*

This title is also available as a Zondervan ebook. Visit www.zondervan.com/ebooks.

Requests for information should be addressed to:
Zondervan, 3900 *Sparks Dr. SE, Grand Rapids, Michigan 49546*

Library of Congress Cataloging-in-Publication Data

Names: Powell, Kara Eckmann, 1970-
Title: Sticky faith service guide : moving students from mission trips to missional living / Dr. Kara Powell and Brad M. Griffin.
Description: Grand Rapids : Zondervan, 2016. | Includes bibliographical references.
Identifiers: LCCN 2015028392 | ISBN 9780310524205 (softcover)
Subjects: LCSH: Church work with students. | Church work with youth. | Church work with young adults. | Missions — Study and teaching.
Classification: LCC BV4447.P6528 2016 | DDC 259/.23 — dc23 LC record available at http://lccn.loc.gov/2015028392

Cover design: Brand Navigation
Cover photography: © Pixelrobot / Dreamstime.com
Interior imagery: © Frank Fiedler / Shutterstock®
Interior design: Kait Lamphere

Printed in the United States of America

15 16 17 18 19 20 21 22 23 24 25 26 27 28 29 30 /DHV/ 25 24 23 22 21 20 19 18 17 16 15 14 13 12 11 10 9 8 7 6 5 4 3 2 1

CONTENTS

PART 3: DURING: EXPERIENCE AND REFLECTION

PART 4: AFTER: DEBRIEF

PART 5: AFTER: ONGOING TRANSFORMATION

CONTRIBUTORS

Additional contributors to the first version of this project, *Deep Justice Journeys*, included Todd Bratulich, April Diaz, Cari Jenkins, Terry Linhart, David Livermore, Mark Maines, Kurt Rietema, and Rana Choi Park. A few of the original sessions were adapted from two shared projects with World Vision U.S., originally called One Life (2006) and Vision Generation (2007).

Special thanks to Laura Addis and Matt Laidlaw for offering critical input to the revised version, to Art Bamford for research assistance on updates to this version, to Matthew Schuler and Macy P. Davis for help reimagining the creative design, and to all of the leaders and students who have helped make this resource better by using it in their ministries and offering helpful feedback.

KEY TO ICONS

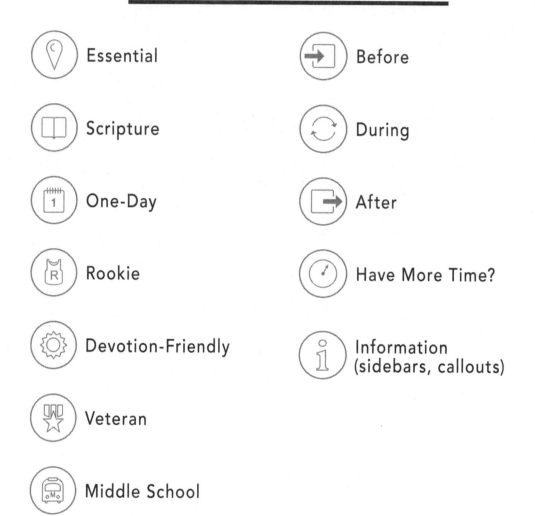

Essential

Scripture

One-Day

Rookie

Devotion-Friendly

Veteran

Middle School

Before

During

After

Have More Time?

Information
(sidebars, callouts)

PART ONE

PREPARING FOR SERVICE THAT LEADS TO STICKY FAITH

CHAPTER ONE

INITIAL STEPS

GETTING THE MOST OUT OF YOUR SERVICE TRIP OR LOCAL PROJECT

YOUR SUMMER MISSION TRIP TO MEXICO is four months away. Your Saturday breakfast for families who are homeless is four weeks away. Your talk on the importance of service is four days away.

This book is for you.

If you're like most youth workers, you want your students to get a taste of service that leaves them hungering for more. Because you know service changes people, your ministry calendar offers a buffet of opportunities—a short-term mission trip here and a half-day convalescent home visit there. But if you're honest with yourself, you sometimes wonder if your students are feasting on all God offers or merely scraping up the crumbs.

You're not alone. About one-third of US congregations sponsor international mission trips each year, sending over 1.6 million churchgoers overseas.[1] But does the impact of these trips *stick*? Recent research suggests service trips and experiences might not produce the spiritual and relational "bang" we expect—at least not in the long term. Consider these research findings:

- The explosive growth in the number of short-term mission trips among both young people and adults has *not* been accompanied by similarly explosive growth in the number of career missionaries.

- Participating in a service trip does not seem to reduce participants' tendencies toward materialism.[2]

- It's not clear whether participation in service trips causes participants to give more money to alleviate poverty once life returns to "normal."[3]

- Fewer local congregations and their individual attendees are serving the poor. One study found that those who reported having participated in "any human service projects in the past twelve months" declined around 8 percent over the past half decade.[4]

ARE WE MAKING A DIFFERENCE?

Given the mandate throughout Scripture to care for the poor, believers' commitment to serving people in impoverished communities is admirable. And on some level, largely thanks to the work of global development nongovernmental organizations, extreme poverty around the world is decreasing. Over the past three decades, the percentage of people in the developing world living on less than $1.25 a day has dropped by 25 percent. While that's something to celebrate, there are still 1.9 billion people living in extreme poverty.[5]

Even more powerful than these statistics are the real faces, names, and stories of those who are impacted by poverty. Giving our young people a chance to interact with real people and real challenges is part of what is so powerful about short-term service trips. But most service trips away from home—whether domestic or international—also tend to create an aura of what's been called *mission tourism*. We want to see and experience local culture, but we can easily romanticize the poor and make them objects for our own growth or, worse, the targets of consumer experiences that make us feel like "good Christians." Research suggests that our trips could be far more helpful if we focused less on "doing" and more on listening and building relationships, and stepped up our intentionality in what happens post-trip.[6]

Experts Steve Corbett and Brian Fikkert critique the majority of short-term work as being too focused on "crisis relief" types of projects in communities where what's really needed is help with rehabilitation or community development. North American congregations are often too impatient and controlling to enter into the messier relationships and processes that *help* without *hurting*.[7] Along the same lines, urban ministry veteran Robert Lupton notes, "Our memory is short when recovery is long. We respond with immediacy to desperate circumstances but often are unable to shift from crisis relief to the more complex work of long-term development."[8] Sadly, short-term teams may not be willing to listen to local voices when more thoughtful rebuilding strategies are needed.

We also tend to create work where work isn't needed. Lupton notes some of the more grievous examples from short-term missions teams: "like the wall built on an orphanage soccer field in Brazil that had to be torn down after visitors left. Or the church in Mexico that was painted six times during one summer by six different mission groups. Or the church in Ecuador built by volunteers that was never used as a church because the community had no need for it."[9]

Why do things like this happen? If we are really honest, many of us do service trips not because of their benefits for those we serve but because we believe they transform our students. While that's understandable, it makes us all the more likely to unintentionally exploit the poor for the sake of our own spiritual growth, which is an injustice in itself.

To find out more about research-based resources from the Fuller Youth Institute or to sign up for the free *FYI E-Journal*, visit fulleryouthinstitute.org.

THE GOOD NEWS IS ALL THE BETTER

As we come to terms with the bad news that our service is less transformative than we would hope, we become more eager for tools that help us make a deeper impact on our students and our world. We have been addressing this need for the past decade at the Fuller Youth Institute (FYI). A few years back, our FYI team collaborated with David Livermore of the Cultural Intelligence Center and Terry Linhart of Bethel College (Indiana) to convene two summits with short-term mission and youth ministry experts.[10] Building on our exploration of deep theological and sociological questions of the role of justice in our faith and ministry practices,[11] we set out to answer tough questions like these:

- How do we move service beyond spiritual tourism?
- How can our service work be part of God's kingdom justice?
- What are the most important theological threads that should weave their way through our service?
- How does service contribute to teenagers' identity development?

- What does it look like to transform rhetoric into true reciprocal partnership with those we're serving?

With the help of some sharp minds and a lot of prayer, we wrestled with those questions and tried to pin down at least a few answers. Those answers were translated into a host of learning activities that were field-tested by youth leaders and their students across the country and originally published as *Deep Justice Journeys*.

What's more, we simultaneously have been working for nearly a decade on a research initiative that morphed into a movement called Sticky Faith (see stickyfaith.org for a summary of Sticky Faith and hundreds of free resources). We explored why one out of every two youth group graduates walks away from faith after high school, and what families and congregations can do to turn that tide. One of our discoveries is that service—both locally and away from home—is correlated with lasting faith in young people.

Here's more good news: the students in our study told us *they want to serve even more*. We asked graduating high school seniors what they wished they'd had more of in youth group. Of the thirteen options we provided, their second and third top choices were mission trips and service projects (time for deep conversation was first).

Along a similar vein, 60 percent of the seniors we surveyed were motivated to come to youth group because of the ways youth group has helped them learn to serve.

In the midst of students' desire to serve, we also found that that desire is more likely

17

to become a reality when service hits close to home. It needs to be in the home *literally*—as we invite parents to exemplify by encouraging and participating with their own kids in righting wrongs around them. It needs to hit close to home *thematically*—as we help teenagers understand how particular injustices relate to their lives. It needs to hit home *personally*—as we expose young people to real individuals who have been oppressed, thereby giving injustice a face and a name. And our acts of compassion need to hit home *relationally*—as we help them serve others in partnership with their friends.[12]

As gang worker Father Gregory Boyle writes, "Serving others is good. It's a start. But it's just the hallway that leads to the Grand Ballroom."[13] That grand ballroom is one where we see others as our brothers and sisters and work side by side for kingdom purposes. And that's the ballroom we want to lead our students into when we plan out our long-term service and mission strategy.

Based on our work with churches implementing Sticky Faith and Deep Justice principles over the past several years, we revised the book you have in your hands and also redeveloped a parallel student journal.

THE MODEL IN THE DRIVER'S SEAT

As we researched what helps service stick, one theme repeatedly emerged everywhere we looked: We need to do a better job of walking with students before, during, and after their mission experience.[14]

Let's be honest. Our "preparation" before

the usual short-term mission trip often consists of M&Ms: money and medical releases. Our "reflection" during the trip boils down to a few minutes of prayer requests before our team tumbles into bed exhausted. And our "debrief" after we get home is little more than organizing the media show and the testimonies to share in "big church." While these steps are good, they're not enough for the kind of impact we hope for.

If we want greater transformation, we need a completely different time frame for our service. Perhaps instead of viewing a weekend trip to work with homeless people in the inner city as a three-day commitment, we need to view it as a three-month process. Instead of looking at a week in the Dominican Republic as seven days, we need to think of it as a seven-month journey. Instead of thinking of service as discrete chunks of time we slide in and around the rest of what we do in youth ministry, it's time to revise our schedule to give service a more organic ebb and flow.

WHAT DO WE DO WITH ALL THAT TIME?

So what do we do with those extra weeks before and after our service experience? And how do we squeeze every ounce of impact out of the time we spend doing this important work?

The many hands and brains that have poured into this curriculum recommend an experiential education framework originally proposed by Laura Joplin[15] and later modified and tested by Terry Linhart[16] on youth ministry trips.

THE STICKY FAITH
SERVICE MODEL

STEP 1. BEFORE:
Framing

A successful service or mission experience starts when we help students *frame* the sometimes mind-blowing and other times menial experiences that await them. Getting ready for a mission experience involves much more than just helping them raise money, learn a drama, or know what to pack. Research indicates that *our job as youth workers is to facilitate a series of gatherings and events that prepare students emotionally, mentally, spiritually, and relationally for what lies ahead.* If we don't, we're cheating them out of all God has for them.

During this framing time, you might want to nudge your students to start journaling about their thoughts and feelings as they think about what lies ahead, and the *Sticky Faith Service Guide Student Journal* is designed to help you do just that.

Admittedly, getting students to show up for pre-work can be a challenge. It might require a major paradigm shift for your ministry since students and families aren't used to doing much "pre-work" for church-based projects. Hopefully the activities in this book can help with that framing, but don't be surprised if buy-in doesn't happen right away. Note that you will likely need to do a fair amount of framing for the *adults* participating in the experience as well, so they can lead the way in modeling trip preparation.

BEFORE	DURING	AFTER
1 FRAMING	2 EXPERIENCE & REFLECTION	3 DEBRIEF
	S U P P O R T	F E E D B A C K
		4 ONGOING TRANSFORMATION

STEP 2. DURING: Experience and Reflection

The main component in students' learning during their actual service is the cycle of *experience and reflection*. In this ongoing feedback loop, you and your students are placed in situations and activities that purposefully stretch you. Maybe you'll use new skill muscles in a cross-cultural setting unfamiliar to you. Or your group will get tired, cranky, and hungry—and the glue that has united your team up to this point will start to dissolve.

Whatever young people are experiencing, they are constantly assigning meaning. Though they may be unconscious of it, your teenagers are continually engaged in a highly personal, ongoing "conversation" in their own minds about who they are in relation to themselves, others, and God.

The barrage of experiences on a typical service adventure comes so fast and furious that participants often feel as if they're sprinting through a museum, only barely viewing its masterpieces out of the corners of their eyes. As leaders, *our job is to give space for both students and adults to catch their breath and ask questions that help decipher the deep meaning behind their observations, thoughts, and feelings.*

If you are serving with students who struggle to process their feelings and experiences (can anyone say "middle school boys"?), then your first attempts to help young people reflect on their experiences may get just a few bites of conversation. Answers may range from "I don't know" to "What he said." That's okay. Sometimes it takes months—or

years—to get to the point where students are able to truly join in the reflection. In the meantime, we have the opportunity to model patient listening and simply being there with them. Further, adults who model their own meaning-making process help young people participate in it more fully when they're ready.

STEP 3. AFTER: Debrief

At the end of your trip, as your students' minds and your ministry's minivans are starting to head home, you've now entered the third step: *debrief.* Maybe it's the last day of your trip as you take a bit of time to relax and have fun. Or perhaps it's when you hit a coffee shop together right after you've visited patients at the local children's hospital. Either way, the goal is to gather your team together just after the "work" is completed to start thinking about the even harder work of long-term change.

STEP 4. AFTER: Ongoing Transformation

For our short-term work to translate into impact that sticks over the long haul, we need more than just one touch point following our service. If most youth groups lack an effective pre-service framing time, even more have difficulty facilitating proper *ongoing transformation.* Two realities fight against effective learning transfer. First, most of the significant growth in a service experience takes place in an environment very different from the home communities of students. Second, the students themselves don't know how to translate the learning to their own

lives. That's why we need to help them connect the dots between having lunch with a homeless man in Detroit and having lunch with a new kid in their school cafeteria one month later.

THROUGH IT ALL:
SUPPORT AND FEEDBACK

Right about now, this is probably sounding like a lot of work. You're right. But it's not work you should do alone. In order to facilitate the experience-and-reflection cycle, our students need to be surrounded by walls of *support and feedback*. While these two expressions of care are vital throughout the process, their importance peaks during the time you're actually serving. Support and feedback are such sticky factors that we've devoted chapter 2 of this book to helping you develop this philosophy and a great support structure.

You might assume support and feedback would flow most naturally from the other adults and students on your team. While that is often true, the best networks stretch far beyond the immediate team. Research shows a strong correlation between individuals' success in a cross-cultural experience and the emotional and tangible support they receive from friends and family at home. Be sure you're building a support team to hold up the team members who are serving. Support can include the financial, logistical, and emotional assistance provided by a sending church, denomination group, or short-term missions agency. Plus, let's not forget support from the people in the community we're serving. Many of them can wrap your students in the type of

love that both comforts and convicts.

One primary purpose of such feedback is to nudge group members beyond their initial conclusions into deeper insights. For example, your group may be serving in an under-resourced community plagued by poverty. While serving, students may notice a lot of people smiling at them. The "fast" conclusion can be, "Even without much money or stuff, these people are happy." Are they? Maybe—but maybe not. Perhaps the locals are simply being polite, just as you would be if you were hosting newcomers. Whatever the case, proper feedback helps us avoid settling for the superficial or becoming knee-jerk experts.

STICKY FAITH SERVICE:
NAVIGATING THE ROAD

If the model we've just outlined is in the driver's seat, the following assumptions can help you navigate the road—pointing out when your group should turn left, when you should turn right, and when you should make a U-turn and head in the opposite direction:

1. *As your students serve, they have opportunities to learn about themselves, their youth group, their God, and their world.* Because of this, both this leader's manual and the student journal work through the steps of before, during, and after in three dimensions: *God and Me, God and Us* (meaning the youth group), and *God and Locals* (meaning the people we serve and those who live in our host community). So you can pick and choose exercises that help students grow in their understanding of their lives, their youth group, and their role as world Christians.

ⓘ We've included a session to help you discuss support and feedback with your team, called "If You're Happy and You Know It … Smile," on pages 137–139.

2. *A good curriculum is easy to use, but it's also customizable.* After all, we know students, but we don't know *your* students. We know something about service, but we don't know all the details about *your* upcoming adventure. While we've given you these learning exercises in an order that feels logical to us and that worked well for the youth groups that tested this curriculum, you might want to pick and choose items off the menu in a different order. You're the expert on the young people and families in your community, and these resources are designed so you can adapt them to what God is doing in and through your service.

Further, we learned from the first edition of this resource that all kinds of teams beyond church-based youth ministries found these tools helpful: college groups, Christian schools, adult mission teams, families, and parachurch ministries. Please adapt the language used here as necessary for your unique context.

3. *The stickiest projects help students move past service that addresses symptoms in order to examine the justice issues that might be the root causes of the needs they are addressing.* Here's one way to think of the difference between service and justice: we *serve* when we give food to people in need; we *engage in justice* when we address why people don't have the food they need, and

then work with those people to change the situation so they can get the food they need in the future. We want to help the students in our ministries dive past service into the deeper, and often murkier, waters of justice—into places where they can find lasting solutions to systemic problems. Suburban, urban, rural, or something in between, our prayer is that this curriculum helps your ministry name the injustices around you so you can unearth the hope and freedom Jesus offers to the world. If you want to frame this difference with your students right at the start, see "Parable of the Cracked Roads" on pages 76–81.

4. *Thoughtful ministries engage in "cultural intelligence" as they serve.* Virtually every service trip involves cross-cultural relationships in which you interact with people from a different background, ethnicity, geography, or economic status (or sometimes all of those combined). As described by expert Dr. David Livermore, one of the contributors to this curriculum, cultural intelligence (or CQ) assumes that you and your students are constantly engaging in a process of observing and responding to cultural cues and encounters. Similar to IQ or EQ (emotional intelligence), your group's CQ is strengthened by the God and Locals exercises that help you reach across cultural gaps in ways that are appropriate, respectful, and even—dare we dream?—transformative.[17]

5. *Wise youth leaders know why their students are involved in service and justice work.* Before you ask yourself the important questions (What do we want to do? Where do we want to do it? And how in the world are we going to pay for

it?), there's a more fundamental question you need to tackle: *Why are you involving your youth ministry in service and justice work?* Because you've always done it? Because other youth ministries do it? Because your students/church leaders/parents/bosses/deacons expect you to do it? Because Jesus expects you to do it? Because your own life was impacted by service and justice work when you were a teenager? Because you want to stretch your students? Because you want your students to be exposed to the multicultural reality of our world today? Take some time, both on your own and in conversation with the other adults and students on your team, to prayerfully prioritize the main reasons you feel called to go. (Here's some good news: The learning activity "Why Go?" on p. 62 helps you and your team pinpoint in just a single sentence why you're doing this work.)

6. *The young people who really "get" service and compassionate action usually have families who get it.* Parents generally have more influence with students than youth workers do. In fact, one major Sticky Faith principle is that parents tend to be the most significant influence on their kids' faith, *even through adolescence.* Because of that, chapter 3 offers tips for engaging parents who aren't going on the trip, and chapter 4 offers ideas for including parents and whole families in your actual service. Research shows that families who serve together grow in faith together in a host of other ways as well.[18] As leaders, we are in a unique position to create contexts for students and parents to serve side by side.

7. *Service is a church family affair.* The church family also has an important part to play in students' service. Your church is more than just an audience for your post-trip slide show, or a group to hit up for money. Sticky Faith research reveals the power of intergenerational relationships in the faith development of young people, and we've gathered a host of great ideas from dozens of churches who are involving other generations in support and even the service itself. We hope you consider, and then implement, some of these proven ideas from chapters 5 and 6 with your whole church.

8. *Don't underestimate the power of partnership.* Many youth ministries have found that effective partnerships make the difference between a *good* service experience and a *great* service experience. While much of this book explores how to develop a true partnership with the people you're serving, a second important partner many youth ministries rely on is a short-term missions agency that helps coordinate the trip. Consider the values, theology, ministry philosophy (with your team and with the local community), staff support, longevity in the community, and participant costs as you choose. To find out more about how to select an agency partner wisely, check out the Seven US Standards of Excellence in Short-Term Mission at soe.org/explore/the-7-standards/.

9. *Consider the terms we use as we talk about all of this.* As we developed and tested this curriculum, we realized there are some inherent problems with the terminology we often use to describe our efforts. Here are some questions that just wouldn't go away:

As we move beyond service to justice, what verbs in addition to *serve* can we use to describe what we do? ("To just" isn't a verb.)

Does the word *serve* imply some sort of unequal need? In other words, does such language suggest that the people doing the service are somehow subtly superior to those who receive the service? Does "shared work" translate well?

Does the designation "short-term mission trip" contradict a more holistic vision for viewing mission or missional living as a lifestyle?

How do we talk about the people in the communities where we're serving? We commonly use the terms *locals* and *hosts* in this curriculum, but in no way do we mean *locals* to be pejorative. So if in your particular context that term comes across negatively, please swap it out for a better one.

In the midst of these tensions, we've tried our best to use language that is both clear and accurate. We're not sure we always succeeded. Please adapt according to your own context and convictions.

BUT DOES IT WORK?

You may be wondering by now whether all of this work will pay off. Does more intentional investment before, during, and after your service really make a difference in students' lives? While we have not conducted longitudinal research ourselves on this question, the research within the service learning field backs the Sticky Faith Before-During-After Service Model we're using here. What's more, Diana Garland and a team of Baylor researchers explored faith transformation related to service and found the following factors to be closely related to faith maturity:[19]

1. Volunteers are well prepared ahead of time.
2. The service experience provides opportunity for a relationship to grow between those serving and those served.
3. The approach is "doing with," not just "doing for" recipients—asking for their input as well as serving side by side.
4. Working with those who are different stretches volunteers' empathy and compassion muscles.
5. Volunteers grow by working through conflicts rather than quitting.
6. Volunteers feel challenged and that their gifts are used well.
7. Leaders make time afterward for reflection and debrief.

Good news: these factors sound a lot like the values that guide the ethos of this project and the specific exercises you will find ahead.

CREATE YOUR OWN PLAN: HOW TO GET THE MOST OUT OF THIS TOOL

Now we're handing the keys over to you. How do you get the most out of the pages that follow?

1. *Give your students time and space for their own reflection before, during, and after your work.* Based on the feedback we have received from

youth workers, we developed the *Sticky Faith Service Guide Student Journal* as a companion piece to this leader's manual. The journal gives your students an easy space and place to reflect and respond during their personal devotions or in the midst of your team discussions. Plus, your students are much more likely to keep their journals for years to come than they are a stack of handouts. Many—but not all—of the exercises in this guide have parallel reflection exercises in the journal.

2. *Schedule time to meet with your group before, during, and after you serve.* Don't skimp on this. Even if it means you do two fewer Bible studies or three fewer worship team practices, you and your students will be better off if you give yourself plenty of time to frame, discuss, and debrief your service. We suggest that you plan out the dates and times of *all* of your before, during, and after meetings at the same time you plan the dates of the actual experience.

When we tested this curriculum with youth ministries around the country, a consistent theme in leaders' feedback was that they weren't used to scheduling meetings *after* their work experiences. But when leaders made the effort to meet with their students afterward, they felt the seeds God had planted during the actual service went deeper and bore greater fruit.

If you're planning a one-week trip to an urban community two hours away, your journey time frame might look something like this:

BEFORE	DURING	AFTER
three months	one week	three months

If you're planning a three-hour visit to the local rescue mission, your time frame might look more like this:

BEFORE	DURING	AFTER
one hour	three hours	one hour

By now, you might be wondering if the Sticky Faith Service Model is something you progress through *once* during the many months involved in your service experience or if it's something that you progress through *many times*. The answer is *both*. Part of the beauty of the Sticky Faith Service Model is that you can walk through it in a morning, in a week, or during a year-long emphasis on service or missions. We hope you will use this approach over and over again, and that there are enough exercises in this guide to help you for the next few seasons of service with your ministry.

3. *Tentatively plan the exercises you'll do during those meetings, being sensitive to the various topics and codes for each exercise.* To help you organize your teaching, we've done a bit of organizing for you already:

■ *God and Me, God and Us, God and Locals.* We've already told you about these three content categories that weave their way throughout the entire book. In general, try to emphasize all three categories roughly equally. For instance, if you have three sessions before a trip, try to choose one from each category of Me, Us, and Locals. Then do the same during the trip and after.

■ *The Order of the Exercises.* The exercises placed earlier in each section of the book (Before, During, and After) often lay groundwork for future exercises. Since you probably won't be able to complete all the exercises in any one section during a single experience, you might want to focus your attention on those placed first. But obviously, you know your students and your project better than we do, so please flip through all the exercises before zeroing in. We've marked some as essential, because if you have to choose to do only one or two, we think these are the most critical.

■ *Time.* Most exercises can be done in twenty to forty-five minutes, assuming you are working these discussions into meetings that require other elements. For those of you who prefer longer discussions, we've marked additional ideas as "Have More Time?"

■ *Integrating Scripture.* Some exercises center more on Scripture or incorporate some level of engagement with a Bible passage. We've indicated these with a Scripture icon.

■ *One-Day Projects.* If you are incorporating one or more of these exercises into a local half- or whole-day service project, please look for the One-Day symbol for ideas you can use without a "trip."

■ *Devotion Friendly.* Since many of you will want to lead daily group devotions with your students or give them time with God on their own, we've marked several exercises in the During section with this icon that can easily be used for this purpose. If your students are using the *Sticky Faith Service Guide Student Journal*, you can direct them to exercises for their personal reflection or group discussion. We've given you a list of these exercises on page 117 near the beginning of the During section. Otherwise, you will probably need to give some verbal instructions, make copies of the handouts in this book, and/or point students to the relevant Scripture passages so they can reflect and pray on their own.

■ *Rookies and Veterans.* Some of these sessions are better suited for less experienced students and teams, while others may be better for seasoned veterans. Similarly, if you are leading a middle school group, we have noted some sessions as particularly friendly for younger students. Look for the middle school symbol.

We are thrilled to navigate these journeys into service, compassion, mission, and justice-seeking with you. We can't wait to hear how God leads you and your team, so please share your stories with us at fyi@fuller.edu.

In the *Sticky Faith Service Guide Student Journal*, we have provided a number of additional options for your students to journal, including both guided exercises and blank pages. These can be used for morning or midday personal devotion time, evening quiet reflection before bed, or whenever you'd prefer based on your schedule. Specifically, here are the options that are ideal for participants' individual reflection times:

BEFORE

- "My Gifts"

DURING

- "Daily Journal" (Five days of journal entries based on daily reflection questions)
- "Your Kingdom Come"
- "Remaining in Christ"
- "Prayer of Review"

AFTER: DEBRIEF

- "Reflect Back"
- "Initial Debrief: Sharing the Highlights"
- "Sharing the Journey"

AFTER: ONGOING TRANSFORMATION

- "Paying Attention to the Presence of God"
- "What Now?"
- "Extra Journaling" (additional pages at the end of the *Student Journal*)

Other *Student Journal* entries are designed to be used with the group sessions included in this manual but could also be treated as stand-alone journaling and reflection exercises.

THE STICKY FAITH
SERVICE MODEL*

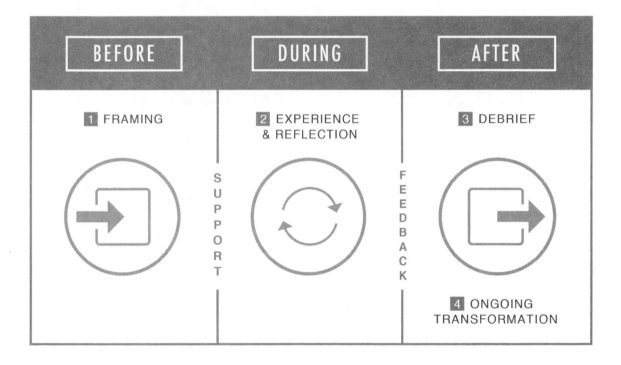

BEFORE   **DURING**   **AFTER**

1 FRAMING   2 EXPERIENCE & REFLECTION   3 DEBRIEF

SUPPORT   FEEDBACK

4 ONGOING TRANSFORMATION

---

*This model is built on an experiential education framework originally proposed by Laura Joplin and later modified and tested by Terry Linhart on youth ministry short-term mission trips. See Laura Joplin, "On Defining Experiential Education," in K. Warren, M. Sakofs, and J. S. Hunt Jr., eds., *The Theory of Experiential Education* (Dubuque, IA: Kendall/Hunt, 1995), 15–22; and Terrence D. Linhart, "Planting Seeds: The Curricular Hope of Short-Term Mission Experiences in Youth Ministry" *Christian Education Journal* 3 (2005): 256–72. For the purposes of this curriculum, some of the terminology in the model has been modified. Used by permission.

CHAPTER TWO
JOURNEYING TOGETHER

CREATING STICKY WALLS OF SUPPORT AND FEEDBACK FOR STUDENTS

FOURTEEN-YEAR-OLD AMANDA WAS A participant in a short-term mission trip I (Brad) once took. Amanda stood out because she walked into our church's trip more obviously broken than most kids and seemed more than a little hesitant about the cross-cultural realities we faced every day. To be honest, I was more than a little hesitant about her, and not long into the trip, I heard another leader mention that Amanda seemed really disengaged.

But Amanda didn't walk alone through her experience. Laura was there too—an adult who had been Amanda's small-group leader and was intentionally tracking with Amanda during this experience.

Our daily work was focused around teaching sustainable microgardening in our host community. I didn't really think the shoveling and planting was having much of an impact on Amanda. Yet the night before we packed up to head home, Amanda shared about a profound faith encounter. "Last night I talked with God," she relayed in our group debrief. She had lain awake for several hours praying and wrestling with God's presence in all she'd

seen and experienced—and then offered her life to God. She confessed to us that she was anxious about what that might mean for her back at home. Laura sat by her as she shared. Our team prayed with her, reminding her she was not alone in her faith journey.

Two months later Amanda stood in front of our congregation and shared about God's movement in her life before and since that trip, and was baptized as a public declaration of her faith in Christ. But Amanda didn't make that declaration alone; Laura was there with her, participating in Amanda's baptism. And we were there too—adults and students who pledged to keep walking with Amanda.

Amanda's story represents two fundamental pieces of the short-term project puzzle: *support* and *feedback*. Laura consistently offered Amanda a sounding board for her questions, and our team provided a safe place for her to be vulnerable about her stumble toward faith. Friends at church and the youth pastor added further pieces to the puzzle, voicing their encouragement and being patient with her struggles.

As we explained in chapter 1, the model

behind this process is the experiential education framework originally proposed by Laura Joplin[20] and later modified and tested by Terry Linhart.[21] In the center of the model is a cycle (Joplin pictured it as a hurricane) of challenging experience paired with reflection.

Note that this cycle of experience and reflection does not exist in a vacuum. Surrounding experience and reflection are *support* and *feedback*, two parallel walls that buoy the process. *Support* provides safety for students to keep trying even when they flounder, and *feedback* helps students form appropriate judgments and offers new insights to their experiences along the way.

Here's how it works: As young people are being purposefully stretched by their encounters, they are constantly assigning internal meaning to those experiences. The conversations in their heads never stop as their brains work overtime to process the often-disjointed perspectives of reality they tumble through each day. While the goals of *reflection* and *debrief* are to help decipher these messages and give them lasting meaning, *support* and *feedback* provide the backdrop for this whole drama. As it unfolds, trusted adults are somewhat like stage managers, giving cues and offering encouragement.

SETTING UP SCAFFOLDING

Lev Vygotsky was a developmental theorist who studied the social processes of development in children and adolescents and came up with a very helpful term: *scaffolding.*[22]

Scaffolding serves as the safe structure around the emerging adolescent that supports growth and fosters colearning with adults and other kids. Adults become the steadying force that is carefully added (when young people are most in need of that support) and removed (when they need to be set free to try on their own).

Please don't miss the imagery here: just as scaffolding is made up of many interlocking pieces in order to balance the weight and surround the building, no single adult can provide all the scaffolding a teenager needs. To truly thrive, every adolescent needs an interlocking network of caring adults. This is especially true when we ask them to serve others. In the midst of experiences that challenge and stretch them, young people need safe people and places in order to process the new experiences they face.

This developmental research echoed loudly throughout our Sticky Faith findings as we also observed the power of intergenerational relationships in helping faith stick long term. Based on research, we believe that each adolescent needs a team of at least five adults surrounding them with a web of support. Those adults aren't all paid youth leaders nor are they five small-group leaders. These five "team members" include relatives, neighbors, teachers, mentors, other students' parents, and the volunteers on your next mission trip.

Keeping this imagery in mind, we recommend the following four tips to help build webs of support around students during their service:

1. Maximize Support Channels

One mistake we often make when creating support structures around students is failing to capture the potential available to us. Support can take many shapes and sizes, and part of our role as leaders is to maximize this network for our students before, during, and after the trip.

Support can come from other people sharing in the experience—other students on the team, adults, local hosts—or it can come via the church family back home. Support comes in multiple forms, including finances and prayer as well as verbal and emotional footings. Knowing that their community has invested money, trust, and prayer into the ministry of their team is a compelling witness of God's faithfulness to young people in the midst of their work.

We also limit the support channels provided for students when we cling to a narrow perspective of who makes a "good" adult volunteer on a mission trip. As in other aspects of youth ministry, youth workers often look for only the youngest and hippest prospects to help lead trips. But in following this strategy, we may miss out on people who bring not only different life experiences but also a different level of safety for students.

Grandparents are one example. It had never occurred to me to invite grandparents along on a student mission trip until Julie asked if hers could join us for two weeks in Costa Rica. In many ways, Bob and Jean were the heroes of that trip. They offered an ultrasafe presence to teenagers and adults alike, and their years of wisdom steadied us without smothering us. Don't be afraid to step outside the realm of "normal" when you begin to build a support team for your next service trip—you might be surprised by who you find ready to journey alongside your students! In fact, the best adult support teams bring a mix of skills needed for the tasks at hand. One leader might have the technical skills needed to show a student how to hang drywall; another may model remarkable flexibility in the face of changing plans.

2. Create Opportunities for Risk

Whole books have been written about learning through our failures, so we probably don't need to convince you of that truth. But as leaders we sometimes forget to give young people the chance to risk failure as part of the learning process.

Our role as adults who provide support and feedback includes creating space for risk. In order to be willing to step into a space of risk, students have to feel safe. One of my early mentors in leading wilderness trips trained me to assess continually where participants fall on the *OSV* scale as a way to gauge our environment for healthy risk-taking. OSV stands for *oriented*, *safe*, and *valued*. I encourage adult leaders to periodically ask (sometimes out loud but often internally) the following:

1. *Is each person oriented?* Does she understand where we are, where we're headed, and what's going on?
2. *Does each person feel safe?* Physically, emotionally, spiritually, and mentally, have we pushed too far beyond the bounds of comfort for anyone (or everyone)?
3. *Does each person feel valued?* Have we communicated in any way that anyone's voice is not important or that his safety doesn't matter? Have we devalued the image of God in anyone by our actions, words, or attitudes?

These three simple guidelines help us assess whether we are creating safe and supportive environments for students to take healthy risks as they interact cross-culturally and make efforts to serve others. That doesn't mean we need to give young people every detail in order to orient them well. For example, one leader relayed that he tells students they're never allowed to ask, "What's for lunch?" or "What are we doing later today?" because (1) often it would change, and (2) he wants them to focus on the moment at hand and to learn to trust God during moments of uncertainty. Look for the balance between overfocusing on the person's desire for orientation while gauging the actual need for a sense of safety.

3. Reflect Back What You See

As young people dive into cross-cultural experiences or take on near-heroic tasks ("Let's build a house in a week!"), they need accurate information about not only what they're seeing but also what they're *doing*. Sometimes the most important insights you can share with a student are your observations about how that person is working, interacting with others, or exhibiting particular character traits.

When reflecting, it is important to be as specific as possible. It's more valuable to hear, "Tim, your encouraging comment to Sandy about the way she led games with the kids showed real selflessness, especially since you had wanted to be the game leader," than to hear, "Tim, you're a really nice guy."

4. Level the Playing Field

Feedback is best received when what Joplin calls an "equalization of power" exists between the participant and the leader. This doesn't mean we should negate our leadership in the midst of stretching experiences, but it might mean revisiting how we lead during those moments.

Students will be more likely to hear and apply our feedback when we *share power* with them as much as possible. This might mean we bring a few students into the decision-making meetings about the work project at hand. It might also mean we spend as little time as possible during our trip doing "leader-type" things and way more time doing servant jobs. When young people see us digging the sewage drain, mixing the concrete, or washing the dishes after a meal, they gain a new perspective on what it means to lead. Such leveling of the playing field often renders students more likely to hear us when we offer the feedback they so desperately need.

WHAT SUPPORT IS NOT

Recently a friend told me about a mom and son he'd seen at an airport. They were eating, and the son was being spoon-fed by his mother. But the boy was not an infant—he was an early adolescent, perfectly capable of feeding himself. His mom was feeding him because the young man was too busy playing a video game to stop and eat lunch. Seriously.

That mom needs some help with boundaries. And perhaps she needs help understanding the difference between support and, well, perpetuating immaturity. In other words, support is *not* an escape hatch for reluctant young fledglings to duck back in the nest and hide, comfortably sucking on worms. It's more like a safety net ten branches down, carefully positioned to catch if necessary, but only after the little bird has actually jumped and stretched its wings a bit.

During your justice work, you (or other adults on your team) might be tempted to bail out young people whenever they hit a challenging moment, a cultural wall, or the consequences of a bad decision. While there are certainly times we *should* bail out our students—especially if their or others' safety is jeopardized—we must walk a fine line between being the safety net and being the spoon-feeding parent.

THE RECOVERY TENT

If you've ever been part of a long-distance running race, you're probably familiar with the "recovery tent." Race planners with any kind of experience know that once runners hit the finish line, all kinds of (often painful) things can happen to their bodies and minds—cramping, nausea, disorientation, chills, and sometimes even more drastic experiences like heart failure. So the recovery tent is designed to supply post-race athletes with appropriate food, foil blankets, lots of water, and medical attention.

In a similar way, after a day—or a week, or three weeks—of serving cross-culturally, students need a recovery-tent environment to catch their breath, find some nourishment, and attend to their wounds. We have the *responsibility* to build a team of trusted adults who can create that type of recovery-tent environment around the students in our care. When we do, the Amandas on our teams will have opportunities to experience significant healing and growth in the recovery tent at the end of the day. Hopefully it will be one of the ways our young people will come face-to-face with God during their journeys.

CHAPTER THREE
PARTNERING WITH PARENTS
IN STICKY SERVICE
AND MISSION

IF YOU'RE LIKE MOST OF US IN YOUTH ministry, where do you turn when you need money to fund your service events? Your students' parents. And who do you assume will transport your students to and from your next project? Their parents.

While it's great to have the financial backing of families, and we all love those parents who let us borrow their big SUVs for a few hours or a couple of weeks, stickier service will come only when we view parents as more than just checkbooks and chauffeurs.

One of the best ways to partner with parents in sticky service is to empower them through good communication. Let's take some time to think about how our service can stick with parents before, during, and after a mission experience.

BEFORE: THE INFO MEETING

For major trips, many leaders find it helpful to host a parent meeting once the trip location and dates have been announced and before students sign up or apply to go. You can make this a forty-five-minute meeting after worship or at the end of a typical youth group gathering in order to make it as convenient as possible for parents.

The goal is to value parents by inviting them into the early communication about the what, why, when, and how of your trip, including the level of commitment you expect from their kids and from the parents themselves.

Make sure you set a warm and friendly tone by arranging your chairs in a circle and offering *adult* snacks (more than a bag of crushed tortilla chips and stale cookies).

This is a great time to provide as thorough a description as possible of your work's logistics, including the following:

- Why you chose this place for your service, and how it fits into your overall vision for compassionate action and seeking justice.

- Your partners (any agencies or churches with whom you're working).

- The other adults who will be going on the trip as leaders, and whether there are more spots available for parents to go as volunteers. Be sure there's time in the

gathering for parents to meet the leaders who are already in place.

- The student application and/or registration process, and by what date you will need a final commitment.
- What you'll actually be doing during your work.
- Food and lodging arrangements.
- Funding needed and the amount each student/family is expected to contribute, and by what dates.
- Fundraising strategies and how students and families are expected to participate.
- Transportation details (if you don't know them yet, hold this for the second pre-trip meeting).
- Safety precautions.
- Medical release forms and insurance (health or otherwise) needed.
- A schedule of additional meetings both before and after your service.
- What students need to bring with them. You'll have to repeat this list a few times, but now's a great time to start.
- Your plan for technology and communication. It will be helpful for parents to know ahead of time if, for example, you are collecting cell phones at the start of the trip and not returning them until the ride home. Parents who are used to being in constant communication will appreciate a heads-up about this and about your plan for communicating updates during the trip. (See p. 44 for ideas about communication so you can plan a strategy ahead of time.)

Allow time for parents' questions, and anticipate their concerns about safety by showing the work you've done to determine that this trip will be appropriate for the ages of students involved. If you have photos, video, or anything that might be helpful to give more context for the location and the partners with whom you will serve, share these too.

BEFORE:
The Pre-trip Family Meeting

We encourage you to schedule a ninety-minute meeting with students and their parents once the team has been determined and students are committed to the trip. The goals of this meeting are to engage parents more deeply in the "why" of the trip and to invite parents and students to develop a covenant of support.

You will most likely have students whose parents cannot (or don't want to) come. Please let these students know they are welcome to invite another adult, and if that doesn't work out, you or a volunteer can play the part of their parent for the evening.

YOU'LL NEED

- ☐ Copies of the "Family Covenant" handout (pp. 43–44)
- ☐ Pens
- ☐ Poster paper
- ☐ Markers

Before the meeting begins, hang four large pieces of poster paper along the walls of your meeting space. Write one of the following four headers on each piece of paper: STUDENTS' DREAMS FOR THEMSELVES, PARENTS' DREAMS FOR THEMSELVES, OUR DREAMS FOR THOSE WE SERVE, and OUR DREAMS FOR OUR FAMILY AND OUR CHURCH FAMILY.

Once people arrive, welcome everyone and ask the students to introduce their parent(s). Depending on the level of vulnerability in the group, you might ask students to share something unusual about their parents or one thing they've appreciated about their parents recently.

Ask parents:

Why are you excited for your kids to be part of our upcoming service experience?

After several parents have answered, explain:

Many people in churches (not our church, of course, but other churches!) tend to think that when it comes to service, something is better than nothing. In other words, any service is better than no service. I wish that were the case, but it's not.

Share some of the relevant research insights described in chapter 1 of this curriculum (p. 15). Explain:

As someone who wants to ensure that our service work makes a lasting impression on these students, on our church, and on the locals we'll be partnering with, I'm pleased to say we are working

diligently on a deeper approach to our service work.

At this point, distribute copies of the Sticky Faith Service Model found on page 28. Walk students and parents through the method, drawing from the explanation given on pages 19–21 of this curriculum. Along the way, share examples of ways you're planning to engage students before, during, and after the trip. If parents in your context are already familiar with Sticky Faith, you may want to mention that this helps further several of the research-based aspects of ministry that are correlated with faith that sticks beyond high school.

Continue:

We can't do this without you. In every aspect of your kids' growth and discipleship—including this one—we want to partner with you. I've shared the steps we as a youth ministry are planning to deepen the impact of this service on your kids and on the world. Now I'm hoping you'll think tangibly about your own role in this work. We would like you to take some time as a family to think through a few commitments you are willing to make to one another.

Distribute copies of the Family Covenant and pens to the parents and students, and let them know how much time you are giving them. Eight to ten minutes should be enough; you don't want to drag this out and have it get awkward. Make sure to point out that parents can either give specific goals ("I will pray for your service project every day for five

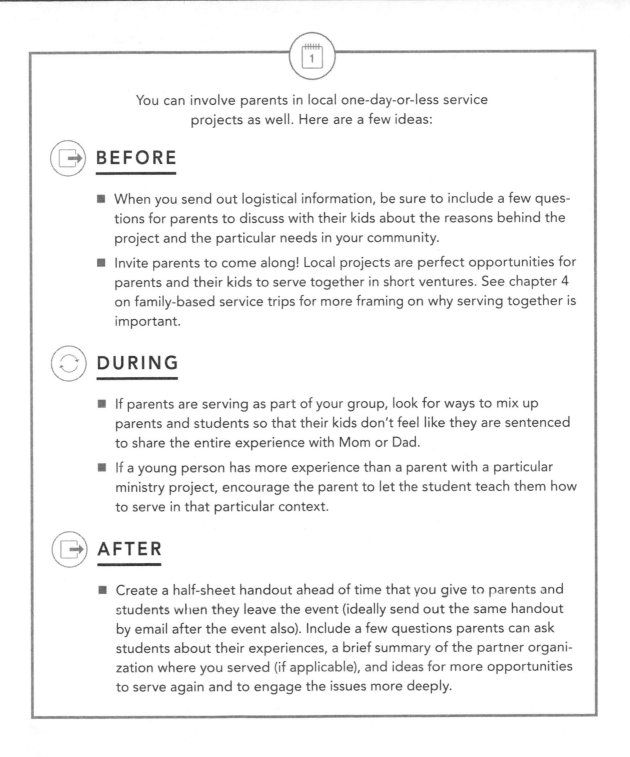

You can involve parents in local one-day-or-less service projects as well. Here are a few ideas:

BEFORE

- When you send out logistical information, be sure to include a few questions for parents to discuss with their kids about the reasons behind the project and the particular needs in your community.

- Invite parents to come along! Local projects are perfect opportunities for parents and their kids to serve together in short ventures. See chapter 4 on family-based service trips for more framing on why serving together is important.

DURING

- If parents are serving as part of your group, look for ways to mix up parents and students so that their kids don't feel like they are sentenced to share the entire experience with Mom or Dad.

- If a young person has more experience than a parent with a particular ministry project, encourage the parent to let the student teach them how to serve in that particular context.

AFTER

- Create a half-sheet handout ahead of time that you give to parents and students when they leave the event (ideally send out the same handout by email after the event also). Include a few questions parents can ask students about their experiences, a brief summary of the partner organization where you served (if applicable), and ideas for more opportunities to serve again and to engage the issues more deeply.

minutes") or more general goals ("As I think of this upcoming service, I will pray for you all"), and the same for students. You definitely don't want to create an atmosphere of competition among parents or cause parents to think they'll somehow be judged based on their level of commitment. We recommend that you let families keep their copy of the Family Covenant after they've filled it out so you don't even see what they've written. Encourage families to post the covenant in a central place at home where they will be reminded of these commitments to one another.

The "post-service support" category in the handout is one you should think about ahead of time. How do you hope parents will stay engaged after this project? At the very minimum, we strongly encourage you to schedule a sixty-minute post-event meeting for students and parents (see pp. 40–42). In addition, you can invite students and parents to any *ongoing transformation* activities you plan. Share as much detail as possible about those post-service activities *now* so parents can think about and write down what they'd like to commit to.

After families are finished, explain:

I'd like us to close our meeting by taking some time to dream and pray. As you can see, we've hung four different sheets of poster paper around the room. The first says STUDENTS' DREAMS. **I'd like students to walk up to this paper and use markers and write out (or draw) their dreams for how our service will impact them.**

The second poster paper says PARENTS' DREAMS. **As you can probably guess,**

I'd like parents to use markers to write out (or draw) on this sheet their hopes for how the youth ministry's service will impact you as parents.

You might want to give a few examples of the type of dreams parents could write, such as praying for God to do great work and then celebrate the answered prayers with their kids, or being more informed about and involved in issues of poverty and justice. (Note: To avoid bottlenecks, you might hang up multiple sheets of poster paper for each category.)

The last two sheets of poster paper are labeled OUR DREAMS FOR OUR FAMILY AND OUR CHURCH FAMILY **and** OUR DREAMS FOR THOSE WE SERVE. **On each piece of paper, as a family please write (or draw) the ways you hope this service impacts your family and our church, as well as the people you'll be serving. These might be new dreams that will hopefully emerge from the service, or they might be dreams you're already pursuing that hopefully the service will fuel.**

Here again, you might want to give some examples. A family might hope to sponsor a child or a family through monthly donations or more diligently clean out closets and donate clothes and household items to those who are poor. Dreams for those we serve might include providing new venues for ongoing education or creating job skills and greater job-placement opportunities.

Give plenty of time for families to write on all four sheets of poster paper, and then

call the group back together. Briefly recap the responses by reading out loud from each sheet. Finally, close in prayer. You can pray as a group (perhaps holding hands and inviting parents to pray for the youth ministry's service) or you can ask each family to huddle and pray together.

Make sure you save all four pieces of poster paper. They will come in handy during your post-service parent meeting.

DURING: Simple but Sticky Ideas That Engage Parents

While your energy during your actual service will be focused on your students and the locals you're serving, don't make the all-too-common mistake of neglecting parents back at home. Here are a few simple but sticky ideas to engage parents during your service work (you can also use these ideas to communicate with your whole church, but more on that coming up in chapter 5):

1. Encourage parents to gather together to serve in your community while your team is serving elsewhere. Then make sure to have parents and students each share about their experiences afterward.

2. During your service experience, invite parents to meet together at your church or a home to pray for your group regularly—maybe even daily.

3. Create a team blog in which you load daily photos and reflections and on which parents can comment with prayers and encouragement. Ask a few more mature

students if they would write brief reflections during the trip that you can post as you're able to do so.

4. If you are in a location where cellular service is available, use a group text service to send daily updates and photos to parents.

5. If you have convenient Wi-Fi access, consider providing a forum in which students can send email to parents and vice versa. Or designate a contact parent who will receive emails and pass them on. We only recommend this for trips longer than one week, as you want to be careful not to create a platform where students can dive back into home life or parents can hover inappropriately.

6. Consider inviting some parents to come along as leaders (if this is your first time inviting parent-leaders, check with their kids first to gauge how comfortable they are with this). See chapter 4 for specific ideas on helping whole families serve together.

AFTER: The Post-service Parent Meeting

When meetings for parents are held after a service experience, many youth workers find that few parents attend—and those who do come are usually the parents who are already committed to the type of conversations you're hoping to facilitate. (In other words, they're the ones who *least* need such a meeting.)

Given that, it's tempting to give up trying

to engage with parents after the service. Please resist that temptation.

Hopefully you were able to announce your plans for post-service activities when you held your pre-service parent meeting, and parents were able to commit to those activities in their Family Covenant. Even if that's not the case, we encourage you to consider the following ideas for engaging parents after your trip:

■ Create time for students to write letters to parents during your initial debrief, and mail those letters to the parents with an accompanying letter from you that celebrates all the Lord (and the students!) did.

■ Invite parents to some, or all, of your ongoing transformation activities after your work.

■ Schedule a local parent-student service activity in which your students and their families can serve side by side. Perhaps you can even find the same kind of activity the youth group did on their trip, allowing students to teach parents the skills they learned.

■ Give each parent a copy of any media presentations (e.g., videos, slide shows, PowerPoint presentations) you make.

■ Plan a one-hour post-service parent meeting. Consider providing a meal after worship and making provision for the whole family to attend (e.g., provide child care for younger kids or create an environment in which younger kids are welcome).

YOU'LL NEED:

■ The poster papers from the pre-service meeting where students and parents listed dreams for the students, parents, families and church family, and the community being served

Welcome participants and then ask students to introduce their parents. As part of the introductions, you might invite parents to share what they were doing while their kid(s) were serving. If some parents served with you, be sure to share that as they are introduced.

Explain:

Hopefully by now you parents have had a chance to hear how the Lord worked in and through our youth ministry as we served—at least from the perspective of your own son or daughter. Let's take some time to compare some of our early dreams for ourselves with what actually happened.

One at a time, invite students to find their own writing (or drawing) on the poster paper marked STUDENTS' DREAMS FOR THEMSELVES and read aloud what they wrote. Ask each student to comment on how those dreams matched, or didn't match, what really happened.

After all students have finished, ask the parents,

Q: **What themes did you hear in our students' responses?**

Q: **What, if anything, surprised you about what students shared?**

Explain:

Now it's time for the parents. Instead of doing this as a group, we'll do this sharing as families. Parents, I'd like you to find the dreams you had for yourselves from this poster paper labeled PARENTS' DREAMS FOR THEMSELVES and then huddle up with your kids to talk together about how those initial dreams matched, or didn't match, what really happened.

After families have completed that discussion, ask them to find what they wrote on the poster papers labeled OUR DREAMS FOR OUR FAMILY AND OUR CHURCH FAMILY and OUR DREAMS FOR THOSE WE SERVE and discuss if those dreams still seem to fit. Each family should discuss the new dreams they might have for themselves, the church, and the locals that emerged from, or were fueled by, the service. If they want to add to or revise their dreams, they can feel free to, if necessary, cross out what they originally wrote and rewrite (or redraw) their new dreams. If appropriate, emphasize that God's plans often unfold differently than we expect, so it's okay if our dreams weren't quite realized as we imagined.

Once families are finished, go around the group and ask each family to share one dream they wrote for their family and/or your church family as part of a closing prayer. After each family has finished, the rest of the group should say a one-sentence prayer out loud:

By the grace of our God, may it be so.

FAMILY COVENANT

We acknowledge that the upcoming trip requires energy, work, prayer, and commitment on the part of both students and families. Each of us would like to commit to the following together over the course of this project (please write a goal for any appropriate categories):

PRAYER SUPPORT

(Examples: commit to pray daily for the trip; invite others to pray on their own or join with me for particular prayer times; pray as a family before and after the trip)

PARENTS:

STUDENT:

LOGISTICAL SUPPORT

(Examples: drive my kid to meetings; try to avoid schedule conflicts with meetings; participate fully in meetings)

PARENTS:

STUDENT:

FINANCIAL SUPPORT

(Examples: give a certain amount of money before, during, or after the trip)

PARENTS:

STUDENT:

COMMUNICATION SUPPORT

(Examples: stay on top of communication from the youth ministry; share my own thoughts and concerns directly with youth ministry leadership; communicate with each other in the family about needs and emotions surrounding the trip)

PARENTS:

STUDENT:

POST-SERVICE SUPPORT

(Examples: figure out how to be involved in justice work at home; engage in service and justice as a family)

PARENTS:

STUDENT:

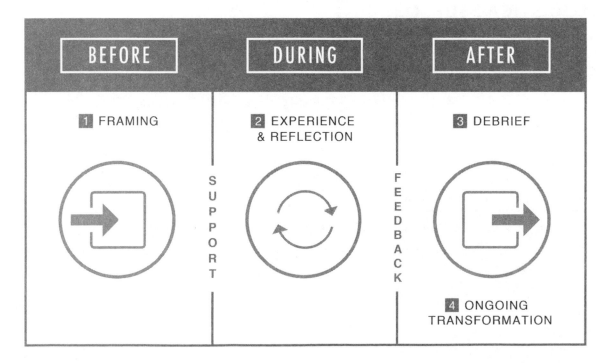

CHAPTER FOUR
CRAFTING A FAMILY SERVICE TRIP THAT STICKS

ONE WAY MINISTRIES ARE MOVING INTO stickier service is by organizing projects designed for families to serve side by side.

Here's where our work as researchers, youth workers, and parents collide. Each of us has a spouse and three kids. We also both believe in serving others in the name of Jesus inside and outside the church. This value works its way through our marriages and parenting, but we've noticed something striking: when our families of five serve, we usually serve in separate rooms or on separate trips. For both the Griffins and the Powells, all five family members are serving in various ways, but we often don't serve at the same time through the same experience.

We've also both led a lot of youth ministry service trips, so believe us when we say there's a lot of value in sixteen-year-olds side by side hammering nails or teaching the Bible

If you are looking for predesigned trips whole families can experience together, YouthWorks has a host of options. (See youthworks.com.)

to children. We wouldn't have written this resource if we didn't think that was true.

While serving alongside peers can be transformative, a unique strength emerges when family members serve as a team. Research has found that families who serve together grow in a host of other ways in their faith too. As one mom told us in an interview for our recent project, *The Sticky Faith Guide for Your Family*, "While I wish this wasn't the case, when I talk with my boys about how I hope they are willing to serve the Lord, they sometimes roll their eyes. When we actually serve the Lord together as a family, they never roll their eyes."[23]

We have seen this in our own families. Serving together sparks all kinds of great conversations that may never have emerged otherwise. For example, serving recently in an evening outreach program sponsored by my (Brad's) church to local immigrant families helped open our kids' eyes not only to the needs around them but also to their own privilege and access to resources they take for granted. Being there as a parent to be part of those experiences and insights (that frankly I've often had with *other* people's kids as a leader when they weren't around) was priceless.

What's more, when we interviewed fifty families from across the country about how they nurture Sticky Faith, we found that families who serve together tend to have churches who catalyze that service. Your church's gateway to family engagement may be one of the most important ways you support parents.

That's why we are excited to partner with YouthWorks, a short-term missions organization committed to building Sticky Faith, to help create a family trip model that has been tested and refined over the past few years. Out of that work, we share the following tips with you for developing your own family trip.

BEFORE

In addition to the parent meetings described above, you will want to communicate a few additional guidelines when families serve together.

1. *Create clear expectations about time and work.* Parents often care about the details of your plans for each day, including how long you will be working and logistics related to meals and housing. You will save yourself both time and failed expectations if you make an effort to communicate these logistics ahead of time and at the start of each day. If you are opening the trip to entire families and including younger kids, think carefully through the schedule implications for that shift (including shorter work hours, flexible afternoons for naps, and earlier bedtime options).

2. *Frame the parent's role as companion and fellow traveler.* In order for service to stick in the hearts and minds of their kids, parents need to assume a different posture than they probably do at home. As companions and fellow travelers, parents don't need to be experts. They simply need to share the experience alongside their kids, remaining open to how they might grow through it. Giving families opportunities to process together during the trip (see below) will help facilitate this.

DURING

1. *Help parents learn to notice, talk, and relax.* These three skills will help parents navigate a shared service trip with style. Share with parents the following tips:

- *Notice.* One of the best ways to get the most out of this trip is to *pay attention*. Remind yourself throughout each day to pay attention to what's going on with your kids — their emotions, energy, and reactions — and to what God might be doing in your midst.
- *Talk.* Take advantage of the moment, any moment, when you have a window to ask a question, point something out, or notice God together. Be sure to share your own reflections and not just to interrogate your kids in these moments.
- *Relax.* You are not a Super Christian Parent. You're probably going to blow it in some way on this trip, and so will your kids. Let Jesus work through the real you and your real kids, and don't sweat a little failure on both sides.

Give parents a copy of the "Questions to Ask along the Way" handout on page 48 to tuck in their pockets or Bibles, and be sure to bring extra copies for parents who lose their first one (or two).

2. *Give parents and kids space to work both together and apart.* Few teenagers want to spend the entire day—or week—side by side with their parents. Depending on the duration and nature of your trip, consider mixing up work teams, tasks, and meal arrangements so parents and kids have a balance of together time and time with other parents and students.

3. *Create fun, memorable experiences together.* Part of the memory-making for parents and kids on a trip like this might include a pickup soccer game after the workday is done, late-night card competitions, or relaxing somewhere fun at the end of the trip. Look for easy wins for fun connections.

 AFTER

1. *The post-meeting guide shared on pages 40–42 above can be adapted for a shared trip that includes parents.*

2. *Invite parents to one or more meetings using the ongoing transformation activities found in the final section of this book.*

3. *Give parents copies of the Post-trip Discussion Guide on pages 49–51 for families to use together immediately after the trip as well as a few weeks later.*

4. *Consider holding a separate debrief with parents a month or so after the trip.* Gather parents' impressions of what went well, what surprises they encountered, and what to consider for next time. Get their input on planning the next family trip, and consider asking a parent or two to spearhead that planning for you.

QUESTIONS TO ASK ALONG THE WAY

The best conversations with our kids often happen on the fly. But sometimes we need good prompts to kick-start those conversations. Keep this list of prompts handy and consider tapping into them before bedtime, in the car on the way to or from the work site, or over lunch. Don't ever try to blitz through all of them; just pick one or two at a time. Be sure you share your own answers too!

- What was most life-giving for you today? (or for younger kids, What was the best thing about today?)

- What was most draining today? When did you feel overwhelmed, frustrated, or undone today? (for younger kids, What was the worst part of the day?)

- What person or experience was most significant for you today? Why?

- How did you grow today? How are you being stretched?

- Where did you notice God today?

- What are you most thankful for right now?

- On a scale of 1 to 5, what overall rating would you give to today? Why?

- What unexpected gifts did you receive today?

- What are you asking of God for the coming day?

- How can I pray for you today?

FAMILY POST-TRIP DISCUSSION GUIDE

Whether you're a mile away from the work site or already back at home, you can use this resource to help you leverage what happened on your family trip to catalyze stickier service and mission as a family every day.

The good news is that families who serve together also tend to engage faith in lots of other ways. According to research by Diana Garland with over seven thousand Christians, families who serve together also "pray, read their Bibles, attend worship services, share their faith with others, promote justice, and give more financially than those not serving." Serving "is *the most significant and powerful contributor* to faith for teenage and adult Christians."[*] The more serving becomes part of the DNA of your family, the more likely you'll experience growth in all areas of spiritual formation.

HIGHLIGHTS FOR HOME

This list of reflection questions could be used on the drive home, over a meal stop, or once you return. You might want to break them up into a few different debrief conversations. Either way, they are meant to be shared fairly soon after your trip.

- What was one highlight from our trip for you—an experience, a relationship, or something that made you feel fully alive?

- Where did you notice God as we served?

- What's something new you learned about God?

- What was a lowlight for you—something that was frustrating, disappointing, or not what you expected?

---

[*]Based on surveys from 7,300 church members. Diana Garland, *Inside Out Families: Living the Faith Together* (Waco, TX: Baylor University Press, 2010), 42.

■ What did you learn about yourself?

■ What did you learn about our family? Did anything surprise you, make you laugh, embarrass you, or make you feel proud of our family?

■ What did you learn from people in the community or someone else on the trip?

■ Who do you want to remember from this trip?

■ What ideas do you have for how our family can serve together back at home?

■ Would you want to do this kind of trip again? Why or why not?

FAMILY DREAMING

A few weeks after your trip, set a time to gather for a family night to revisit the trip and think about connections with your life at home and your ongoing commitments to serve others. Look back at your pictures and videos from the trip and ask each person to share one story they most remember.

Hand out one sheet of paper to each family member, and give each person a few moments to start listing ideas for how they (and all of you) might serve others in the future. These ideas should be separated into three lists:

■ Dreams for myself

■ Dreams for our family

■ Dreams for those we serve

Encourage family members to think about ways to serve locally as well as beyond your community, whether across the state or across the globe. You may also want to talk about involvement in advocacy on behalf of others (e.g., raising money and awareness to help free child slaves) and specific people or groups your family wants to keep in prayer. While you may never travel to the Horn of Africa together, for example, your child's passion to support famine relief and basic health care might catalyze your family to pray and respond in other significant ways.

Take some time to debrief these new lists. Consider:

- What simple or wild ideas do family members have for serving together?

- What ideas resonate most with everyone?

- What could be some next steps for pursuing at least one of those ideas and developing a plan to put it into action?

- Who is the best point person for carrying out this first idea?

Be sure to keep the lists in a safe place or post them in your home so you can refer back to them and check in on progress toward your goals. Or you may want to create one "master" family list of goals you all agree to work toward together.

CHAPTER FIVE
YOUR CHURCH

DISCOVERING UNTAPPED RESOURCES FOR STICKY FAITH SERVICE

FOR MANY YOUTH MINISTRIES, THE SUM total of the church's support of your mission work is to listen patiently to a few student testimonies and then murmur, "Isn't that sweet?" Moving beyond this shallow (and somewhat patronizing) level of church engagement takes thought, perseverance, and a bit of diplomacy on your part. Here are a few ideas to catapult you and your students into a deeper relationship with your congregation.

→ BEFORE

- Meet with your church's missions committee so its members understand the goals of your service. You may want to invite a few students to attend the meeting with you. Consider inviting the missions committee members to participate in the trip as volunteer leaders.

- Ask your senior pastor if you can invite the church to pray for you and your students. Provide a list of specific prayer requests and pictures of your students in your church bulletin.

- Find out about any missionaries or leaders your church already supports in the region you're serving so you can connect with them before and during your work.

- Figure out creative ways to invite the congregation to support your trip financially. Consider selling $25 or $50 "shares" as a way to invest in students' transformation, or partnering with adult or children's ministries to make fundraising a shared effort.

- Ask the leader who works most closely with the children in your church if your students can pair up with one or more children and ask those children to pray for them. Make sure your students bring back a small gift for those children. Meet with your senior adult ministry and do the same thing.

- Invite a pastor from the community in which you're serving to come to your church and give a short profile, or even an entire sermon, on their community and what God is doing there already.

- Ask your church or specific classes or small groups to volunteer to mentor your students. See the Prayer Partner Guide (pp. 82–86) for ideas on how to help those mentors connect in meaningful ways.

- Make sure any means of communication you're sending from the trip (email, blog, etc.) are communicated to the whole church (in the weekly email, weekend bulletin, or a link from the church website).

- Ask for a sending/commissioning prayer from the congregation the weekend before you leave for your trip.

DURING

- At any church gatherings or services while you're gone, see if the parents of one or two of your students can lead your congregation in prayer.

- Any weekend you're away, give some sort of report at church services through phone calls, video conference calls, emails, or social media posts (depending on the technology available).

- Ask adult classes and small groups to spend a few minutes praying for your ministry. (When you get back, be sure to let them know how God answered their prayers!)

- Find out if there will be any prayer gatherings occurring during your service experience and ask the leaders to pray specifically for your students.

AFTER

- Report the work God did in and through your students to the entire church. When you share, be sure to highlight what you learned from the people in the community where you served.

- Teach your church any worship songs or rituals you learned from your hosts.

- Invite the locals you served to share (in person or by video) how God is working in their community and how your group participated in God's work.

- Invite adults who can help your students become justice advocates back home to meet with your students. There might be a city council member or community leader in your church; if not, someone in your church is likely to know that type of leader.

- Write a formal report for church leadership that includes participant numbers, financial cost analysis, hours of work served, a few stories of transformation, lessons learned, hopes for the future, and photos.

- Set up a meeting in which the students and adults who participated in the trip can discuss the experience with your church missions committee. Make sure the agenda includes discussing next steps for the church's participation in future service opportunities.

CHAPTER SIX
INTERGENERATIONAL SERVICE PROJECTS AND TRIPS

IF YOU WANT TO CREATE EVEN STICKIER intergenerational relationships, think about inviting adults in your congregation to *serve with* your youth ministry. Serving together beyond the church can be a powerful catalyst for relationships. Whether these are weekly or monthly experiences in your community or short-term mission trips out of the country, following are a few helpful tips based on what we've learned from experienced leaders:

1. *Start small.* While we know several youth pastors who canceled their typical summer youth mission trip so they could host an intergenerational trip, few leaders attempt that kind of leap as a first step. Look for a local opportunity to serve alongside adults in your congregation or jump on board with something another ministry is already doing. Serving with your children's ministry can also be a great first step.

2. *Give lots of framing.* Many leaders have found that they need to frame the "why" of serving together both for young people and for adults. You might want to share the insights from *Sticky Faith* that point to the importance of intergenerational connection. For example, share that every young person needs a web of

support that ideally includes at least five non-parental adults. Teenagers with such a web in place tend to stick with faith and church into adulthood.[24] Serving together creates a natural context for building these kinds of supportive relationships.

3. *Mix it up.* As soon as you have opportunity to do so—whether at a pre-trip planning meeting or at the start of your service day—mix up the generations with get-to-know-you games, table assignments, or mixed work teams. Be sensitive to the level of awkwardness that everyone can handle at first. Ideally, any mixed group should include at least two students who know each other.

4. *Spread out jobs evenly.* Look for opportunities to level the serving field to set up young people to contribute in significant ways that might surprise adults. For example, you might invite a teenager to lead the morning devotions while a middle-aged CEO is placed in charge of filling water coolers for the day. This can be fruitful for both of them. Also be sure students don't get let off the hook on tasks like cooking or cleaning up after meals. Create mixed teams for these tasks as much as possible.

5. *Create skill-building opportunities.* Keeping the above in mind, if someone is skilled in a particular area and another person wants to learn that skill, pair them up. The motivation to learn can help relationships grow. And note that it might be a teenager who is teaching that skill to an adult!

6. *Look for the little wins.* When you get adults and young people serving side by side, celebrate that as a win! Then look for every little win you can find. A smile, a conversation, an approving nod, a teenager choosing to sit by an adult for lunch without being asked. Treasure these moments, and make sure someone is capturing photos so you can talk up these stories in your congregation later.

7. *Debrief together.* During any debrief or reflection time, make sure both adults and students participate. Listen for insights that are both similar and different across generational perspectives. As time allows (or over meals or while traveling), invite the older generations to share about a meaningful experience they had when they were younger. Then let the younger participants speculate about what they want to be like when they are older.

8. *Don't stop now!* If you've been able to get adults and young people serving together once, that's a great start. Gather input from all age groups who participated, and start planning your next shared experience.

Since intergenerational service can feel daunting to those of us who have built our ministries around youth-based projects, we thought we'd close with an inspiring story shared by our friend Keegan, a Sticky Faith leader who has been leading intergenerational trips for the past handful of years:

We began experimenting by mixing our traditional youth summer mission trip with an equally traditional adult summer mission trip. This was a huge change, and one of the important components of those trips was to be intentional about intergenerational connections. I did not realize how difficult this was going to be for us. We have become so accustomed to segregation by ages in the church that we do not know how to engage relationally with one another. People tend to think that if all ages are in the same space together it's an intergenerational gathering. This couldn't be further from the truth, because more often than not none of those age groups is actually talking with another.

In the months leading up to the trips, I would remind the adults, "We are in this together." I would even say they could get work done faster without the teenagers, but if they would take the time to teach the skills and be present with the teenagers, they would be offering more than just skills in building a park or church office.

After two months of our pre-trip meetings, I finally got them to split

up and sit in mixed groups. We offered specific questions to get conversation going. About the time we left for the first trip, a few adults actually began to interact with students. Slowly the walls began to come down.

After the first trip, life on Sunday mornings back at church began to change. Students would call the names of adults from across the patio and run for a hug. People began to notice this change, even Vic, the general contractor on our work sites both years.

By the third year, Vic couldn't wait to go on our summer trip again. He became known that as "the guy who would buy ice cream every day after work." It was one way he could relate with the kids.

The students fell in love with Vic too. When we came home one summer, I asked several students what they thought about Vic joining our volunteer staff on a regular basis. They thought it was the best idea! The coolest part? Vic was sixty-six years old.

Sitting down with him and inviting him to share his life with students wasn't that hard because he'd already told me how great they were. It was affirming for him to hear appreciation from teenagers too. Vic became an amazing ministry volunteer.

Getting adults and teenagers to learn to serve with each other—and like each other—was hard work. But our church is less fragmented today than we were before we started this journey. That's another step in the right direction.

BEFORE: FRAMING

Prepare students—and yourself—for all that awaits you in your journey. Use these exercises as part of your pre-trip meetings or before short local service experiences.

BEFORE: GOD AND US
PRAYING FOR EACH OTHER

ESSENTIAL · ONE-DAY · MIDDLE SCHOOL

HEADS-UP TO LEADERS!

One of the learning exercises we suggest you might use after your work ("The Hope of Glory," pages 186–187) will work *way* better if you do a bit of setup before your work begins. Plus, it's always a good idea to get students praying for each other.

And if you are using this idea as part of a one-day service experience, you might need to do this exercise pretty quickly—maybe even as you are driving to your service site. If you're short on time, you might want to ask students to list one prayer request instead of two. You might also need to do a fairly short prayer time (like thirty seconds), but it's still wise to take a few moments beforehand to nudge students to pray for each other throughout the day.

To get participants connected and praying, consider doing the following activity.

Before your mission begins (ideally early in your preparation process), pass out index cards to all trip participants and ask them to write their names at the top of their cards. Then invite each person to list two personal prayer requests for this trip. Be sure to let them know before they start writing that these requests will be shared with other participants (you can decide whether adults and students will be mixed for this activity), and that they will be praying for one another using these cards.

Then gather the cards and redistribute them to participants, either randomly or intentionally (just be sure no one ends up with their own card!). You may want to redistribute them in gender-specific ways so guys only pray for guys and girls only pray for girls. Instruct each student to pray for the person whose card they receive throughout your team's preparation and during your trip. Invite students to keep these cards by their beds or in their Bibles—wherever they will see the card frequently and be reminded to pray. If you'd like, you can either ask them to keep their prayer partners a secret or to encourage each other by letting their partners know they are receiving prayer.

WHY GO?

ESSENTIAL   SCRIPTURE

BIG IDEA

Youth ministries engage in service projects, mission trips, and other kinds of justice work for a variety of reasons. Early on in the experience, our group should determine exactly why we're going and state that reason in one clear sentence we can share with others.

YOU'LL NEED

☐ Poster paper and markers. Ahead of time, tape pieces of poster paper on different walls around the room.

☐ Optional: Copies of the *Sticky Faith Service Guide Student Journal*

Start by saying,

> Most of us do things every day that we simply don't put much thought into. We might call them "no-brainers"—we just do them, seemingly without even thinking—for example, brushing our teeth, putting on deodorant (hopefully!), breathing, and tying our shoes.

> Think for a minute about something you've always done but you're not really sure why or when you started. Would anyone like to share one of those no-brainers with us?

Q: Why do we do those things so thoughtlessly?

Q: Can you think of things we do pretty thoughtlessly that we probably should think harder about?

Examples might be posting on social media or thoughtlessly checking our phones or other devices in the midst of conversations or even important gatherings like this one.

> As we get ready for our upcoming service work, we need to be careful that this experience is not just another no-brainer.

Preparing for and entering our trip on cruise control could lead to a number of negative outcomes: we might get frustrated with one another, ourselves, and our hosts; we might do more harm than good in our host community; and we might not experience the transformation we hope for through this experience—either for ourselves or for the community we're serving.

Today we're going to take some time to guard against a no-brainer approach to preparing for our trip together. We're taking some time to get at an important question: Why are we going?

At this point, invite your students to walk around the room and write on the poster paper at least one of the reasons they are involved in this work.

There are, of course, a number of reasons groups do short-term missions, and even more reasons why individual students choose to go. Some of the reasons students list might include: "We've always gone"; "Other youth ministries do it"; "Church leaders/parents expect it"; "To get service hours for school"; "To be stretched or changed"; "For multicultural exposure"; "To bring justice where we see injustice"; "To serve the poor"; "To be with friends"; "To get away from home": or "To spread the gospel." It's important to clearly understand early in the process all the motives on students' and leaders' minds.

Have a different student read the writing on each poster paper aloud, then ask the group:

Q: What are some of the themes you notice in our reasons? How do you feel about those?

Q: Looking at the motives we all wrote, is there anything we've missed that we might want to consider? Are there any motives you think we might want to change?

Q: How do you think the people who will host us might feel about these motives?

Q: Are there ways we could be more God-honoring or more sensitive to the reasons God might want us to be involved in this justice work?

Many private and public schools require some sort of "community service hours," so you may have some students participating in your event partly to meet this school requirement. If this is the case, be mindful that the goal of those questions is not to shame these students but to invite them to be open to something more that God might have in mind for this experience.

After you have had some good discussion about the "whys" of your trip, note to the group that asking, "Why are we going?" begs a related question:

Q: Why are we going *together*?

Explain:

While we often focus on our personal relationships with Jesus, the Bible indicates that the ways we relate to one another are also important.

In fact, some of the passages in the New Testament that we often interpret as applying to "me" really apply to "us." The New Testament uses a "you" that is plural—really a "you all" (similar to *ustedes* for any Spanish speakers out there)—to communicate some important truths about the value of doing life, service, and even short-term mission trips with other believers. Let's look at a few of those Scripture passages together.

Divide students into smaller groups and have each group look up one of the two passages below. Ask them to discuss how these words of Jesus might shape the way we do work as a team.

1. MATTHEW 5:13–16

Q: When you hear this passage, what ideas come to mind about what it means to be "salt" and "light" today as followers of Jesus?

Q: The "you" in this passage is really a "you all." How does knowing that change the way we think about what it might mean to be "salt" and "light"?

ⓘ In Jesus' day, salt was used to flavor foods and as a preservative, especially for meat.

Q: Thinking specifically about our trip, how could these words of Jesus shape the ways we serve as a team?

Q: How can we be on the lookout for ways "salt" and "light" are already being shared among our local hosts?

2. MATTHEW 28:16–20

Q: When you hear this passage, what ideas come to mind about what it means for you to "go and make disciples of all nations" today as a follower of Jesus?

Q: The verbs in this passage are all plural— they imply "you all" together, not just "you" individually. How does knowing that change the way we think about what it might mean to be called to "go"?

Q: Thinking specifically about our trip, how could these words of Jesus shape the ways we serve as a team?

Q: What could it mean for us to be the ones who are being discipled just as much as—or maybe even more than—the people in the place where we'll serve?

Bring the smaller groups back together to share their insights with the whole group, and then move on to the final part of the discussion.

Continue:

It is unlikely that each of us would write the exact same statement about why we're going on this trip, but perhaps we can work together to create a statement

expressing a common purpose and vision. A clear statement of our mission can help guard against the no-brainers that could sabotage our attitudes and our service.

Of all the reasons we've discussed that we might use as the primary focus of our trip, what do you think is the *best* reason? Can we summarize this best reason in one sentence?

Work together with students to complete the following sentence, hopefully right there in your meeting. You might need to look at each part of this sentence separately, perhaps listing possible answers below each line, and then deciding at a later time on your final statement. Use this sentence or some variation of it to help your group create a clear purpose:

We're going to _____
(place)

to _____
(what we think we're going to do there)

because _____.
(why we feel compelled to go)

HAVE MORE TIME?

One link that's often missing in youth short-term missions is the buy-in and full support of the church. Once your group has determined a clear purpose statement for your trip, you might want to take it to the church missions committee and/or senior leadership for their review, input, and support. Ideally they would be in on the process before you get to the point of forming a student team, but we know church processes don't always work that way! The point is to take the "extra" time to be sure the wider church family is on board with what you're doing. That support will go a long way in the lives of your students and their families.

Another idea would be to start this entire process with the church mission statement or purpose statement and then work backward to why, on a large scale, your youth ministry is doing this service. This could then become the context for all the ideas listed by the group and could draw them more deeply into the life of the congregation.

Close by thanking God together for calling you to serve and to act with justice. You might want to use an open-ended prayer in which students can speak sentence prayers in response to your prompts, including possibly:

- prayers of thanksgiving for the opportunity to serve and bring justice;

- prayers of repentance for the ways we have served out of self-focused or harmful motives;

- prayers for God's vision and purpose to guide our group's vision and purpose; and

- prayers of praise in advance for what God will do through our willingness to serve.

Note: You may want to start future pre-trip meetings by reviewing this statement as a way to keep everyone focused on the big-picture "why" of your work.

STICKING TOGETHER IN UNITY

ESSENTIAL   SCRIPTURE   MIDDLE SCHOOL

BIG IDEA

When we are unified as a group, we are more open to the work of God's Spirit in us and more able to allow Christ to work through us as we serve others.

YOU'LL NEED

- Intro Option A:
  - Play the Gettysburg speech clip from the movie *Remember the Titans*. As of this printing, it can be found online at youtube.com/watch?v=E_HFCYz4x6o, titled "Remember the Titans—Coach Boone Speech."
- Intro Option B:
  - Large open area (indoor or outdoor)
  - Masking tape (indoors) or cones (outdoors)

- Bicycle tire tubes or hula hoops (at least one for every two to four students)
- Bibles
- Poster paper or whiteboard
- Markers
- Ball of string, twine, or yarn
- Optional: Copies of the *Sticky Faith Service Guide Student Journal*

Intro Option A: Greet your students and set up the clip from the movie *Remember the Titans* by explaining:

Remember the Titans is a movie depicting a true story about a high school football team in the 1960s that deals with issues of race in a newly integrated school. The tensions between the racial groups rise as the players try to claim spots on the team during training camp. This clip begins as Coach Boone (played by Denzel Washington) wakes the entire team in the middle of the night for a surprise training run.

Play the movie clip and then lead the following discussion:

Q: What are some of the differences that tend to divide people in your school, family, community, country, and world?

Q: Why do you think it is so difficult for people to see past those differences and be unified?

Q: What are some of the differences among us on this team?

Q: In what ways have you noticed our differences affecting the way we interact as a group?

● ● ●

Intro Option B: Mark off a large circle with cones or tape. Have two to four students come to the center and stand inside the same bicycle tire tube (or hula hoop) with the tube at their waists, forming a circle facing outward. Explain that they are going to play tug-o-war, but in this game, it's every person for themselves. The object of the game is to be the first person to get across the outside circle (cones or tape) while remaining inside the bicycle tire tube. You may need to try this out first in order to make sure your circle is wide enough and tubes are strong enough. If your tubes break, simply add another one to double the resistance and strength. After you play a few rounds, gather everyone to debrief the game.

Explain:

Sometimes in life it seems everyone is moving in his or her own direction, and it's tough to make any progress. Even as we serve together, we all have different individual goals for what we want to learn and accomplish as well as our own ways of doing things.

Q: Have you ever been part of a group or a team in which it felt like everyone was doing their own thing? Talk about that experience.

Q: What would happen if we all operated like this on our service experience?

● ● ●

Continue:

Today we're going to talk about unity as a team and as the body of Christ. It might seem obvious we should be unified, but unity is often difficult to achieve, especially in an unfamiliar environment in which all of us likely have our

own goals and perspectives. So the first thing we need to do is ask, "Why do we need unity in the midst of our work?"

Write students' suggestions on a whiteboard or poster paper.

Continue:

Those are all great reasons to strive for unity. Jesus seemed to care a lot about unity among his disciples, as well as among those who would follow him in the future. Let's explore and find out why. In the Scripture passage we're about to read, Jesus has just told the disciples he is about to be arrested and crucified. He's praying for all his disciples—both then and now (which means he's praying for you!).

Read John 17:20–23 aloud.

In John 17:21 Jesus prays that his disciples through all time will be one just as he and the Father are one. That means our goal isn't uniformity (after all, Jesus and God aren't absolutely identical) but rather a unity of purpose and mission.

Q: Why did Jesus care that his disciples were unified?

Q: With whom did Jesus want his disciples to be unified?

Q: What other people outside of our team do you think God might want us to be unified with on this trip?

Hopefully students will mention your local host community, as well as others in your own church who aren't going on the trip. If they don't, please mention them yourself.

Q: What might hinder us from being unified with God, one another, or any of these other people we have mentioned?

Q: What are some ways we can seek to be unified as a team during our service?

Write students' ideas on poster paper or a whiteboard.

Affirm students' ideas and explain that you have an activity that will help you start to feel the power of unity.

Team Exercises: (Choose one of the following, or do one now and another in your next meeting.)

1. *Connected to the web.* Share hopes, fears, and expectations together as a group by being united by a ball of string, yarn, or twine. Begin by having a volunteer share a hope, fear, or expectation for your service. When that person finishes sharing, tell her to hold on to the end of the string and then throw the rest of the ball of string to someone else she would like to have share, ideally someone sitting across the circle. Continue this process until everyone has shared and you end up with a web of string spanning the circle. If the string is fairly strong, you can have everyone stand up and lean back a bit. At that point, share that

when we are bound to one another in unity, we can hold one another up as we learn, grow, and face our fears. Then take a pair of scissors and cut the string in a few places, which will cause the circle to collapse. Explain that when we are disconnected and left to ourselves, we may not experience all that Christ desires to do in and through us. As the string demonstrates, we are stronger together than we are on our own.

2. *Group covenant.* Write a covenant together to clarify the expectations for how your team members will treat each other. Begin with general brainstorming, making sure to create a safe environment in which every idea is heard and acknowledged. Once your students have had a chance to share their ideas, go back through the suggestions and see if your students can agree on which expectations are most important to your team's unity. Write those expectations on poster paper and invite students to sign their names at the bottom of the poster paper. Afterward type up (or ask a student to type up) the covenant and distribute it to your team members, as well as to their parents and church leaders.

3. *Subteams.* Now or later you may want to divide into subteams, especially if you have a large group. It's best if you do the dividing ahead of time and announce the teams rather than have students choose their own teams. These teams might be work project groups, shared-chore groups, daily debriefing groups, or all of the above. Encourage them to come up with a team name. This can give everyone a sense of belonging and help them learn about working together in unity to accomplish shared goals.

Close with a prayer for unity, inviting students to repeat one phrase at a time after you:

> *God, we thank you for creating us*
> *to be in relationship with one another.*
> *We confess we often do our own thing,*
> *seek our own interests,*
> *and miss the blessing*
> *of sharing in unity with one another.*
> *Help us depend on you*
> *and offer ourselves to one another.*
> *Unify this team, Lord,*
> *and make us a witness*
> *to your love for the world.*
> *Let your Spirit work in us*
> *and through us as we serve.*
> *Amen.*

WHAT DO THEY NEED MORE?

SCRIPTURE   ROOKIE   MIDDLE SCHOOL

BIG IDEA

The gospel invites us to focus on people holistically and participate in kingdom work that serves both spiritual and other (physical, relational, economic) needs.

YOU'LL NEED

- A photograph of someone experiencing deep poverty—either from your host community or from some other part of the world. You can easily download images from organizations which serve the poor, such as World Vision or Compassion International. You only need one picture, but it helps if you have a specific name and a bit of information about the person and their context to share with the group. The point is to put a face and a name to physical needs. See the "Have More Time?" idea below for an alternate way to open this activity.

- Whiteboards or poster paper and markers
- Bibles
- Index cards
- Pens
- Tape
- Wall on which students can tape index cards. If that's not possible, use poster paper or a whiteboard to create a large area that will work.
- Optional: copies of the *Sticky Faith Service Guide Student Journal*

HAVE MORE TIME?

Have students visit a local homeless shelter, nursing home, or food pantry/soup kitchen ministry in your community. Be sure to get permission ahead of time, and send students in pairs with video cameras or voice recorders to interview care-givers they encounter. Encourage your students to ask questions about needs on various levels. Debrief the experience as part of this lesson, discussing the different ways we—and others—perceive needs. You might even use these interviews as an opener to the discussion.

Begin by asking students to share some of their needs this week—big or small. Ask how those needs are being met or going unmet, and how that is impacting their week. It might be appropriate to pause to pray for one another and lay your needs corporately before the Lord before you go on.

Next invite students to view the photograph you've brought of the person experiencing deep poverty. If it's someone from the host community you'll visit during your upcoming trip, you can tailor the conversation directly around that community. If it's someone from another location, you can use this as a case study to help your group think together about holistic ministry and then apply it to your host community and the work you hope to do there.

Describe the person and share as much as you know, then ask:

Q: **What do you think might be some of _____'s needs?**

Depending on the situation, the tangible support might be more obvious than others—medicine, food, education, shelter, or other needs can be mentioned here specifically.

Q: **Suppose we knew that _____ had never heard about Jesus. How many of you think _____'s biggest need is hearing about Jesus? How many of you think his/her biggest need is tangible physical support?**

It's inevitable that some students will say this person needs both, but don't let them choose that middle ground. Ask them to choose the one need they think is most pressing.

Divide students into two groups based on their answers and ask them to discuss the reasons for their answers.

After four or five minutes, bring the groups back together and ask them to share their ideas.

Q: **Having heard these ideas, which seem especially powerful?**

Continue:

Let's see how Jesus handled an encounter with a paralyzed man in Mark 2:1 – 12.

For variety's sake, you may want to ask for two volunteers to read the story — one student reads Jesus' words while the other one reads everything else.

Continue:

Homes in first-century Palestine were different from most of our homes today. A typical peasant's house was a small, one-room structure with a flat roof. Some homes may have included an outside staircase that led to the roof. The roof itself was usually made of wooden beams covered with thatch and compacted earth to keep moisture from entering the house. Sometimes tiles

There's been great debate about Mark 2:5, where Mark writes, "When Jesus saw *their* faith." Does "their" refer to the faith of the four friends, or the faith of the four friends plus the paralytic's faith? The original Greek doesn't definitively answer this question. Given what you know about Scripture, what do you think?

were laid between the beams and thatch for even greater protection.

In this passage the four men, upon seeing the crowd in the one-room house, probably carried the paralyzed man up the outside staircase, dug through the thatch and earth, and lowered him between the beams.

Q: **Does Jesus choose to help this man's soul or his body?**

If Jesus weren't really the Son of God, then the teachers of the law in verse 7 were right — Jesus would have been blaspheming. In Jewish teaching, even the Messiah couldn't forgive sins; only God could. The teachers weren't just being mean to Jesus; they were trying to protect their people's understanding of God.

The answer is both.

Q: **Do you think there's any significance to the fact that Jesus forgave his sins first, before healing him? Why or why not?**

Draw a horizontal line on the whiteboard and explain:

We've been talking about two types of needs — physical and spiritual. Most people tend to think of these needs as unrelated, or as two different ends of a continuum.

At this point, write PHYSICAL/PRACTICAL NEEDS on one end of your line and SPIRITUAL NEEDS on the other end.

As we see from Jesus' interaction with the paralytic, the two types of needs don't lie in opposition to each other. The reality is that God's kingdom helps meet both types of needs. Instead of a line, God's kingdom is more like a circle. (Draw a circle and write both SPIRITUAL NEEDS and PHYSICAL/PRACTICAL NEEDS inside the circle.) All types of needs are crucial to the kingdom, and they are interconnected in all kinds of ways.

Q: As we consider this image of a circle, let's think about Jesus. If Jesus were to encounter _____ and his/her family, what do you think he'd do? What do you think he'd say?

It's likely many of your students might say Jesus would try to "convert" this person by convincing them they needed eternal life. You may want to help them focus not only on Jesus' words about salvation but also on his hopes and dreams for this person—and for others who live in despairing circumstances. Help your students think about how Jesus might want this person to experience the kingdom—not just in the ultimate new creation but also in their life and relationships here and now.

If your students are still feeling the both-and tension in this exercise, that's okay. In fact, it's probably a good thing. Living in the midst of that tension is the key to kingdom thinking that pulls both together.

Continue:

As we keep wrestling with this both-and kingdom concept, we can actually look back to the cross for a model. Jesus' death on the cross is the ultimate example of the gospel's power to meet all our needs. His death not only rescued our souls but also impacts our entire lives—including our relationships, our bodies, and our emotions.

Now we are kingdom people who are called to follow Jesus' example. The Bible calls that justice—following Jesus' example of righting wrongs around us whether they be spiritual, physical, emotional, or all of the above. What do you think about that explanation of justice?

Using these index cards and pens, I want you to write down the ways you see our ministry (and particularly our upcoming project) helping meet people's various needs. Please write one need we will try to meet on each card.

Give students a few minutes to complete this. You may want to have a few examples ready to prime the pump, and you might consider giving prompts students can complete, such as "Our ministry will impact souls by . . ." or "Our ministry will impact physical needs by . . ." or "Our ministry will impact relationships by . . ."

ⓘ Although God's kingdom is active in the world, there's also a lot of sin in the world around us. But in the midst of sin's darkness, God's kingdom is light. Jesus himself says so in John 8:12: "I am the light of the world. Whoever follows me will never walk in darkness, but will have the light of life." As Jesus is alive in us, we become "the light of the world" (Matthew 5:14).

Continue:

Now I'm going to give you some tape. If what you've written is primarily focused on impacting people's souls, then I want you to tape that card to the left portion of the wall. If you think the impact is primarily on the rest of their lives—such as their bodies, emotions, or relationships—please tape that card to the right portion of the wall.

You might want to label both sides so students don't have to remember which goes where. After students are finished, read aloud the cards on both sides.

Q: Which items appear most frequently on the left? Which items appear most frequently on the right?

Q: What connections do you see between the ways we plan to help people—both physically and spiritually—and our efforts to bring about justice? How are our efforts to help others connected to the way we worship? How are they connected to our salvation?

Q: As kingdom agents, what ideas do you have for what we can and should do differently as we prepare?

Q: How can we develop a plan so we actually act on these ideas and don't just talk about them? Is there someone from our host community with whom we need to consult in order to best honor the community in the midst of trying to understand its holistic needs?

Close by gathering ideas and setting up action plans for moving toward a more holistic, justice-oriented trip. Spend time in prayer together, asking God to reveal the ways he cares deeply about the holistic needs of the people in your host community.

PARABLE OF THE CRACKED ROADS

VETERAN

BIG IDEA

Beyond meeting immediate physical needs, justice invites deeper, more holistic, and more systemic solutions.

YOU'LL NEED

- Whiteboard or poster paper
- Pens
- Bibles
- Copies of "Parable of the Cracked Roads" handout (pp. 79–80) and/or copies of the *Sticky Faith Service*

Guide Student Journal; at least three copies of the handout for your three readers or copies for everyone

- "Have More Time?" option: Copies of the "Service vs. Justice" handout (p. 81)

Ideally you would lead this discussion in a location where cracked roads or cracked concrete is visible (a parking lot, a quiet side street, or a deteriorating sidewalk would work well). If that's not possible, you might want to start by commenting on either the cracked roads you've driven on that day or the cracked roads that crisscross their way through your home city.

Ask for three volunteers who like to read aloud, and give each one a copy of the "Parable of the Cracked Roads" handout. Explain that

each reader represents a different way youth ministries serve others.

After the three readers are finished, lead the following discussion, taking notes on the whiteboard:

Q: How would you describe the Quick-and-Easy Physical Solution of the first youth ministry?

Q: How about the second youth ministry's Warm-and-Fuzzy Friendly Solution?

Q: You guessed it ... What about the third youth ministry's Deeper Solution?

Q: Chances are good that the goal of our upcoming mission isn't to fix cracked roads, so let's translate this parable to what we will be doing. What are the immediate physical needs of the people we'll be serving?

Q: How will we try to meet those needs?

Q: Let's think about some deeper needs of the people we've served. What are their ...
   • emotional needs?
   • relational needs?
   • educational needs?
   • spiritual needs?
   • economic needs?

Q: What deeper structural or systemic problems might have led to those needs?

Q: What is preventing the locals from meeting those needs themselves?

Q: What, if anything, could we do to meet those needs?

HAVE MORE TIME?

Distribute copies of the "Service vs. Justice" handout (p. 81) to your students and review it together. Lead the following discussion:

Q: Which parts of the table don't make sense to you?

Q: Which rows on the table seem most important for us to keep in mind in our upcoming work? Why?

Q: What can we do during our trip to help us be more like the right-hand side of the table?

Q: What can we do here at home, both before and after our trip?

Explain:

One way to think about the difference between service and justice is that we serve when we give water to people in need; we engage in justice when we figure out why those folks don't have the water they need in the first place and then work with those individuals and communities so they have access to clean water in the future.

Another way to say that might be, "Serve the need, and help solve the problem." Both actions are important, and they are dependent on each other.

Often this kind of justice is known as "social justice" because it's about addressing systemic societal issues.

At this point, invite the third reader to reread the final portion of the parable. Then ask:

What would it take for us to move in the direction of the Deeper Solution?

Be careful in the following discussion to caution students against thinking they can solve others' problems without them. At some point you may want to mention that there is no way to know a deeper solution without being there and spending time with local hosts. Our predetermined solutions — even systemic ones — can make it more difficult for us to engage locals, listen well, and partner in reciprocal ways toward kingdom goals.

Q: What would we gain by trying to go deeper? What would we lose?

Q: What would it look like if our goal wasn't to meet the needs of the locals but to help them discover ways to meet their own needs?

Q: Chances are good we won't be able to finish — or maybe even start — the Deeper Solution before we head back home. How does that make you feel?

Q: What, if anything, can we do once we're back home to help the locals in the area we visited keep making progress toward a deeper solution?

Close by giving students a few minutes by themselves to pray individually about the questions and feelings that have emerged as they've contemplated asking the deeper "Why" questions. Or, you might ask them to sit together or walk together but to remain in silent prayer.

PARABLE OF THE CRACKED ROADS*

READER 1

Once upon a time, three youth ministries decided to address an unusual—and dire—problem permeating [*name of the city or town in which you'll be serving*]. Somehow, the streets and sidewalks in this town had fallen prey to alarming cracks that crisscrossed the entire town. These cracks were two to four inches wide and several feet long, making the roads dangerous and virtually undrivable. No one knew the exact cause of the cracks, yet residents felt trapped in their homes and ventured to work, school, and church only when necessary.

In an effort to fix the town's problem, the first youth ministry surveyed the damage and came up with a Quick-and-Easy Physical Solution. Their plan was to use a thin layer of topcoat to cover the cracks and render the roads drivable and the sidewalks walkable. Residents stood and watched as the adult leaders and students poured out of their minivans, mixed up the topcoat, and spread it across the cracks like a layer of chocolate icing on a cake. Pleased with the quick repair, the townfolk hugged the young people and cheered as the youth ministry drove off in minivans.

The topcoat worked.

For a few weeks.

But the weight of the cars, the heat of the sun, and the pounding of the rain soon eroded the topcoat. The cracks reappeared, and residents retreated again to their homes. Some thought the cracks were not as severe as they'd been before the topcoat, but no one could be sure.

READER 2

The second youth ministry, after examining the town's broken roads, adopted a different strategy. Recognizing that there was a lot they didn't know, the students figured they'd better learn more about the town's needs and neighbors before making things right. They divided up into teams, some interviewing the residents and others visiting home improvement stores to learn about the type of cement that would best address the problem.

The neighbors had ideas for road repairs that the youth ministry never would have thought of. As a result, the youth ministry was able to develop a Warm-and-Fuzzy Friendly Solution in which the youth ministry and the neighbors worked side by side filling in the cracks with a customized cement.

---

*Adapted from Chap Clark and Kara E. Powell, *Deep Justice in a Broken World* (Grand Rapids: Zondervan, 2008), 11–12.

The cement worked. For six whole months. But then, to the students' dismay, a new series of cracks began to crisscross the roads. Their new friends told them that even though the Warm-and-Fuzzy Friendly Solution had fixed the old cracks, an entirely new set of cracks had emerged, making the roads almost as hazardous.

READER 3

The third youth ministry, having heard about the first two well-intentioned-but-failed strategies, knew that neither topcoat nor a brand-new cement would make things right. Like those in the second youth ministry, these students spent several days interviewing neighbors and hearing stories and dreams about crack-free driving as well as the pain and fear caused by the unsafe conditions. Wanting to avoid the mistakes of the first two youth ministries, the third youth ministry adopted a more radical repair strategy.

The students decided to divide into two teams. The first team was tasked with repairing the current cracks. Recognizing that the very foundation of the city's roads was not right, the team members worked with their new friends to jackhammer large sections of road, dig up the resulting rubble, relevel the foundations, and then lay a brand-new asphalt surface for the roads.

In order to prevent the cracks from reappearing, the second team investigated a few deeper and more complex questions. First, the students looked into why the faulty roads had been built in the first place and lobbied at City Hall to change the construction code so defective roads would never be built again. Second, they asked the local people why they'd been unable to fix the roads and then raised funds to provide the training in construction and asphalt-laying that their neighbors would need to keep the roads shipshape in the future.

This Deeper Solution did the trick. Thanks to the new, stable foundation and the neighbors' new training, the broken roads were fixed—for good.

SERVICE VS. JUSTICE*

SERVICE	JUSTICE
Service can make us feel like "great saviors" who rescue the broken.	Justice means God does the rescuing but often works through the united power of a diverse community to do it.
Service often dehumanizes (even if only subtly) those who are labeled the "receivers."	Justice restores human dignity by creating an environment in which all involved "give" and "receive" in a spirit of reciprocal learning and mutual ministry.
Service is something we do *for* others.	Justice is something we do *with* others.
Service is an event.	Justice is a lifestyle.
Service expects results immediately.	Justice hopes for results but recognizes that systemic change takes time.
The goal of service is to help others.	The goal of justice is to remove obstacles so others can be empowered to help themselves.
Service focuses on what our own ministry can accomplish.	Justice focuses on how we can work with other ministries to accomplish even more.

*Adapted from Chap Clark and Kara E. Powell, *Deep Justice in a Broken World* (Grand Rapids: Zondervan, 2008), 15–16.

PRAYER PARTNER GUIDE

ESSENTIAL

MIDDLE SCHOOL

BIG IDEA

For trip-based experiences, students need a support network. Ideally that network includes prayer partners who meet with them before and after their trip.

YOU'LL NEED

- An adult prayer partner or couple for each student and a plan for helping the student and adult(s) meet. Consider asking students to identify these adults themselves based on existing relationships, asking their parents for help, or to look for mentors who might already be in place (Confirmation sponsors, etc.).

- A copy of the "Prayer Partner Guide" handout (pp. 85–86) for each adult. If you'd like, you can also make copies of the handout for students or use the similar questions in the *Sticky Faith Service Guide Student Journal.*

- Optional: Consider bringing all the adults and students together for one kickoff meeting and providing a meal. If you're meeting as a whole group, be sure you have breakout space where students and adults can talk one-on-one by pulling two chairs close together.

- If students are meeting with prayer partners outside the context of your group time, review with the adults your church's guidelines for appropriate adult-youth relationships (e.g., whether they should meet in a public place, whether adults can allow students to ride in their cars).

YOU'LL NEED (CONT.)

- If your church requires background checks before setting up relationships like this, start that process in advance.

- Consider connecting specifically with senior adults in your congregation who may have more available time to listen to and pray for students and who have exceptional wisdom and life experience to offer.

While we all know the importance of adult relationships in young people's lives, some adults don't know what to do or say when they meet with students. We hope this starter guide gives your adult prayer partners ideas to help students prepare for their upcoming work.

In the introductory section of this book, we explained the important role support plays in the Sticky Faith Service framework that shapes this curriculum. (See chapter 2 to review why.) Adults provide essential scaffolding around students by listening well and reflecting back to students what they hear and see. We recommend that students begin meeting with prayer partners early in the preparation process and that students and adults meet several times both before and after the trip. We also recommend that you think broadly as you recruit prayer partners; adults who might seem to be unlikely youth workers can make

wonderful mentors, and good mentors come in all ages, shapes, and sizes. Involve students by asking them to suggest prayer partners and maybe even inviting them to find their own. And be sure to involve parents, either in the selection process or by introducing parents and prayer partners early on in the Before phase.

After you have recruited adults, offer copies of the "Prayer Partner Guide" handout to help them get started.

You might want to host an initial gathering for all students and prayer partners to help make the introduction to the process as easy as possible. If you have the capacity to do this over a community meal, that's even better. Here's a potential format for your meeting:

Bring everyone together and lead the following discussion.

Q: **Why is it a good idea to pray before, during, and after our service experience?**

Q: **Can you share a time when you've seen God answer a specific prayer?**

A prayer partner is a type of mentor. To find out more about mentoring, as well as ways to avoid some of the common mistakes people make in youth ministry mentoring, visit fulleryouthinstitute.org and search for articles using the word *mentor*.

To see how we hope these prayer partner relationships continue *after* your trip, see pages 197–201.

This question could also be shared around tables or in smaller groups.

Q: **When and where are you most likely to pray?**

Ask the students:

What are some of your hopes for this prayer partner relationship?

Ask the adults:

What are some of your hopes?

At this point, break out into groups, inviting prayer partners and students to work through a few of the questions on the "Prayer Partner Guide" handout.

When they are finished, close by coming back together for a time of worship and prayer. Make sure you thank the prayer partners for their investment in students, and encourage the students to do likewise.

PRAYER PARTNER GUIDE

Congratulations! You have been given the opportunity to help a student process his or her experience of serving others and seeing God's justice done on earth. Get ready for an exciting journey!

A FEW SUGGESTIONS

- *Do not be afraid!* You might be a bit intimidated by this experience, and maybe by the person in front of you. Remember that the most important thing you can offer is your attentive presence.

- *Listen, listen, listen.* Don't feel compelled to give lots of advice, and don't be scared by occasional periods of silence. Simply be a safe place for your student to speak whatever is on his or her heart.

- You first. Remember that the person in front of you is probably scared too. Be as transparent as possible about your own questions and fears when it comes to service and justice, and be prepared to share first if you ask tough questions.

- *Pray, pray, pray.* Pray before, during, and after meeting with your student, and before, during, and after the trip. Be sure to tell your student you are praying regularly for him or her.

STARTING POINTS

The following list of ideas and questions might help you start conversations that prepare the young person you're mentoring for what lies ahead. You might pick out one or more questions to use per session, depending on how many times you will be meeting. These are simply *prompts*, not scripts, and the goal is to help your student share what he or she most needs to share.

QUESTIONS FOR BOTH OF YOU:

1. Tell me your story. What's important for me to know about who you are, where you've been, and what God is doing in your life?

2. How do other people describe you, or what do you think your friends would say about you if I asked them to describe you?

3. Read John 15:1 – 5. What does it look like practically to "remain" in Christ from day to day? What do you think it might look like on this trip?

4. Read Micah 6:8 together. When you think of what God requires of believers, what comes to mind? Does the list in Micah seem like "enough"? Does it seem like "too much"? What are some ways you might act justly, love mercy, and walk humbly with God through this mission experience?

5. Read Luke 9:21 – 27 together. What do you think it means to take up your cross every day to follow Jesus? What do you think it means for you at your school or at home or at your job? What do you think it might mean during your service work? How do you feel about being asked to make sacrifices for the sake of Christ?

QUESTIONS FOR THE STUDENT:

1. What draws you to be part of this team/experience? What is it you're hoping for or anticipating from this experience?

2. What do you think life is like in the place you're visiting? How do you think it might be different from — or the same as — life here? If you were growing up there, how might you be different? How does that make you feel?

3. What do you fear about this project? Where do you think those fears are coming from? What do you tend to do when you're afraid? How can I pray for you about your fears?

4. How do you hope to be changed by your work? How do you hope others will be changed?

5. How can I pray for you? What are a few specific things I can pray for as you prepare for the trip? What are the ways I should pray for you during the trip? How can I pray for you when you come home? How do you think I can pray for your family?

WHERE I COME FROM

ROOKIE

BIG IDEA

Before we attempt to serve in another cultural context, it's important to "culturally locate" ourselves.

YOU'LL NEED

- Whiteboard or poster paper and markers
- A blank piece of paper and a pen for each student
- Copies of the "Where I Come From" handout (p. 91) and/or copies of the *Sticky Faith Service Guide Student Journal*
- Bibles
- Maps or aerial pictures of your community. (You can print these out ahead of time using an online mapping system. If you know exactly who will be participating, you can print an aerial picture of each student's neighborhood. If not, simply print out multiple copies of whatever geographical boundaries will feel like "home" for your students.)

In many ways, culture is like the *social air we breathe*: most of the time we don't notice it, but it deeply shapes the ways we think about ourselves, others, God, and pretty much everything else! Family systems and traditions are one great example of a type of subculture that can be vastly different from one home to the next on the same block.

Welcome your students and have them turn to one person next to them and ask:

"Where are you from?"

Give students time to ask and answer this question before continuing:

Q: When someone asks where you're from, what do you say?

Q: Do some of you have a hard time answering that question? What makes it difficult for you?

Likely there are students in your group who have moved a lot, or who were born in one place but have mostly grown up in a different state or country.

Q: Where do we get our ideas about our roots? Who or what tells us "who we are" and "where we're from"?

Q: What's behind the question, "Where do you come from"?

Give students time to share ideas, and then point out we often ask this question to help us culturally locate someone—whether that is because that person has a different accent than ours, looks different in some way, or we just want to understand them more fully by knowing where they grew up.

Continue:

Most of the time we ask about someone's roots when they seem "different" from us. When have you experienced a moment of cultural awareness like this?

Q: In what ways would you guess the people we'll encounter in our service work are most different from us? In what ways are they most similar?

Write their answers on your whiteboard. Continue:

As we prepare to interact with people from a culture that may be different from ours, it's a good idea to look at our own cultural location—the ways in which we are shaped by where we're from.

Ask this question:

If you were to draw a map of your life, what might it look like? Think about the geography of your family, your beliefs, the places you've lived, the events and people significant in shaping you.

Pass out copies of the "Where I Come From" handout for students to complete on their own. Then have students get in groups of three and share insights from their handouts. Get everyone back together to debrief that experience:

Q: **How did it feel to think more about your cultural location? What new insights do you have about who you are and how that shapes the way you interact with others who are different?**

Q: **What are some important things we might want to learn about the cultural location of the people we will serve during our work? If some of the teenagers from our destination filled out this same list of descriptors about themselves,** how do you think their lists might be similar or different from ours?

If it's not already obvious from the sharing around the room, you'll want to note that there is often quite a bit of diversity among people who live in the same location, even though an outsider might be tempted to lump everyone together based on a set of stereotypes. Just as you cannot assume everyone in your youth ministry is the same, you can't assume that getting to know one local person in your host community will mean you understand everyone.

Q: **How can we honor those we visit without being spiritual tourists who ooh and aah over their different culture and setting?**

HAVE MORE TIME?

Often our cultural location determines the power we have over others or the power others have over us. It is helpful to have students think through ways their particular heritage and set of circumstances might put them in a role of power. You might ask questions like:

In what ways do we (or might we) participate in the oppression of others because of who we are and where we're from? What should we do about that?

One example might be wearing clothes made in sweatshops where labor environments are harsh, workers are underpaid, and in some cases people are forced to work as slaves. Youth ministries have begun to speak out against such injustices, and some have begun purchasing non-sweatshop clothing or even making some of their own clothes.

Q: If the people we serve are living in poverty and we are not, how can we move beyond simply thanking God that we're not "like them"?

At this point, distribute maps or aerial photos of your area as a prompt for the closing prayer. Invite students to pray that the Lord will help them be mindful of their own cultures and appreciate all they can experience by interacting with a different culture.

HAVE MORE TIME?

Have students create videos, slide presentations, posters, or culinary dishes that share about their cultural identity with the rest of the team. Give them one or two weeks to learn as much as they can about their ancestry, their family history, and their current "cultural location" and creatively share that with the rest of the group. Talk together about the ways our unique cultural heritages shape — but do not have to dictate — our interactions with others. Celebrate whatever diversity might exist among your students, and encourage one another as you continue to learn to relate to those who are different. Alternatively, encourage team members to look up recipes for local food where you will be serving and to make dishes for future team meetings.

WHERE I COME FROM

What makes you "you"? If you were a map, how would you draw you (go ahead and give it a try on the back of this handout!)? How do your history and cultural context shape the way you think, feel, and interact with others? The prompts below will give you a starting point. Try to answer each one briefly, then keep this page and return to it later as you get more thoughts and perhaps find out the answers to more questions!

- I was born in …

- I have lived in …

- My family is made up of …

- My parents grew up in …

- My ancestors came from …

- I describe my race/ethnicity as …

- My house/apartment is like …

- My parents work as …

- My family likes to eat …

- My favorite food is …

- I spend most of my time …

- When I can choose, I usually spend my free time …

- My favorite place to go is …

- The music I listen to is …

- The clothes I wear are …

- My clothes come from …

- I spend money on …

- I get money from …

Now share this list with someone else, and ask them to point out how your story shapes who you are and the unique perspective you bring to the group.

FINDING OURSELVES IN GOD'S STORY

SCRIPTURE   ROOKIE   MIDDLE SCHOOL

BIG IDEA

We find our ultimate motivation for justice when we find our place in God's story.

YOU'LL NEED

- Six pieces of poster paper, hung next to each other

- Pens

- Bibles

- In advance: Meet with seven students and/or volunteers so they can help you explain the six movements of God's story. Copy and cut out the seven parts of the script found in the "Finding Ourselves in God's Story (Readers)" handout on pages 97–98 to give to them.

- Print copies of the second "Finding Ourselves in God's Story" handout for all participants on pages 99–100, or use copies of the *Sticky Faith Service Guide Student Journal*.

Welcome students and explain:

Understanding and embracing God's role in our upcoming work begins with understanding God's role in our lives and where our work fits into what God is doing in the world. One way to think about that is to view Scripture as one big story about God's love for the world and to acknowledge the joy God experiences as we serve in his kingdom.

Today we're going to look at God's story of interacting with people throughout Scripture. As we understand this story, we'll understand more of how God feels about us and why and how God wants us to be involved in serving others and working toward justice.

At this point, you can pass out copies of the "Finding Ourselves in God's Story" handout.

The story starts ... well ... in the beginning. In the first chapter of Genesis, we learn that we were created special, that we were created in God's image, which means that we were created good.

At this point, ask Reader 1 to read Genesis 1:26–27 and write the word GOOD in large letters at the top of the first sheet of poster paper.

> Then God said, "Let us make mankind in our image, in our likeness, so that they may rule over the fish in the sea and the birds in the sky, over the livestock and all the wild animals, and over all the creatures that move along the ground."

> So God created mankind in his own image,
>   in the image of God he created them;
>   male and female he created them.
>
>   *Genesis 1:26–27*

Now comes the bad news. Our inherent goodness from being created in God's image has been marred by what happened in the first garden when humans chose to disobey God. All of us have been tainted by guilt because of sin, and it impacts us every day.

Ask Reader 2 to read Romans 3:10–12 and write GUILT in large letters at the top of the second sheet of poster paper.

> There is no one righteous, not even one;
>   there is no one who understands;
>   there is no one who seeks God.
> All have turned away,
>   they have together become worthless;
> there is no one who does good,
>   not even one.
>
>   *Romans 3:10–12*

Next ask Reader 3 to walk up to the third sheet of poster paper, write the word GRACE in large letters at the top, and then sit down. Give students some time to sit in silence, staring at the word. After at least sixty seconds, ask Reader 3 to return to the front of the room and read Romans 3:23–24.

> All have sinned and fall short of the glory of God, and all are justified freely by his grace through the redemption that came by Christ Jesus.
>
>   *Romans 3:23–24*

After another pause, have Reader 4 read Ephesians 2:6–10.

> And God raised us up with Christ and seated us with him in the heavenly realms in Christ Jesus, in order that in the coming ages he might show the incomparable riches of his grace, expressed in his kindness to us in Christ Jesus. For it is by grace you have been saved, through faith—and this is not from yourselves, it is the gift of God—not by works, so that no one can boast. For we are God's handiwork, created in Christ Jesus to do good works, which God prepared in advance for us to do.
>
> *Ephesians 2:6–10*

Q: **When you think of grace, what images or phrases come to mind?**

The main point you want students to grasp is that through the life, death, and resurrection of Jesus, God has extended grace to us to make things right and restore us to relationship with God and one another. It all comes as gift, not something we earn.

Now ask Reader 5 to share Ephesians 2:19–22 and write GOD'S PEOPLE on the fourth sheet of paper.

> Consequently, you are no longer foreigners and strangers, but fellow citizens with God's people and also members of his household, built on the foundation of the apostles and prophets, with Christ Jesus himself as the chief cornerstone. In him the whole building is joined together and rises to become a holy temple in the Lord. And in him you too are being built together to become a dwelling in which God lives by his Spirit.
>
> *Ephesians 2:19–22*

Continue:

As we experience grace, we are adopted into the body of Christ, embodying God's reign in the world. We join the mission of God, participating in the work of God happening through God's people.

At this point, Reader 6 can come up to the fifth piece of poster paper and write the word GRATITUDE, reading Colossians 2:6–7.

> So then, just as you received Christ Jesus as Lord, continue to live your lives in him, rooted and built up in him, strengthened in the faith as you were taught, and overflowing with thankfulness.
>
> *Colossians 2:6–7*

Explain:

Out of this gift of grace, we respond in gratitude toward God. This is the well out of which our obedience—those behaviors—flows. In other words, the gospel doesn't begin with behaviors, nor is it dependent on behaviors. The behaviors are like a big thank-you note we offer back to God in response to grace. As we grow in trust, we naturally grow in obedience as a response to grace.

As Paul says in the verses we just heard, we continue to live our lives in Jesus, rooted and built up in him, strengthened in the faith, and all of this is done out of the overflow of thankfulness.

Q: **What difference does it make whether we obey God out of guilt or out of gratitude?**

If students don't make this connection, help them see that responding in gratitude to God means that our obedience—including serving others—flows from a place of freedom rather than a place of shame and the feeling that we "should" do something good so God will like us more. Because of grace, we don't have to work for God's favor. We receive it as a gift and offer any good work back as a gift.

Next ask Reader 7 to go to the final piece of poster paper and write, GOD'S VISION. Then have him or her read Revelation 21:1–5:

> Then I saw "a new heaven and a new earth," for the first heaven and the first earth had passed away, and there was no longer any sea. I saw the Holy City, the new Jerusalem, coming down out of heaven from God, prepared as a bride beautifully dressed for her husband. And I heard a loud voice from the throne saying, "Look! God's dwelling place is now among the people, and he will dwell with them. They will be his people, and God himself will be with them and be their God. 'He will wipe every tear from their eyes. There will be no more death' or mourning or crying or pain, for the old order of things has passed away."
>
> He who was seated on the throne said, "I am making everything new!"
>
> *Revelation 21:1–5*

Explain:

Gratitude for God's grace isn't the very end of the story. We are living in between Christ's first coming and his second coming, when he will make everything new. Service work and the ways we seek justice on behalf of the poor and oppressed are part of the in-between story that God's kingdom is growing right in front of us. We get to participate in something Jesus has started and that ultimately Jesus will finish.

HAVE MORE TIME?

If you need to take more time to explore how Jesus is working in us now in order to build God's kingdom, 2 Corinthians 5:16–21 might be a helpful passage. It centers the work of Jesus in God's new creation, where God is reconciling the world to himself through Christ and invites us into that ministry. "We are therefore Christ's ambassadors, as though God were making his appeal through us" (v. 20).

At this point, help students connect the 6-G story to your work by moving to the first piece of poster paper and asking:

Q: How does the first part of this story that tells us that everyone was created good in God's image relate to our upcoming service?

Jot down their answers on the poster paper. Encourage students to consider how the fact that those we serve are likewise created in God's image affects your upcoming work.

Continue this pattern with the other sheets:

Q: How does guilt—including our own sin, the sins people have committed against us, and other sin that shapes our world—affect our work?

Q: In 2 Corinthians 5:17, Paul writes, "Therefore, if anyone is in Christ, the new creation has come: The old has gone, the new is here!" How does the grace that makes us a new creation relate to our upcoming mission?

Q: What does it mean that we—and those in our host community—are part of God's family together?

Q: What would it look like for our service to be offered as a thank-you note back to God?

Q: How does knowing the end of the story—that ultimately Christ will make all things new—shape our approach to our work?

Close by inviting team members to pray for each other in pairs or small groups, thanking God for the chance to act out this story in your upcoming work as well as in your daily lives.

HAVE MORE TIME?

Divide students into pairs and have them practice sharing the *Good/Guilt/Grace/ God's People/Gratitude/God's Vision* story with each other. After each person shares, the other should affirm what the speaker did well and offer suggestions for how that person can more effectively share this story in the future.

FINDING OURSELVES IN GOD'S STORY

READER 1

Then God said, "Let us make mankind in our image, in our likeness, so that they may rule over the fish in the sea and the birds in the sky, over the livestock and all the wild animals, and over all the creatures that move along the ground."

So God created mankind in his own image, in the image of God he created them; male and female he created them.

Genesis 1:26–27

READER 2

There is no one righteous, not even one;
there is no one who understands;
there is no one who seeks God.
All have turned away,
they have together become worthless;
there is no one who does good,
not even one.

Romans 3:10–12

READER 3

All have sinned and fall short of the glory of God, and all are justified freely by his grace through the redemption that came by Christ Jesus.

Romans 3:23–24

READER 4

And God raised us up with Christ and seated us with him in the heavenly realms in Christ Jesus, in order that in the coming ages he might show the incomparable riches of his grace, expressed in his kindness to us in Christ Jesus. For it is by grace you have been saved, through faith—and this is not from yourselves, it is the gift of God—not by works, so that no one can boast. For we are God's handiwork, created in Christ Jesus to do good works, which God prepared in advance for us to do.

Ephesians 2:6–10

READER 5

Consequently, you are no longer foreigners and strangers, but fellow citizens with God's people and also members of his household, built on the foundation of the apostles and prophets, with Christ Jesus himself as the chief cornerstone. In him the whole building is joined together and rises to become a holy temple in the Lord. And in him you too are being built together to become a dwelling in which God lives by his Spirit.

Ephesians 2:19–22

READER 6

So then, just as you received Christ Jesus as Lord, continue to live your lives in him, rooted and built up in him, strengthened in the faith as you were taught, and overflowing with thankfulness.

Colossians 2:6–7

READER 7

Then I saw "a new heaven and a new earth," for the first heaven and the first earth had passed away, and there was no longer any sea. I saw the Holy City, the new Jerusalem, coming down out of heaven from God, prepared as a bride beautifully dressed for her husband. And I heard a loud voice from the throne saying, "Look! God's dwelling place is now among the people, and he will dwell with them. They will be his people, and God himself will be with them and be their God. 'He will wipe every tear from their eyes. There will be no more death' or mourning or crying or pain, for the old order of things has passed away."

He who was seated on the throne said, "I am making everything new!"

Revelation 21:1–5

FINDING OURSELVES IN GOD'S STORY

GOOD

Then God said, "Let us make mankind in our image, in our likeness, so that they may rule over the fish in the sea and the birds in the sky, over the livestock and all the wild animals, and over all the creatures that move along the ground."

So God created mankind in his own image,
in the image of God he created them;
male and female he created them.

Genesis 1:26–27

GUILT

There is no one righteous, not even one;
there is no one who understands;
there is no one who seeks God.
All have turned away,
they have together become worthless;
there is no one who does good,
not even one.

Romans 3:10–12

GRACE

All have sinned and fall short of the glory of God, and all are justified freely by his grace through the redemption that came by Christ Jesus.

Romans 3:23–24

And God raised us up with Christ and seated us with him in the heavenly realms in Christ Jesus, in order that in the coming ages he might show the incomparable riches of his grace, expressed in his kindness to us in Christ Jesus. For it is by grace you have been saved, through faith—and this is not from yourselves, it is the gift of God—not by works, so that no one can boast. For we are God's handiwork, created in Christ Jesus to do good works, which God prepared in advance for us to do.

Ephesians 2:6–10

GOD'S PEOPLE

Consequently, you are no longer foreigners and strangers, but fellow citizens with God's people and also members of his household, built on the foundation of the apostles and prophets, with Christ Jesus himself as the chief cornerstone. In him the whole building is joined together and rises to become a holy temple in the Lord. And in him you too are being built together to become a dwelling in which God lives by his Spirit.

Ephesians 2:19–22

GRATITUDE

So then, just as you received Christ Jesus as Lord, continue to live your lives in him, rooted and built up in him, strengthened in the faith as you were taught, and overflowing with thankfulness.

Colossians 2:6–7

GOD'S VISION

Then I saw "a new heaven and a new earth," for the first heaven and the first earth had passed away, and there was no longer any sea. I saw the Holy City, the new Jerusalem, coming down out of heaven from God, prepared as a bride beautifully dressed for her husband. And I heard a loud voice from the throne saying, "Look! God's dwelling place is now among the people, and he will dwell with them. They will be his people, and God himself will be with them and be their God. 'He will wipe every tear from their eyes. There will be no more death' or mourning or crying or pain, for the old order of things has passed away."

He who was seated on the throne said, "I am making everything new!"

Revelation 21:1–5

OBSTACLE COURSE

SCRIPTURE   MIDDLE
SCHOOL

BIG IDEA

We reach our full potential as the body of Christ when we work together and use our unique gifts.

YOU'LL NEED

- Copies of the "Obstacle Course" handout (p. 105)
- Some type of blindfolds for several students, depending on how many you assign to be "blind" during the obstacle course (see below)
- Whiteboard or poster paper and markers
- Optional: Copies of the *Sticky Faith Service Guide Student Journal* for each participant (the exercise related to this session is called "My Gifts"; see pp. 43–44)

Before your meeting: Make copies of the "Obstacle Course" handout and cut along the designated lines so you have one task to give to each person.

Then create an obstacle course all of your students will go through together. Some of the students will be blindfolded and others will need to be carried, so it's wise to plan

an obstacle course that is not terribly difficult. The best obstacle courses involve walking, crawling (e.g., under tables or chairs), and going up or down stairs. Whether you're meeting at your church or a home, you can design the course to include both an inside and outside component.

After students arrive, greet them and explain:

Today we're going to start off with a short obstacle course. Our goal is for everyone to finish the course.

It's important that you clearly explain once and only once *that the goal is for everyone to finish the course.* Describe the actual path of the obstacle course, drawing it on the whiteboard or poster paper so students can visualize where they are supposed to go. It would be best if students didn't use their cell phones or other devices to take pictures of what you draw.

Continue:

I'm going to give out the tasks each of you gets to do during the obstacle course. Do not show anyone else the task I give you. You are not to act out your task until you officially begin the obstacle course.

Distribute one task to each student, making sure no one else sees it. Be strategic (but subtle) in the way you give out tasks; assign your most outgoing students "You are mute and cannot speak at all." Give students who tend to be leaders the assignment "You offer all sorts of suggestions, none of which is helpful and some of which impede progress." Give students who are physically smaller and lighter the task "You can't move your arms or legs at all. In fact, when the game starts, just sit down."

Remind students that they shouldn't tell anyone their assignments nor should they act them out until the obstacle course begins and they pass a beginning point that you have

designated (e.g., they walk through a particular door or into a particular room). Ask students to get in a line at the start of the course, and send them off.

During the obstacle course, you should traverse the route so you can note how students are doing, but do *not* help anyone. Do *not* remind students of the simple goal you gave them earlier—that *everyone* finishes the course. If time runs too long, you can give them a five-minute warning and then end the exercise, even if they did not complete the challenge.

Afterward, lead the following discussion, adding other insights or examples you noticed after students share:

- How did we do?
- What were some of the feelings you experienced during the course?
- What did I say the goal was? How did you interpret that goal?

Most students hear "everyone" and think "everyone individually" instead of "everyone together."

- In what ways did you do a good job of accomplishing that goal? Can you think of specific moments when people worked together to accomplish the goal?
- What are some examples of our group failing to work together to accomplish that goal?
- What does this activity show us about our team?

- What does our team do well?
- What areas might our team need to work on?

Transition to Paul's teachings about different gifts within the body of Christ by asking:

Q: What Scripture passages come to mind as you think about our experience together on the obstacle course?

Chances are good that students will mention something about the body of Christ or spiritual gifts. If not, you can mention it and invite students to turn to 1 Corinthians 12:4–11.

Give a bit of the history of the church in Corinth:

The church of Corinth in the first century makes our obstacle course seem like a piece of cake. As Paul learned from some members of the household of Chloe (see 1 Corinthians 1:11), the believers were fighting with each other. While the church was definitely gifted (see 1 Corinthians 1:4–8), it was spiritually immature and full of conflict.

HAVE MORE TIME?

Invite one volunteer to read Romans 12:3–8 and another to read Ephesians 4:11–13. Ask:

What are the various spiritual gifts Paul describes in these passages?

As students name the gifts, write them on the whiteboard. You might want to make sure you're familiar with your own and your church's position on prophecy, miracles, and speaking in tongues if (or perhaps we should we say "when") students have questions.

Do these lists from Paul give us an exhaustive list of the spiritual gifts? In other words, are the gifts Paul mentions in these passages the only *real* spiritual gifts? Since the lists are not identical, some scholars have suggested that while these lists may name many (and perhaps most) spiritual gifts, they are not exhaustive. It's often proposed that other spiritual gifts exist, such as the gifts of worship and hospitality.

Invite a volunteer to read 1 Corinthians 12:4–6, and then ask:

Q: **How would you summarize these verses in your own words? If we really believe the Spirit distributes the various gifts and talents we all have, how should that affect the way we work together?**

Read 1 Corinthians 12:7 and then ask:

Q: **What do you think Paul means by the "common good"? What does the "common good" look like for our upcoming justice work?**

Next have someone read 1 Corinthians 12:8–11.

Q: **Many people refer to the gifts and talents Paul describes as "spiritual gifts." Remembering that Paul emphasizes that these gifts are for the common good, how would you define spiritual gifts?**

Q: **What other kinds of gifts do we all have that are also valuable?**

Personality, skills, financial resources, and other talents are all important to name as good gifts that we might bring to the body.

Q: **How do you think these spiritual and natural gifts can help us work better together as the body of Christ in our upcoming work?**

Q: **Paul uses the Greek word *charismata* (pronounced care-is-MAH-tuh) to describe the gifts.**

The word *charismata* is derived from another Greek word, *charis* (CARE-iss), meaning "grace." How might thinking of your (and other people's) gifts as starting from grace affect how you view these gifts?

Chances are good your group members will not all be aware of their own gifts, so ask:

Q: **For those of you who aren't sure what your gifts are, how can our upcoming work give you a better sense of what they might be?**

Now invite someone to read 1 Corinthians 12:14–27 and ask:

Q: **If we took this seriously, what would happen to any "gift envy" we might feel toward others who seem to have more, or cooler, gifts than we do, especially when we're serving together?**

Q: **Likewise, how might we care for one another differently when we consider that each of us also brings weaknesses to our group?**

Close in prayer, perhaps inviting students to join hands as a reflection of the desire to work together and use their gifts more effectively in kingdom work.

OBSTACLE COURSE

You are mute and cannot speak at all.

You offer all sorts of unhelpful suggestions, some of which impede progress.

Your arms and legs are stiff and you can't bend them at all.

You are blind and cannot see at all.

One of your legs doesn't work; you have to hop. (You can switch which leg works from time to time so you don't get too tired.)

Your arms don't work at all.

You can't move your arms or legs at all. In fact, when the game starts, just sit down.

You are mute and cannot speak at all.

You offer all sorts of unhelpful suggestions, some of which impede progress.

Your arms and legs are stiff and you can't bend them at all.

You are blind and cannot see at all.

One of your legs doesn't work; you have to hop. (You can switch which leg works from time to time so you don't get too tired.)

Your arms don't work at all.

You can't move your arms or legs at all. In fact, when the game starts, just sit down.

You are mute and cannot speak at all.

You offer all sorts of unhelpful suggestions, some of which impede progress.

Your arms and legs are stiff and you can't bend them at all.

You are blind and cannot see at all.

One of your legs doesn't work; you have to hop. (You can switch which leg works from time to time so you don't get too tired.)

Your arms don't work at all.

JESUS ACROSS CULTURES

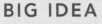

ROOKIE

BIG IDEA

God communicates his love most fully through Jesus, but God also communicates through each of us and across our cultures.

YOU'LL NEED

- Three stations in your meeting space, representing different things you'll be doing during your service.

  - Station 1: Food—You'll need some unfamiliar foods, preferably from the region where you're going, as well as some familiar foods your students love. In addition, have some hand sanitizer and bottled water available as well as a flip chart or poster paper with the phrase EATING ACROSS CULTURES written across the top.

- Station 2: Travel—A flip chart or poster board with the phrase TRAVEL ACROSS CULTURES written across the top

  - Station 3: Work—If available, use some black construction paper or poster board with the phrase WORK ACROSS CULTURES written across the top, and some glow-in-the-dark pens. If not, just use a regular flip chart or poster board.

- Pens
- Bibles
- Paper

Welcome your students. Explain that one of the reasons we're spending time thinking about the culture where we'll be serving is because we're trying to follow what Jesus did when he came to earth.

Q: **Imagine being God (yes, that's quite a stretch!). In what ways would you, as God, try to communicate who you are to the world? Be as creative as you can. Remember, you're God.**

Write students' responses on the whiteboard. If students are stuck, throw out the following possibilities: God could have bellowed it from the sky; God could have put a preprogrammed chip in all of us; God could have made his message the only thing coming across television and the Internet.

Q: **What are some of the ways God reveals himself—both in the past and today?**

Some ways we know about from Scripture include: visions, prophets, nature, a talking donkey, a pillar of fire, and, most vividly, Jesus.

Ask a volunteer to read Hebrews 1:1–2. Explain:

The author writes to fellow Jews a few years after Jesus' death and resurrection. The author reminds them what they know well: their God, Yahweh, has always communicated to them in very personal ways. But now God has best revealed himself through his Son, Jesus.

> *(i)*
>
> In many English translations, Hebrews 1:2 refers to Jesus as coming "in these last days." That phrase in Greek is more literally translated as "on the last of these days," a phrase indicating that Jesus' arrival on earth marked the end of one age and the beginning of a new era altogether.

Continue:

Jesus gives us an "up-close" view of God and, in doing so, allows us to grow closer to God ourselves. Today we want to spend some time practicing what it looks like to give people an "up-close" view of Jesus during our service work. The three stations we've set up represent the kinds of situations we'll encounter during our trip.

Divide students into three groups and have each group start at a different station. Give them three to five minutes at their first station, with the goal of thinking about what it looks like to reflect Jesus in that context, and how we might see Jesus in the locals. After they are finished, ask the groups to rotate and repeat the brainstorming at their new station, adding to the list of ideas that the previous group made. Do the same process a third time to complete the rotation. If possible, have an adult leader at each station to facilitate the exercise.

STATION 1: FOOD

As students are trying both familiar and unfamiliar foods, ask them to eat in ways that best reflect Jesus in the midst of new (and maybe yucky-tasting) experiences. Ask students to discuss what it will mean to the locals we're serving if we eat their food, as well as the messages communicated if we don't (or if we hold our noses and groan as we do). Similarly, distribute hand sanitizer and bottled water and have students practice how to use both inconspicuously. Wonder about how we might see Christ through the ways our hosts share food with us.

STATION 2: TRAVEL

How will our behavior while traveling to our destination and while traveling from place to place reflect Jesus? Students might need to be prompted to think about things like volume level, how we interact with strangers, and when and how to take pictures. How can we be on the lookout for how Christ is revealed in the communities we encounter and the people we meet?

STATION 3: WORK

How can the work we do give others (and ourselves) accurate pictures of what Jesus is like? Topics to discuss here include laziness or being too focused on tasks, excluding the locals from joining us, and complaining. How could Christ be revealed to us through working alongside our local hosts?

When the three groups have finished all three stations, spend time as a large group debriefing the exercise.

Q: **In which of these areas will it be most challenging for you personally to live out Jesus' example across cultures? Which will be easiest?**

Q: **How can we help one another reflect Jesus throughout our experience?**

Close in prayer by walking with your students to each of the three stations and spending a minute or two at each, together asking that people would get an "up-close" view of Jesus in the way we love and serve the locals (as well as one another), and that we would see Jesus more clearly as we interact with them.

SHAPED BY CULTURE

ESSENTIAL   SCRIPTURE   VETERAN

BIG IDEA

Our culture shapes what we view as "normal" and how we view the world.

YOU'LL NEED

- Copies of the "Info Form" handout (p. 112)
- A few 3 x 5 white index cards with green marker lines drawn on each of them in random patterns (go crazy, you creative types)
- Whiteboard or poster paper
- Pens
- Bibles
- Information about the culture/people you'll be visiting (from websites, books, magazines, or tablets or laptops with Internet access)

Welcome your students and distribute the "Info Form" handout to them, asking them to follow your instructions very carefully. Give the green-and-white cards to a select few. Read the following instructions:

1. Write from right to left.
2. Write as clearly as possible.
3. Fill in every blank.
4. Do not fill in #8 unless you received a green-and-white card.
5. You have four minutes to complete this.
6. You can't ask any questions.

Repeat the instructions one time and then have the students begin.

After you've given them four minutes, lead the following discussion, writing students' responses on the whiteboard:

Q: How did you feel as you filled out this form?

Q: What frustrated you about this form?

If students talk about it being "wrong" or "backward," challenge their assumptions about why writing from left to right is the "right" direction. (Point out that more than half the Bible was originally written in Hebrew, which is read from right to left.)

Q: For those of you who didn't receive index cards, how did it feel? What about for those of you who did receive the cards?

Talk about how "random" opportunities are given, and how that creates instant advantages (or in some cases, disadvantages).

Q: What confused you about this form?

Explain that the options for "Grade in School" are based on the system many other countries use (primary 5 and 6, secondary 1–4, and junior college 1 and 2).

Q: How did it feel to be given options that don't fit what you're used to?

In 1 Corinthians 9 Paul refers to two types of law: The "law" in general (sometimes called "God's law"), which refers to the Old Testament law and practices, as well as "Christ's law," likely meaning Christ's teachings and their implications.

Explain:

Understanding the way culture shapes how we and other people see the world is an important part of seeking justice and sharing the good news globally. Missionaries and justice workers have been talking about the importance of adapting to culture for two thousand years.

As we look ahead to our experience, we want to adapt as needed in order to love and serve well. Let's look closely at how one of Scripture's best-known leaders approached culture.

As you listen to this passage, write down the cultural groups Paul "became like" in 1 Corinthians 9:19–23. You can use the back of your Info Form.

Invite a volunteer to read the passage out loud as the rest of the group writes down the various groups with whom Paul interacted.

Q: Some people claim that this passage means it's okay to become a chameleon, going with the flow of whatever the people around you are doing. How would you respond to that?

Q: If we could ask Paul when it's okay to adapt to the culture of others and when it's not okay, what do you think he would say?

Refer back to the frustration students may have felt in filling out the Info Form and then ask:

Q: In light of what we just learned about the culture where we're heading, what things might be frustrating for us there?

Q: If we want to learn to appreciate cultural differences rather than see them as wrong or abnormal, what should we do?

Q: In what ways might our own culture seem awkward or frustrating to others?

Conclude by reminding students that we don't have to wait for our service experience to notice different cultures and the way culture shapes people's behavior. Encourage your students to become more aware during the next week of the different cultures around them, such as ethnic groups or different social groupings at school.

As you close in prayer, invite students to write down the name of one other person at school who is from a different culture. Ask God to allow them to become all things to this person they'll encounter this week—as well as to those they'll be interacting with during the upcoming trip—for the sake of the gospel.

HAVE MORE TIME?

Q: Let's apply this to our own upcoming project. What do you already know about the culture in which we'll be serving?

Continue:

Let's divide into groups of two or three and spend ten to fifteen minutes finding out as much as possible about the culture we'll be encountering.

Distribute any books, magazines, and travel information, as well as tablets or laptops with Internet access if possible.

When groups are finished, ask each group to report on the three or four most interesting insights they discovered about the culture where you're headed.

INFO FORM

_____ EMAN .1

_____ EGA .2

_____ ELAM _____ ELAMEF :REDNEG .3

_____ HTRIB FO YTIC .4

LOOHCS NI EDARG .5
____2J ____1J ____4S ____3S ____2S ____1S ____6P ____ 5P

_____ PIRT EHT NO OG OT TNAW UOY NOSAER .6

_____

_____ CIBARA _____ NAMREG _____ IAHT :NEKOPS SEGAUGNAL .7

_____ REHTO

_____ YTIVITCA ETIROVAF .8

MISSING HALF THE STORY

VETERAN

BIG IDEA

True partnership means understanding the ministry strategy of the people in your host community.

YOU'LL NEED

- A way to play a few short clips from several currently popular television shows. You can create your own mash-up by recording clips from a handful of different shows. The goal is to find clips that wouldn't make sense if you hadn't been following previous episodes or even earlier parts of the series. If you'd like, you can show movie clips instead.

- Ahead of time, figure out a way you can ask (by email, phone, or video call) some of the local leaders in the community you'll be serving the questions students will suggest during this meeting.

- Whiteboard or poster paper

- Pens

- Optional: Copies of the *Sticky Faith Service Guide Student Journal*

Welcome students and explain that you have some clips to show them from a few recent shows. Play about thirty seconds of your first clip and then ask:

Q: How many of you watch this show? How many of you don't? For those of you who don't, what do you think is going to happen during the rest of this episode?

Let a few students who don't watch the show guess what's going to happen, and then let students who watch the show explain what really happens. Continue this exercise for your remaining clips.

Then lead the following discussion:

Q: What did those of you who watch the various shows know that the rest of us didn't?

Explain:

I don't know about you, but I really hate it when I miss the first few minutes of a movie. I feel behind and wonder if I'm going to be able to really understand the rest. It's awfully hard to jump into the middle of a story. In what ways is our upcoming work similar to jumping into the middle of a story?

Q: What disadvantages might the locals experience since we are jumping into the middle of their story?

Q: What advantages, if any, might there be to us showing up without knowing the full story of the local people?

Q: What questions would you want to ask the locals about their story?

Write down your students' suggestions on the whiteboard.

Q: God is constantly at work all over the world. What questions would you want to ask about how God is at work in our hosts' community and through their ministry?

Similarly, write down student suggestions on the whiteboard.

Explain your plan for asking these questions of some of the local leaders. If it's possible to set up a way to talk to some of the local leaders by phone or video call right then and there, that would be ideal. If not, make a commitment to report the answers back to your students at a future meeting.

Even better, consider bringing a leader from the host community to talk with your group. This is likely a big investment, but it might be worth it—both for students and for the host community. If it seems appropriate, invite a few students to take responsibility for asking the questions or to share that responsibility with you.

PART THREE

DURING: EXPERIENCE AND REFLECTION

Use these exercises to help your students—and yourself—to pause once or twice each day to pay attention to the insights emerging from your journey. Build these spaces into your daily schedule ahead of time.

HEADS-UP: *You may want to look ahead to the "Creating a Shared Rule of Life" (After) exercise on page 207 as you are creating your trip's daily schedule. It might be helpful to build in some particular rhythms of community life and prayer to which students can refer in the course of their service.*

DEVOTION AND JOURNALING OPTIONS

ESSENTIAL   DEVOTION-FRIENDLY

BIG IDEA

Daily devotion times can give us a little breathing room to reflect separately on our experiences outside of group processing times.

YOU'LL NEED

- Copies of the *Sticky Faith Service Guide Student Journal* for every participant

As a reminder, in the *Sticky Faith Service Guide Student Journal*, we have provided a number of additional options for your students to journal, including both guided exercises and blank pages. These can be used for morning or midday personal devotional time, evening quiet reflection before bed, or whenever you'd prefer based on your schedule. Specifically, here are the options that are ideal for participants' individual reflection times:

DURING:

DURING: GOD AND US
DAILY DEBRIEF QUESTIONS

ESSENTIAL   ONE-DAY   DEVOTION-FRIENDLY   MIDDLE SCHOOL

BIG IDEA

Ongoing reflection on a few basic questions can give our trip a sense of cohesion and everyone a sense of God's ongoing transformation.

YOU'LL NEED

- Copies of the "Daily Debrief Questions" handout (p. 119). You may also want to point students to the "Daily Journal" entries in the *Sticky Faith Service Guide Student Journal*, which utilize similar questions.

This book is designed to give your team members all sorts of creative ways to interact with one another as you discover what God is showing you during your service work. But the reality is that sometimes it's better to keep it simple. If your group is running low on either energy or time, choose just a few items from the "Daily Debrief Questions" handout as a basic but effective tool to process all you're experiencing as individuals and as a group.

The youth ministries that tested this curriculum during its development found that choosing a few questions and asking them regularly throughout their journey gave students helpful reflection anchors. Even on short trips or one-day service events, building a consistent reflection pattern is helpful. You may simply want to ask the same questions over and over again. In fact, you might build these questions into regular group meeting times—either small groups or your large-group gathering—to make this kind of reflection a normal part of young people's rhythms year-round. You could also accomplish those goals by periodically repeating with your team the "Prayer of Review" exercise on pages 120–122.

DAILY DEBRIEF QUESTIONS

Note: There's no need to ask (or respond to) all of these questions every day! Pick and choose a few at a time based on what resonates most.

- What was most life giving for you today?

- What was most draining, frustrating, or overwhelming today?

- Where did you see or experience growth today?

- How did you experience Christ today?

- Where did you see God at work today?

- When did you feel overwhelmed, frustrated, or undone today?

- What person or experience was most significant for you today? Why?

- How are you being stretched?

- For what are you most thankful right now?

- On a scale of 1 to 5, what overall rating would you give to today? On what basis?

PRAYER OF REVIEW

ONE-DAY   DEVOTION-
           FRIENDLY

BIG IDEA

God is constantly present with us. From time to time we can stop and prayerfully review God's presence in our lives and the ways God shows up through others.

YOU'LL NEED

- Just this prayer
- Optional: Copies of the *Sticky Faith Service Guide Student Journal*

In the midst of our journey, many factors can work against fruitful reflection times — the schedule itself, cross-cultural adjustment, and even group dynamics prevent us from moving with students into deeper and more insightful reflection. This prayer exercise is adapted from a prayer of review that has been faithfully practiced by Jesuit Christians for centuries. It is intended to help slow down participants' minds so you can all sift through the noise of the day's experiences and become more aware of the ways God has been present to you, perhaps through others.

Begin by asking:

Would a few of you be willing to share brief descriptions of what you experienced today?

Continue:

For most of us, today was probably a sprint through a host of unfamiliar experiences. In order to help us sift through the noise of the day's encounters and become more aware of how Christ has been present to us, we're going to walk together through a prayer of review. We will begin by recalling people, places, and events. As we do, I want us to take note of our feelings.

For the next several minutes, I want to invite us all to slow down, close our eyes, and focus on the small or large ways in which God has been present to us. Let's begin our prayer together.[25]

(i)   As a leader, you may find it difficult to know how long to pause in silence after each question or prayer prompt. The silence may seem awkward at first, but giving enough time between questions gives enough space for you and your students to think and recall the day. To help, we've provided you with a suggested guide for counting after each question or prayer prompt. If you'd like, you or someone else can gently strum a guitar in the background to help focus your students' hearts and minds as bookends to the prayer, but silence is preferable for the prayer itself.

Take a moment now to stop, to become still and focused. (Count to 6 slowly.)

Let your breathing help you relax as you breathe in and out. (Count to 10 slowly.)

As you begin the prayer, ask God to guide your thoughts, feelings, and reactions so you might see God's presence in your life. (Count to 10 slowly.)

And now begin to recall the day:

How did you feel when you woke up this morning and during the first part of the day? (Pause.)

What was happening? (Pause.)

What sort of mood or moods were you in? (Count to 10 slowly.)

How did you spend your morning and the middle of the day? (Count to 3 slowly.)

Whom were you with? (Pause.)

What was happening? (Count to 10 slowly.)

Now let your memory drift over your afternoon and evening, recalling events, people, and places. (Count to 12 slowly.)

With whom did you most connect? Why do you think that was? (Count to 6 slowly.)

How were you feeling at different times? Try to name for yourself the different moods you felt. (Count to 8 slowly.)

As you consider your whole day, when did you notice times of light or life? (Count to 6 slowly.)

What gifts have you received today? (Count to 6 slowly.)

Take a moment to relish these gifts and give thanks to God for them. (Count to 15 slowly.)

If there have been difficult times or difficult people, notice them too, offering them to God that he may send his grace and love into them. (Count to 10 slowly.)

When have you known God today? (Pause.)

When have you seen Christ in others? (Count to 10 slowly.)

Take a moment to talk to God as you would a friend about your day. (Count to 15 slowly.)

As this day comes toward its end and you look forward to the next, is there anything you want to ask of God for the coming day(s)? Take a moment to do this before you bring your prayer to a close. (Count to 60 slowly.)

After the prayer is finished, you have a couple of options. First, you could give students some time alone to journal about how God has been present to them and how they've seen Christ in others. Perhaps students could use that time alone to write a note to a person who has been Christ to them or to seek reconciliation with those with whom they've been in conflict.

A second option is to invite students to share highlights of their personal prayers aloud, including ways they've seen Christ through others in the group. If you choose the second option, prep your adult leaders ahead of time to make an effort to share how they've seen Christ through students who don't get mentioned by other students. If you choose this second option, consider using the following discussion guide:

> As we come back together, let's take some time to share what God revealed to us during the prayer of review and how God has been present to each one of us.

Q: **What things did God reveal to you during the prayer?**

Q: **What unexpected gifts did you receive today?**

Q: **If you feel comfortable sharing about them, what times of difficulty or darkness did you feel today?**

Q: **Where did you see the face of Christ today in others, either locals or your team members?**

Q: **What are you asking of God for the coming day(s)?**

Close by giving students a few minutes to pray silently. Invite them to pray individually or to join with another student for a brief prayer. If they have time after they pray with one student, they can move on and pray with a second student. The goal is to give students freedom to pray individually or to pray with others.

MEANINGFUL MEALS

ESSENTIAL   ONE-DAY

BIG IDEA

Meals as a team can be so much more than functional necessities while we serve; they can become holy moments.

YOU'LL NEED

- A shared meal or a whole week full of them!

You have to eat on your trip, right? Why let mealtimes go to waste? Meals can be great opportunities for processing the day so far, for building team connections, and even for getting to know local hosts. Here are a few suggestions to spice up your meals:

- Make it a practice to gather in a circle and pray before meals. While this may seem like a simple thing, the symbol of the circle itself is important imagery of our unity in Christ. If you repeatedly gather in a circle, try different ways of being connected each time: alternate between holding hands, linking arms, standing shoulder to shoulder, and sitting on the floor. Invite the Lord to bring deeper unity as you begin each meal this way, and point out to students the reason you make circles together.

- Occasionally assign seats or require that students sit next to someone new at a meal. While meals can be important downtime for students to hang with their closest friends, this can also inhibit deeper relationships from forming across group lines. If possible, plan at least a few (if not all) meals for students to intentionally eat with locals as well.

- If your meals are not already set up this way, consider involving students in preparing, serving, and cleaning up after each meal.

- If you usually eat in a private space as a team, consider going to a local restaurant or somewhere you can eat among others in the community. Or find a way to make and serve food for the church or ministry you are working with as an expression of gratitude and solidarity with your hosts.

- Occasionally make new meal rules, like restricting use of hands during a meal so everyone has to be fed by someone else near them, or that each person can only use the hand that is opposite their normal preference.

- See "Eat It Up" on pages 125–128 and "Finding the Face of Christ" on pages 150–154 for ideas to take your team's reflection on eating even deeper.

DURING: GOD AND US
EAT IT UP

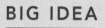

SCRIPTURE   ROOKIE

BIG IDEA

Jesus' eating habits invite us to think more about our own shared meals.

YOU'LL NEED

- Bibles
- Elements for the Lord's Supper— either bread and juice or whatever is available at your site. Try using Communion elements indigenous to where you are serving, like rice or chapattis instead of the traditional bread or wafers your students might be accustomed to. Be sure to work out ahead of time any particular details related to serving Communion within your tradition (e.g., having an ordained pastor consecrate the elements).

This discussion could happen during a meal, immediately after a meal, or even just before a meal if you don't have impatient stomachs on your hands. You could also spread it out over the course of a few meals. In any case, this content will be best digested (so to speak) in the context of a meal.

Open by asking students about the food: their favorite food so far, a local food they're still hoping to try, and maybe what foods from home they are missing. Be sure to be sensitive to the presence of your hosts when you ask these questions. If students have been grumbling about the food, use discretion in whether to ask these questions at all!

Next ask:

Q: What is your favorite thing about meals—here, at home, or anywhere?

Q: How many of you like eating with others? How many would rather eat alone? What makes a difference in whether you would rather eat alone or with other people?

Eating is something we do every day—it's essential to life—but we seldom stop to reflect on how important it is that we eat together. We eat so we can keep living, but when we do it with others, we are reminded of our need to be in community with one another. In fact, when we look closely at Scripture, we see that eating together is important to us spiritually too.

Q: Why do you think eating is spiritually significant? How could sharing a meal be a spiritual encounter?

Note that students may connect the dots differently here, depending on whether you have had many conversations about the interconnectedness of our physical and spiritual lives. If you did the "What Do They Need More?" exercise on pages 71–75, you might refer back to that conversation here and ask whether eating can ever be just physical or just spiritual—or if it's always both.

Q: What examples from Scripture can you think of that describe people sharing meals that had some sort of spiritual significance?

"Table fellowship"—the act of eating together—is a powerful symbol across all cultures, often carrying both social and spiritual significance. In first-century Mediterranean culture, eating together communicated loyalty and intimacy and was an act of reconciliation. The Pharisees taught that the table at home was a representation of the altar at Jerusalem—a holy place for worshiping God. In this context, who you ate with said a lot about the kind of person you were. Despite this fact, Jesus always seemed eager to share a meal with just about anyone—so much so that Luke 7:34 reveals that he was sometimes accused of being a glutton and a heavy drinker!

Likely Jesus' Last Supper will be mentioned, but push them to think about (or suggest yourself) other meals, like Abraham's visit from God (Genesis 18:1–15); the manna and quail God provided for the people in the wilderness (Exodus 16); Elijah's food from ravens (1 Kings 17:6) and from an angel (1 Kings 19:5–8); and Jesus' feeding of the crowds (Mark 6:30–44 and 8:1–13). It has also been noted that Jesus is often eating (or going to a meal, or coming from a meal!) throughout the gospel of Luke.

Then say:

Let's look together at one meal in particular that gives us a picture of Jesus' heart for justice and reconciliation through the way he ate his meals.

Have someone read Mark 2:13–17, and then explain:

By recruiting a tax collector to follow him, Jesus was inviting one of the most hated members of Jewish society to be part of his team. Dishonest tax collectors levied fees against their own people, often taking more than was required by the Roman occupiers and keeping quite a bit for themselves.

Q: What surprises you about this passage?

Q: How do you think these people felt about eating with Jesus? Why do you think the religious leaders were so upset?

You may also point out that tax collectors were not only considered traitors by the people but also declared "unclean" by the Pharisees, which meant they could not attend worship or hang out with other Jews, especially to eat.

ⓘ Levi's decision to follow Jesus likely came with quite a cost. Levi would probably never return to his job as a tax collector, which was a widely sought-after job because it was a sure way to get rich quickly.

So Levi's table, according to this context, was a defiled table—an unholy place. Yet we find Jesus eating there! What's more, the text identifies that "many" tax collectors and sinners followed Jesus. It's one thing to walk behind someone along the road but quite another to sit with him at the table and eat. Jesus' table fellowship with the outcasts of his community was an act of both healing and worship—of making people well and making them holy.

Q: What do Jesus' eating habits reveal to us about Jesus' perceptions of justice?

Q: What do you think our own eating habits on this trip, both individually and as a group, communicate about God's heart for justice?

Q: In light of all of this, what might we want to do differently when we next eat together?

Depending on whether your team eats alone or with locals—or in the case of many mission trips, alone while locals cook and watch—students might bring up uncomfortable feelings or questions about whether it seems just to exclude locals from your table. These are good questions to explore, so be sure you have thought through the implications of changing your eating plans if that's where your group heads in the discussion!

Continue:

Eating together communicates a sense of family-like connectedness. Jesus' common practice of sharing meals with "saints and sinners" alike unveils the value

of table fellowship. The Lord's Supper takes this a step further, making it an act of connection with God the Father, Son, and Holy Spirit, and with other believers as we remember Christ's sacrifice.

Jesus used food—bread and wine—as a picture of his death on the cross. Some Christians believe that every time we eat with other believers, we are announcing Jesus' death and resurrection, and that he will come again. So today we are going to share the Lord's Supper together as part of our meal.

Transition into a time of taking Communion together, or if you are still waiting to eat at this point, begin your meal and then follow

The early church used several names for this special meal. Paul called it the "Lord's table" (1 Corinthians 10:21) or the "Lord's Supper" (11:20); and uses the expression *koinonia* for the cup and bread (10:16). *Koinonia* became *communio* in Latin, which became *communion* in English. So, *koinonia* in the New Testament referred both to Christian fellowship and the Lord's Supper.[26] This combination is important to remember: the act of breaking bread together in table fellowship was both worship and a community ethic, as evidenced in Acts 2:42, 46; 20:7, 11; and 27:35.

it with Communion! At some point during your meal, lead the following discussion:

Psalm 34:8 invites us, "Taste and see that the Lord is good; blessed is the one who takes refuge in him."

Let's think for a minute about this question: Who else needs to be brought to the table? Who do you know who desperately hopes to hear an invitation to find themselves at home with Christ and to taste the new life Jesus offers?

You could try to focus students' answers on the people in the community you're serving, or you could encourage them to think about people back home. Perhaps better yet, invite them to think of people in both settings as a way to connect the dots between their current work and their life at home.

Community—and Communion—are never just acts we do for ourselves; they should always point us outward to love others more faithfully in the name of Jesus. Let's close in prayer for those who need to experience the good news, both here in the community we're serving and back at home. Let's pray that the way we live—even the ways we eat together—might whet their appetites for Christ.

ENGAGING OUR SENSES

ESSENTIAL

MIDDLE
SCHOOL

BIG IDEA

Stopping to notice the sights, sounds, and objects around us can give us new insights into others and ourselves.

YOU'LL NEED

- Six to eight large sheets of paper. Ahead of time, title each paper with a different observation prompt mentioned below (e.g., "The dominant sound I hear is ..."). Substitute some of your own based on your group's experiences.

- Markers
- Pens
- Bibles
- Optional: Copies of the *Sticky Faith Service Guide Student Journal*

Begin by asking your group if there is a particular color they think they've seen more than any other during this trip. Let them take this any direction they want—the color of the dirt, the roofs, the wall you're painting, your group's T-shirts, etc.

Pick one response that names a color they've noticed in the culture (e.g., "red because so many of the roofs are red").

Q: **Why do you think that color is so evident here?**

Explain:

Taking the time to think about the things we're observing is an important part of learning from our work. When we move from observing the color that seems predominant to interpreting why we

129

think that's true, we can't just assume we're right. Instead, we should start testing out our theories; for example, we could ask the locals if they know why there is so much [whatever color was mentioned].

Explain:

Pens and large sheets of paper are scattered throughout the room with different categories written on them. You'll have several minutes to move around to the different sheets to record some of the things you've noticed. Don't overthink your answers. Sometimes your first thoughts are the most profound.

As you write down your own thoughts, note how your response compares with the responses of others. At each paper, feel free to discuss what you and others have written there.

Headings on the papers:

- The main sound I hear is . . .
- One smell I've noticed here is . . .
- Something I haven't seen here is . . .
- Something I see that looks a lot like home is . . .
- People's primary tasks here seem to be . . .
- The most common objects I see are . . .
- The teenagers here are . . .

After giving participants several minutes to go around the room and write their observations, lead the following discussion:

Q: What did you notice about the types of things written down?

Q: What observation by someone else surprised you?

Q: What themes do you see in what we have experienced?

Q: Did you struggle with knowing what to write? Why do you think you struggled?

Q: How well do you think we really know this place and these people? How can we learn more?

Encourage students to take one observation (either their own or someone else's) and focus on it tomorrow. After spending a day focused on that observation, see if that observation still feels accurate. Encourage them to find a way to test out *why* a certain thing is true about this place and/or these people. This will likely involve them chatting with locals about what they've noticed, which will likely lead to a deeper understanding of the community you're serving.

ⓘ Make sure to take down the sheets of paper immediately after your meeting so your local hosts do not see students' raw observations and assumptions, which might be offensive.

HAVE MORE TIME?

Have students journal about one observation they've made of something that seems most different from what they would find at home (e.g., if they felt like the primary color here was red and at home was black). Have them write down the differences and what they think the differences might mean.

Encourage students to begin journaling about things they've observed here that they don't want to forget when they're home—including things they've observed about themselves, your group, God, and the local people.

Explain:

One helpful way to suspend judgment and focus on observing and asking questions is to say to yourself (and others if appropriate), "I wonder why that is?" Keeping that question in mind can help us move deeper in our understanding of culture.

Close by inviting students to choose one of the categories posted on paper and to cluster with other students around that sheet. Allow groups time to pray together for better understanding about that particular element of culture.

WHY ASK "WHY?"

ESSENTIAL   SCRIPTURE   ONE-DAY   DEVOTION-FRIENDLY

BIG IDEA

Truly meeting the needs of the poor means pushing beyond immediate help and asking why they are poor in the first place.

YOU'LL NEED

- Copies of the "Why Ask 'Why?'" handout (p. 136) and/or copies of the *Sticky Faith Service Guide Student Journal.* If being on the field makes this difficult, figure out another way to give each student a copy of the Câmara quotation on the handout. You could possibly read it aloud and ask students to jot it down themselves.

- Pens
- Bibles
- "Have More Time?" option: Copies of the "Service vs. Justice" handout on p. 81

Help students reflect on the day's experiences by asking the following questions:

Q: In what ways have you encountered or experienced poverty before this experience?

Q: What did you see, smell, or hear today that reflected a sense of poverty among the people we met?

Q: When you encounter people who are poor, how do you feel? What do you tend to think about?

Q: What did we do today to help people?

Q: What left you feeling frustrated or helpless today as we tried to make a difference?

At this point, distribute the "Why Ask 'Why?'" handout and lead students through the questions on the handout. Note that you may need to give a brief explanation for the word *communist*, depending on the age and sophistication of your students.

Continue:

Christians sometimes fall into one of two camps. One group emphasizes that Jesus called individuals to follow him and then lead a life of personal purity. These Christians tend to focus primarily on the importance of making a personal decision to follow Jesus.

The second group believes Jesus emphasized serving others and righting wrongs in his name. This group tends to focus on what we can and should do to help those who are poor or marginalized.

Which of these two perspectives best captures what Jesus was about?

Let students wrestle with this tough question. The hope is that your students realize that Jesus was—and is—about both calling individuals to follow and worship him *and* being involved in caring for the least, the last, and the lost. If your students don't arrive at this understanding themselves, try nudging them there yourself. Your goal is to affirm that the real Jesus is beyond *either* personal salvation *or* social reform. He transcends this *either/or* by embodying the *both/and* of the two. In other words, this is a false choice; we don't have to fall into either "camp" but can instead embrace a holistic gospel that lives out both in tandem.

Q: Which of these two positions best describes our church?

Q: What's good about each of these emphases? What do we lose when we focus on one part of Jesus' message and neglect the other?

Explain:

We'd have a much deeper understanding of both sides of the kingdom if we grasped God's plan for his creation. Since the beginning of time, God has wanted to establish *shalom* over all his people and all creation.

Shalom is a Hebrew word often translated as "peace," and while that's not a bad translation, we've tended to focus on only a few angles of the peace God intends. We often think of peace as an absence of conflict or some warm-and-fuzzy feeling that everything is going to work out okay. *Shalom* is far more than that. The type of peace God intends has many forms:

- Peace with God
- Peace with other humans
- Peace with nature
- Peace with oneself[27]

133

HAVE MORE TIME?

Explain to students:

> Just like *shalom*, the Greek word *dikaiosune* (pronounced dih-ky-oh-SUE-nay) has also been misunderstood. In general, this Greek word has been translated in the New Testament Gospels and Epistles as "righteousness." While that's an accurate translation, it misses the full story. *Dikaiosune* also means God's just rule, or God's justice.

> In Matthew 5:6, Jesus teaches, "Blessed are those who hunger and thirst for *dikaiosune*, for they will be filled." In Matthew 6:33, Jesus promises, "But seek first his kingdom and his *dikaiosune*, and all these things will be given to you as well." The North American tendency is to think of that type of "righteousness" as an individualistic form of "right living" or "being good."

Q: What happens when we view *dikaiosune* as God's justice in these two passages?

Give students time to answer the question and then continue:

> Our minds tend to jump to a new form of "right living" that is far more holistic and extends God's kingdom to meet others' spiritual, emotional, social, and physical needs.

Note that injustice often means a disruption in one or all of these relationships.

Q: How, if at all, does that sense of expanded *shalom* relate to Dom Hélder Câmara's quotation on your handout?

Q: Based on a larger understanding of Jesus' gospel and the kingdom *shalom*, what keeps the people we've seen today from experiencing all of God's *shalom*?

Q: What would it look like to ask why the poor have no food in the setting we're in now?

Q: What would we gain by asking why? What might we lose?

HAVE MORE TIME?

If you haven't incorporated it into your discussions earlier, distribute copies of the "Service vs. Justice" handout (p. 81) to your students for discussion.

Q: Based on what we've just discussed, how would you like to deepen our service and justice work in . . .

- the next twenty-four hours?
- the next week?
- the next month?

Close in prayer, giving students a chance to pray that they would have the courage to ask why, and that when they do, others will know that this is a mark of Christ-followers.

WHY ASK "WHY?"

Dom Hélder Câmara was a twentieth-century Roman Catholic priest who showed a relentless commitment to justice work among the poor of Brazil. Câmara is famous for the following quotation:

When I feed the poor, they call me a saint.

When I ask why the poor have no food, they call me a communist.[*]

1. How would you restate Câmara's quotation in your own words?
2. What do you agree with in this quotation? What do you disagree with?
3. If Câmara walked up to Jesus and said these two sentences to him, what do you think Jesus would say in response?

_____

[*] Dom Hélder Câmara, *Dom Hélder Câmara: Essential Writings*, Francis McDonah, ed. (Maryknoll, NY: Orbis, 2009), 11.

- -

HANDOUT

WHY ASK "WHY?"

Dom Hélder Câmara was a twentieth-century Roman Catholic priest who showed a relentless commitment to justice work among the poor of Brazil. Câmara is famous for the following quotation:

When I feed the poor, they call me a saint.

When I ask why the poor have no food, they call me a communist.[*]

1. How would you restate Câmara's quotation in your own words?
2. What do you agree with in this quotation? What do you disagree with?
3. If Câmara walked up to Jesus and said these two sentences to him, what do you think Jesus would say in response?

_____

[*] Dom Hélder Câmara, *Dom Hélder Câmara: Essential Writings*, Francis McDonah, ed. (Maryknoll, NY: Orbis, 2009), 11.

"IF YOU'RE HAPPY AND YOU KNOW IT … SMILE"

ROOKIE   ONE-DAY   MIDDLE SCHOOL

BIG IDEA

When we encounter poverty, we're faced with the challenging task of thinking about the connection between material possessions and happiness in our own lives and the lives of those we serve.

YOU'LL NEED

- Pens
- Bibles
- Optional: Copies of the *Sticky Faith Service Guide Student Journal*

Given the provocative nature of this exercise, it's especially important to read it carefully in advance before leading students through this conversation. You'll want to make sure you understand the twists and turns of the discussion that might emerge as students think more deeply about their typical responses to poverty.

Greet your students and tell them you want to talk about one of the most common statements made by short-term teams who encounter poverty, both domestically and internationally. (If you've heard your own students saying something like the following, you can even reference those conversations):

> These people are so happy despite the horrid conditions in which they live. They sing with joy, they serve us better meals than they eat themselves, and they are so content.

Q: How does this statement relate to your own thoughts and experiences during our service? Have you thought or said something similar to this? Have you heard other people say something like this?

Affirm that it's very important to realize true happiness isn't the result of having a lot of stuff. It's quite possible for people to be happy, even when they might seem to have far less than we have.

Q: Can you think of a time when you felt extremely content and it had nothing to do with money or the things you had? If so, why did you feel content then?

Q: It's been said that true contentment can come only to a person who has a relationship with Jesus Christ. Do you agree or not? Explain.

Stretch your students with a series of questions to help them think more deeply about whether the underresourced people you're with are really "happy." Transition by saying something like:

Let's think a bit more deeply about the people who live here. Would you say the people in this community are happy? Why do you say that?

Students typically respond by talking about the smiles, warmth, and generosity they experience from the locals.

Q: Since we are visitors here, take some time to think about your own experiences when people come to visit you. How might the emotions you show when someone visits your house or community be similar to the emotions our hosts are showing toward us?

The point is to help students realize that just as we and our families might become more positive when guests walk into our lives and homes, the locals might be doing the same thing.

Q: How have you tended to respond to the locals when they smile at us and serve us?

We usually "smile back" and show equal amounts of warmth to the locals.

Q: So do the smiles we give to people we meet definitely mean we are "so happy"?

The point here is not so much to get your students talking about whether they are happy. Instead, the goal is to stretch your students to move beyond the easy assumption that the smiles we encounter are a clear indication that the local people are truly happy. Just as we might assume "Our smiling hosts are happy; therefore poor people are happy," so also the

locals might be thinking, "Our smiling guests are happy; therefore rich people from North America [or your community, or your side of town] are happy." Help them realize that neither conclusion is necessarily true.

In addition, if there's a language barrier, this is a good time to point out that nervous laughter is often a way of dealing with the awkwardness of not being able to do much more than greet one another.

Note: Your point isn't to suggest that the people you encounter in this community can't possibly be happy. They might be happy. But they just as well might *not* be happy. The goal of this discussion is to realize that apart from deep relationship and lots of understanding, we just don't know someone's level of contentment—especially cross-culturally. Just observing smiling faces and hospitality isn't enough to conclude that poor people are happy. Many of them are longing for some kind of economic relief. Some are experiencing broken relationships (just like us). And the pain of life exists here as it does at home.

Q: **If we simply assume people are "happy" because they smile at us when we're here, how might that affect our commitment to seeking justice?**

We can too quickly ease our conscience about responding to poverty if we convince ourselves poor people are happy just the way they are.

Conclude this session by affirming the complexity of all of this. Invite a few students to close by praying that the members of your group as well as those you serve would find their ultimate contentment in Christ. Also pray for discernment whenever locals smile at you, asking that God would help your team to avoid making quick assumptions.

LISTENING TO LOCAL HOSTS

VETERAN

BIG IDEA

We have the huge privilege of building relationships with our local hosts by listening.

YOU'LL NEED

- Copies of the "We Said; They Said" handout (p. 143) and/or copies of the *Sticky Faith Service Guide Student Journal*. If being on location makes carrying or copying these materials difficult, just ask a few students to read the quotations aloud.

- Bibles
- Pens
- Paper

Greet your group and ask:

Q: **As we worked today, what did we hear from the people we served?**

Explain:

Some researchers who study short-term missions suggest that without realizing it, service teams like ours can miss one of the greatest opportunities of being on a trip like this—encountering and listening to the people who live here!

One way to describe this kind of experience is like racing through a museum.

At a museum we look at artifacts from another time through glass but it's hard to really immerse ourselves in what that time period was like. And on a trip like this, we're moving fast through that museum. We can serve and worship alongside our local hosts but never really get past surface interactions.

Q: In what ways does it feel like we're viewing people through a display case in a museum?

During this discussion, push your students beyond quick, easy responses. Wrestle together with whether we can honestly say we're interacting with the local people. Do we know their names? Do we know their backgrounds? Their stories? What have we *really* learned about them?

Distribute the "We Said; They Said" handout and read through it together. After each pair of sayings, discuss the problems evident in the perspectives of the North Americans.

Q: What quotations on this handout might feel similar to things we are thinking or saying as we serve?

Q: How are we acting or talking differently?

Q: What kinds of things can we do to avoid seeming like the people in the quotations on the "We Said; They Said" handout?

Q: In many cultures people would be too embarrassed to tell us explicitly if we're being offensive. So we have to watch for cues. As we interact with the locals here, what clues would tell us we are being sensitive and honoring to them? What clues might tell us we're not?

Q: What kind of advice can the locals here offer us, not just about any tasks we're trying to do but also in light of what they observe in our culture?

Continue:

The reality is that we can't all get to know every single person here really well. So let's each think of one or two local people (not teammates) we've met whom we'd really like to get to know

You might want to offer two suggestions to your group members as they pursue deeper connections with the people you're serving. First, caution them against pursuing deeper male-female relationships, since the lines of appropriate relationships can get blurry, especially when different cultures are involved. Second, discourage your students from making promises to stay in touch unless they're really going to do it.

Be mindful that sometimes certain locals stand out to the group, and most everyone may pick the same person they want to get closer to during the rest of the trip. If this is the case, encourage a bit more diversity beyond the obvious standout.

141

better in the midst of our work. What can we do tomorrow to get to know those people better? How specifically can we begin to practice listening well to them? What obstacles might we face?

Invite students to get into pairs, perhaps even encouraging them to pair up with teammates they don't know well. Ask students to share with each other the names of the local persons they'd like to get to know better, and then have them pray together that God would strengthen those relationships in the days to come. When the pairs have finished praying, ask students to touch base with their prayer partners tomorrow at lunch as a type of accountability for their goal of getting to know a local better. At lunch they can ask their partners if they've had a chance to spend time with that local and identify any other ways they can build a deeper relationship with that local during the rest of the day.

WE SAID; THEY SAID*

NORTH AMERICANS	NON–NORTH AMERICAN HOSTS
"We've got to do something. The window of opportunity is *now*! The time for change is ripe. We must seize this opportunity." —a recurring statement made by short-term missions (STM) teams	"You too quickly get into the action without thinking through the implications for our churches long after you go home." —a recurring concern voiced by local believers who receive STM teams
"They're dirt poor. It just makes me realize how blessed I am to be born in America." —one of the most common statements made by STM teams. It's usually combined with a statement about the happiness of the poor people encountered.	"I can still feel like a stranger in the American church, especially when short-termers return from India bubbling over their accomplishments and describing my birthplace as a land of deprivation." —a comment from an Indian-American woman on the ways STM teams obsess over the poverty of places visited
"It felt really good to work so hard. We gave them some buildings they never would have had without us being there." —a recurring statement made by STM teams	"I found out soon enough that I was in the way. The group wanted to do things their way and made me feel like I didn't know what I was doing. I only helped the first day." —a comment from a Honduran bricklayer who planned to help a team build houses for hurricane victims

*Adapted from David A. Livermore's *Serving with Eyes Wide Open* (Grand Rapids: Baker, 2006).

DURING: GOD AND LOCALS

MAPPING THE COMMUNITY

VETERAN

BIG IDEA

We need to confront any hasty assumptions by learning more about the unique stories that shape and define our host community.

YOU'LL NEED

- Copies of the "Mapping Exercises" handout (pp. 147–149)

- Two or three maps of the area you are serving. If you can't find maps, skip Exercise 1 and focus your team on Exercises 2 and 3.

- One large piece of poster paper

- Pens

- Markers

- Paper

- Host people or translators willing to assist with cross-cultural nuances

- A few hours available for doing the interview exercises

Before your meeting: Arrange for some key people in the community you're serving to join you and to be interviewed by your group for thirty minutes. Exercise 1 works best if the person(s) interviewed has lived in the community long term; Exercise 2 is designed for interviewing church or ministry leaders; and Exercise 3 will work best if the interviewees are successful professionals. Be sure to arrange for translators if needed.

Since we're giving you three mapping exercises, you actually have a lot of flexibility. You can have all of your team do all the exercises over a period of days or some of your team do some of them or all of your team do some of them or ... You get the idea. These exercises also could be done before your work if you prefer (perhaps through the use of email, phone, or video call, depending on geography involved).

Divide your students into smaller teams and give each team one of the exercises on the "Mapping Exercises" handout to complete. Make sure you have at least one host (with translator, if needed) in each team. Give clear time expectations and boundaries if teams are leaving your immediate area for the interviews.

When all the teams are finished, invite them to return and share with the rest of the group what they found. Then lead the following discussion:

Q: What insights stand out as particularly significant or interesting?

Q: What are the implications of our findings from these exercises for our service and any work toward justice we might do?

Q: What can we do during the rest of our time here that will help us continue to learn the story of this community and the people who live here?

To conclude, ask each team to gather again and pray for the community, especially for the needs that emerged during this exercise and the people they met during their study.

Explain:

Today we're going to get to know this community better. How might knowing more about this community help our work?

Q: What might happen if we rush into our work without understanding the community?

Continue:

As you go about these exercises, please be respectful and listen well—let your hosts be your guides. You are not here to "get a job done," but instead to listen and learn. When all the teams are finished, each team will present what they have learned to the rest of the group.

HAVE MORE TIME?

If there are missionaries in the area with whom you are not directly partnering, invite them to talk to your group about their story, their work, and what they've observed about the community. Another possibility is to invite a key leader from a local Christian organization to come and share with your group. You may also want to consider bringing in people from the community you're serving who have been to your own community or country and can talk about the contrasts between their own culture and yours.

Another option is to arrange for your students to spend the night at the homes of the people they interview. This immersion helps make the mapping exercise all the more significant as your students literally walk in the footsteps of your hosts. If you do this, make sure you train your students on appropriate guest etiquette in that culture. In addition, to ensure safety, make sure at least two students and one adult from your group stay at each home.

MAPPING EXERCISES

MAPPING EXERCISE 1:
BIRD'S-EYE VIEW

What is the layout of the community where you're serving? Using two (or more) maps of the area, draw a new map on the poster paper to share with the rest of the group. On the new map, indicate some of the dynamics related to community infrastructure, including answers to the questions you ask your host.

To get this new map completed, you will need to spend some more time with some of your hosts and let them guide you. Instead of those local people just explaining the community to you, it would be best if you went out and walked (or rode) around in order to identify the features of the community yourself. Mark on your map other aspects of the community that will interest your team.

Ask your host the following questions:

1. Where did the town first start, and how did it grow?

2. Are there specific groups of people living in particular sections of the community? Label and mark them on the map.

3. Mark on a map where your host church is (or churches are).

4. Where do people in your community gather? Where is there a lot of energy?

5. Where is housing growing in the community?

6. Where are the poorer areas of this community? What about the more dangerous areas?

7. Where do wealthier people tend to live?

8. What are the locations of the high schools and other schools in the community? What are the differences between the high schools?

9. What other locations are important to the community?

MAPPING EXERCISE 2: WHAT HAS GOD BEEN DOING HERE?

The goal of your team is to "map" the Christian community in the area. You will need to be very sensitive, as there can be deep divisions between churches that stretch back many years (or sometimes even centuries).

Discuss the questions below with church or ministry leaders. You may not be able to hear all sides of the story, and that's okay. Remember, sensitivity and relational trust building are more important than rushing through these questions. If you don't get answers to all the questions, that's also okay.

1. List all the Christian churches (Protestant and Catholic) in your area.

2. What other Christian ministries exist in the area?

3. Are there "groups" of churches that connect well with each other? What are those groups?

4. What percentage of the community attends church services regularly?

5. What stories are told about revivals or key people becoming Christians?

6. What missionaries have come to this community? What missionaries or Christian leaders are still here?

7. Has anyone from this community gone somewhere else as a pastor or missionary? Other than Christian churches, what other religious groups are active in this community? What are these groups like?

MAPPING EXERCISE 3: WHO ARE THE LEADERS?

This exercise invites your team to meet with at least three people from the community who are successful professionals. Each interview should last no more than thirty minutes. Make sure you have a host from your local community with you to help translate and/or pick up on cultural nuances.

As you meet with each person, explain (very briefly) where you're from and what you're doing in the community. When it seems appropriate, move toward interview time, centering on these questions:

1. Can you tell us a little of your story?

2. How did you become involved in your work here?

3. What are some of the unique qualities of this community?

4. What are the economic dynamics of the community?

5. How has the community grown or changed over the years?

6. What are some other changes you would like to see happen?

7. What misunderstandings might guests (such as us) have about your community?

8. What advice would you have for us, as outsiders, as we serve in this community?

When you are done with your interviews, spend some time as a team summarizing your findings and getting ready to share your insights with the other teams.

FINDING THE FACE OF CHRIST

SCRIPTURE   VETERAN

BIG IDEA

Serving others can be a holy experience through which we encounter Christ in those we serve, in one another, and even in ourselves.

YOU'LL NEED

- Paper
- Pencils
- Bibles
- Optional: Copies of the *Sticky Faith Service Guide Student Journal*
- Elements for the Lord's Supper— either bread and juice or whatever is available at your site. Try using Communion elements indigenous to where you are serving, like rice or chapattis instead of the traditional bread or wafers your students might be accustomed to. Be sure to work out ahead of time any particular details related to serving Communion within your tradition (e.g., having an ordained pastor consecrate the elements).
- "Have More Time?" option: Small handheld mirrors for each student (cheaply available at most craft stores), or a way students can pass around a mirror or stand in front of one

ⓘ We recommend that you do this learning activity in two different gatherings (preferably a morning and then an evening), but you could combine the two discussions into one longer exercise. Also, if sharing the Lord's Supper is not an option, you can simply make connections between your team sharing food together and the many, many times Jesus shared meals with others.

PART 1: MORNING CONVERSATION

Begin by asking participants to close their eyes and think about the different faces they've seen in the past twenty-four hours. Then distribute paper and pencils and invite everyone to journal silently about these questions as you read them aloud slowly:

Q: How would you describe the faces you've seen in the past day? What words would you use to describe their appearance? Their emotions? Their expressions? Their reactions?

Q: Whose face made you smile? Why do you think you reacted so positively to that person?

Q: Whose face bothered you the most? Why do you think you reacted so strongly?

Invite a few students to share reflections aloud if they are comfortable doing so. Next ask:

Q: Why do faces evoke so much response in us? What is it about faces that move us so deeply?

If it doesn't come out in the discussion, be sure to point out that we communicate a great deal nonverbally through our facial expressions—sometimes much more than we communicate through our words.

Q: Now think about yourself. What do you think others learned about you through your face?

Q: Now think about that a different way: What do you think others learned about *Christ* through your face in the past day?

Q: How did you experience the face or presence of Christ in others? Why do you think Jesus seemed especially present or powerful in that moment?

Next ask someone to read Matthew 25:34–40, in which Jesus says that when we serve people who are considered the "least" by society, we are actually serving Jesus himself.

Q: Why do you think Jesus was so emphatic that serving people in need is the same thing as serving him?

Q: Think back to the faces you saw yesterday. How does it make you think differently about them when you consider that those faces were the very face of Christ?

Explain:

Throughout the history of the church, certain practices have been considered "sacraments," or holy ways we experience Jesus' presence and grace through acts of worship. The two main sacraments recognized across almost all Christian traditions are baptism and the Lord's Supper (or Holy Communion, or Eucharist). But a number of other experiences also have been considered sacramental in nature. Serving people in need can be one of those kinds of experiences.

Q: How could seeing Jesus' face in the poor—or specifically in the people we are serving—be considered a *sacramental* experience, meaning a worshipful encounter in which we receive God's grace?

Close your morning discussion by explaining:

In the midst of our work today, we are all invited to remain mindful of how our work, and the people with whom we interact, might be sacramental for us. We'll gather together at the end of the day to share what we see.

What makes something "sacramental"? Though denominations and theologians may disagree at points about what constitutes a sacrament, since Augustine, the most commonly held understanding of a Christian sacrament is that it is an "outward and visible sign of an inward and invisible grace." Sacraments are holy practices that embody our commitment and fidelity to God and the community of faith. If your own faith tradition would look down on your saying that seeing the face of Jesus in the poor is a "sacramental" experience, then use other language and don't lose your job. You might simply call it what it is: a great mystery.[28]

Give participants time to close in prayer, perhaps journaling their prayers at the bottom of the paper they've been writing on. Encourage them to draw faces—their own or others they've seen during their justice work—in the midst of their prayer journaling.

PART 2: EVENING CONVERSATION

At the end of the day, gather with your students again and ask:

Q: **What did you experience today that felt sacramental, or holy?**

Be prepared to get the ball rolling by sharing an experience of your own.

Q: **In what ways did the faces of others help you more thoroughly experience Christ?**

Remind students that the Lord's Supper (and here use whatever language your team will be most familiar with) is one of the most commonly practiced sacraments, and then ask:

Q: **How is taking Communion like seeing the face of Christ?**

As we noted earlier, Communion has been an important sacrament of the church since Christ encouraged his followers to celebrate it together. Henri Nouwen, a justice-seeking twentieth-century priest, once wrote that our identity in Christ is like the Lord's Supper. As the Spirit moves in our lives to form us into deeply loved sons and daughters of God, we are "taken, blessed, broken, and given," reflecting the actions of the Lord's Supper.[29] So in a mysterious way, through our faithful surrender to Christ, we become bread for the world as we are taken, blessed, broken, and given by God.

We are now going to share in the Lord's Supper together. As we do, I encourage you to remember that just as these elements of bread and juice represent

HAVE MORE TIME?

As part of this exercise, invite students to look carefully at their own reflections in a mirror. Have them ponder their own faces and consider how the face of Christ might show through their faces, words, and actions. Invite students to pray while looking at their own faces, asking that they might be the very face of Christ to someone in need today (or tomorrow, if you are doing this at night). If you cannot provide a separate mirror for each student, pass one mirror around or invite students to take turns coming forward to look in a mirror during a time of prayer and reflection. You could also weave this into the experience of taking Communion together by placing the elements on a table in front of a mirror.

What's necessary in the act of taking the Lord's Supper? In 1 Corinthians 11:23–26 Paul provides three features: (1) a common meal, (2) remembering the Lord's presence in the act of partaking of bread and wine, and (3) pointing to our future hope in the kingdom of God by continuing this ritual "until he comes."[30] So while our different traditions may place various requirements on the ways this meal should be prepared and taken, these basic features mark the essential spirit of the sacrament.

Christ to us, you and I represent Christ to the world—and specifically right now to the people we are serving.

Share in Communion together, reading from either 1 Corinthians 11:23–26 or Matthew 26:26–29. If it fits your context, you may also want to sing worship songs together. Close your time in whatever prayer format seems most appropriate—in pairs, small groups, or as one large group.

SAYING GOOD-BYE WELL

ESSENTIAL   SCRIPTURE   MIDDLE SCHOOL

BIG IDEA

Saying an appropriate good-bye is an important part of our cross-cultural service experience.

YOU'LL NEED

- Copies of the "Saying Good-Bye Well" handout (pp. 158–159) and/ or copies of the *Sticky Faith Service Guide Student Journal*
- Whiteboard or poster paper
- Pens
- Paper
- Pencils
- Bibles

Divide your group into equal teams of four to ten students and play "The Good-Bye Game." Distribute paper and pencils and explain:

> I am going to give your team three or four minutes to list different words or phrases people have used to say good-bye. You can write down movie or television quotations, songs, words for good-bye from other languages, or catch phrases you've heard. Brainstorm

as many as you can and have one team member write them down.

At the end of three or four minutes, interrupt the brainstorming and explain:

> Starting with the team to my left, and then going around to the other teams one at a time, your team needs to stand and say one of the "good-bye phrases." We'll go around the room until a team

cannot come up with a new phrase, at which time that team is out.

Be sure to keep the game moving from group to group as quickly as possible. You are the final judge as to whether a phrase is acceptable or not. It's okay if teams come up with phrases as the game progresses. Award a prize if appropriate.

> ⓘ Here are some "good-bye" examples for you, the leader: *Later 'Gator; Toodles; Hasta la vista; TTFN; So long; Time to bounce; Let's boogie; See you on the flip side; Catch you later; Aloha; Adiós; Adieu.*

Transition by asking:

Q: **How does your family say good-bye? What about your friends?**

Q: **What are some hurtful ways to say good-bye?**

Continue:

Saying good-bye is not as big a deal in some families as in others. In fact, you may have heard someone say, "I hate saying good-bye." However, in most cultures, saying an appropriate good-bye is an important moment. In your teams, think through the following questions:

1. **What could we unintentionally communicate to others if we do a poor job of saying good-bye at the end of our trip?**

2. **Who are the people here with whom we most need to do a good job of saying good-bye?**

Give your teams a few minutes to huddle up and answer those questions and then ask them to share their responses with the entire group.

Distribute Bibles and the "Saying Good-Bye Well" handouts and invite students to complete the top portion on their own. When they are finished, they can complete the rest in teams.

After each team is done filling out the form, pull everyone back into a large group and have teams share their answers to each question. Make sure to get every group sharing as often as possible, but keep it moving. Write answers to the last question on your whiteboard or poster paper.

> Paul's good-bye to the Ephesian elders in Acts 20:17–38 is similar to the format of many of his letters, in that its body has three main components: the past, the present, and the future. ⓘ

Ask the entire group the following questions:

Q: **How is this scene in Acts 20 the same as saying good-bye to the local people we've worked with on this project?**

Q: **How is it not the same?**

One important difference to note might be that your team's visit probably wasn't the first introduction of the gospel to the community, and you probably aren't spiritual leaders to them like Paul was to the community in Ephesus.

Q: **What does it mean when we're sad to leave?**

Q: **Since we've shared this intense experience, how can we properly say good-bye to our local hosts?**

Conclude by distributing paper and explaining:

> **Working in your teams, I want you to spend the next four or five minutes writing down ideas about how we can say good-bye well on this project. As you're brainstorming, use the three examples in the New Testament listed on your "Saying Good-Bye Well" handout as a springboard for your ideas.**

After five minutes, invite teams to share their answers. If appropriate, see if your group can choose one or two ideas that stand out to them as the best ways to say good-bye. If you feel like you need more time to consider, massage, or nuance your students' ideas, you can say something like:

> Saying good-bye well requires cultural sensitivity. It may be tempting to want to give money or to say good-bye in a way that gets the locals to like you or appreciate you more. It will be very helpful to talk with someone who understands the cultural dynamics about appropriate good-byes.

> **I'll think about all these ideas and get back to you with a few possibilities.**

Lay out some poster paper and distribute pens to your students. Invite them to create a good-bye card or picture to present to the church and/or community you've been serving. Brainstorm any Scripture passages you might want to include. If appropriate, make the card a "thank-you" card for all you've learned from the local people.

Close in prayer, inviting students to lift up the names of the local people to whom it will be hard to say good-bye. Ask God to continue to do great kingdom work in the community you're serving, as well as in your community back home.

157

SAYING GOOD-BYE WELL

ON YOUR OWN

Put an X on the line at the spot that best describes how you feel about good-byes.

●——●

I don't mind them.   I haven't thought   I don't like them.
                            much about them.

    Write down one moment you remember in which you, or someone you know, didn't say good-bye very well. How did people (including you!) feel when that happened?

WITH YOUR TEAM

Read this: Look up the following Scripture verses one at a time and then write down your answers. Each passage reflects a different "good-bye" in the New Testament:

1. Luke 9:61. The word for *good-bye* in this verse means "to dismiss with orders." Write down times when someone might give instructions as part of their good-bye.

2. Philippians 4:4. The word for *rejoice* also was used for *good-bye*. Write down ways a good-bye can be a joyful time.

3. The apostle Paul provides a great example of taking time to say good-bye well. In the midst of his third missionary journey around the Mediterranean, Paul says good-bye to the elders in Ephesus in Acts 20:17–38.

Pick a team member to read verses 17–21 and then discuss:

What did Paul remember about his relationship with the Ephesian elders?

Have someone read verses 22–27 and then discuss:

What was Paul's main concern in the present?

Have another team member read verses 28–32 and then discuss:

How did Paul want them to get ready for the future?

Each person can silently read Acts 20:33–38. Then discuss together:

What does Paul model for us in the way he says good-bye?

PART FOUR

AFTER: DEBRIEF

Take time as your work comes to a close to cement all that you've learned and experienced by doing these exercises in the final hours or days of your trip or project.

DEVOTION AND JOURNALING OPTIONS

ESSENTIAL   ONE-DAY

BIG IDEA

Daily devotion times at the conclusion of the trip can help us process our time away.

YOU'LL NEED

- Copies of the *Sticky Faith Service Guide Student Journal* for every participant
- Pens

Journaling options that will help with your end-of-trip debrief are included in the *Sticky Faith Service Guide Student Journal* for use before you head home. Specifically, here are the options that are ideal for participants' individual reflection times:

AFTER: DEBRIEF

INITIAL DEBRIEF: SHARING THE HIGHLIGHTS

ESSENTIAL   ONE-DAY   MIDDLE SCHOOL

BIG IDEA

Sharing about our experience right away helps us process what we've learned and lets others know what God is doing.

YOU'LL NEED

■ Copies of the "Sharing the Highlights" handout (p. 166–167) and/or copies of the *Sticky Faith Service Guide Student Journal*

■ Pens

Whether you are serving across town or across the globe, the student and adult participants in your work need to think through how they will talk about their experience with others. This processing is part of what helps the transformation stick. While the following exercise ("Sharing the Journey") is more suited for processing longer trips, this current exercise can be used both for half-day service projects as well as multiweek trips.

One way to be faithful with the experiences we have been given is to share our stories with others. In fact, we have a responsibility to tell our stories well and to give God glory for the work itself and for any transformation we have seen or personally experienced through it. You may want to give some of that framing to your team if they wonder why you are taking so much time for processing.

Open this exercise by asking a few general debriefing questions, depending on how much time you have available (these are adapted from the During list of suggested daily reflection questions; the full list is available on p. 119). Adjust the wording based on whether you're talking about a brief experience or a lengthy trip. Also, you might alternate doing this exercise in pairs, small groups, or as a whole team. Make sure adults share as well as young people.

Q: What was this experience like for you?

Q: What was most life-giving for you?

Q: What was most draining?

Q: Where did you see growth? How were you stretched?

Q: When did you see God's presence at work? Where did you meet God?

Q: What person or experience was most significant for you and why?

Q: For what are you most thankful right now?

Eventually transition by saying:

Now that we've had some time to think through our experience and how it has impacted us, let's take some time to think about how we will communicate our experiences to others. It is often helpful to think of a few different types of responses based on the situation in which we will be sharing.

Encourage students to share their thirty-second and three-minute highlights with someone else on the trip, and again with their parent(s) when they get home. It's a great way for students to practice, and it gives parents a chance to hear their own child's stories.

Distribute the "Sharing the Highlights" handout and review it together. Give students a few minutes to write notes on the front or back of the handout that would help them share their thirty-second and their three-minute highlights. Encourage them to take some more time to think about who might benefit from hearing the "whole enchilada." Once students have had a chance to write their highlights (or at least some sort of notes or outline), ask if anyone would like to share their three-minute version with the group.

Close in prayer, thanking God for the ways your stories will bless others and transform you.

SHARING THE HIGHLIGHTS

Thirty-Second Highlight: When people ask the quick question, "How was your trip?" in passing, don't just settle for typical quick responses like "Good," or "It was fun." Think of a two- or three-sentence response that will tell them about something significant you learned or someone significant you met. Your thirty-second response might even spark their interest and cause them to ask more questions!

Three-Minute Highlight: You may be asked to share about your mission experience at youth group, a family gathering, over a meal, or even in a class. If you have only a couple of minutes, it's better to share one meaningful moment or story and what God taught you through it than to rush through all the details of the entire trip or event.

*Adapted from *YouthWorks! 2007 Devotional Journal.* Used with permission.

The Whole Enchilada: Everybody needs at least one opportunity to unload all the details, emotions, funny highlights, and meaningful memories of their service experience. We encourage you to find at least two people (an adult and a friend your age) who were not with you on the trip and invite them into your experience by telling them your highlights and showing them your pictures. Sharing about how your views of God, yourself, and others were changed during your work will help you process your experience and also help those close to you understand how you've been impacted by the experience. It may even help them to see the world, themselves, and God in new ways.

Note: You probably can't write about every-thing here and now, but you can jot down a few words or names that you want to remember to share about later.

SHARING THE JOURNEY

ESSENTIAL   ROOKIE   VETERAN

BIG IDEA

Learning to share what we've experienced is helpful not only for our team but also for others back home.

YOU'LL NEED

- Plain white paper plates or the *Sticky Faith Service Guide Student Journal*. See "Reflect Back" for the drawing exercise portion of this session.
- Crayons or markers

- Copies of the "Sharing the Journey" handout (p. 171) and/or copies of the *Sticky Faith Service Guide Student Journal*
- Pens

Welcome participants and invite everyone to grab a paper plate and a few markers or crayons. Explain:

Today we're going to create pictures of what we experienced during our work. On one side of your paper plate, I want you to draw a picture of the experience from an outside perspective. In other words, think of what you saw, the people you met, and the things you did

that stand out to you. If you want, you could chart your journey like a map by listing or drawing the experiences that most impacted you from start to finish.

On the other side of your paper plate, I want you to draw your experience from an internal perspective. In other words, draw about how your experiences made you feel, the new things you learned about, as well as how God shaped or

HEADS-UP: If you're interested in doing the "Rewind and Fast-Forward" activity on pages 213–215, make sure you record (either on audio or video) at least one of your team's debriefing discussions. You might also keep the paper-plate drawings students make in this exercise as a helpful reminder of how students experienced God's transformation during their journey.

If you are using the *Sticky Faith Service Guide Student Journal*, you'll find two entries related to this session. The first is called "Reflect Back" and mirrors the plate-drawing exercise below along with some initial reflection questions. The second is titled "Sharing the Journey," just like the session in this manual, and mirrors the handout contained at the end of this session on page 171.

changed your heart. If you'd like, you can also chart your own internal experiences by using a map. After we all finish, I'm going to invite all of you who want to share your pictures or maps to do so. You certainly don't have to, so don't let the thought that you might show your picture to others constrain your honesty or creativity.

Give participants ten to fifteen minutes to draw, and let them know at the start how long they will have. You'll also want to give them a two-minute warning as the end approaches. When they are finished, ask if people would like to share one or both of their drawings. Then lead the following discussion:

Q: Did anything surprise you or stand out as you recalled the significant people, places, moments, events, and feelings from our trip?

Q: Right now we're talking about our experiences with others who shared them with us. But as we transition home, we will be sharing our experiences with others who didn't take part in the experience with us. Will that be difficult for you to do? Why or why not?

Continue:

The transition back home from a trip like this can be difficult in many ways, and sometimes the hardest part is figuring out how to share it with others who haven't lived it with us. But figuring out how to share our highlights is important because it helps us process what we've learned and creates opportunities for others to hear what God has done through our experience.

Distribute copies of the "Sharing the Journey" handout and pens to students and let them answer its questions.

When students are finished, continue:

Now that we've had some time to think through our experience and how it has impacted us, let's take some time to think about how we will communicate

our experience to others. It is often helpful to think of a few different types of responses based on the situation in which we will be sharing.

Depending on how much time you want to take with this, you can either have them review the questions they just completed and pull out a few highlights they will want to share with others, or give them the "Sharing the Highlights" handout from pages 166–167 and review it together. Give students a few minutes to write a few notes that would help them share a thirty-second and a three-minute recap of the trip with someone back at home. Encourage them to take some more time to think about who might benefit from hearing their whole story. Once students have had a chance to write their highlights (or at least some sort of notes or outline), ask if anyone

Encourage students to share their thirty-second and three-minute highlights with someone else on the trip, and again with their parent(s) when they get home. It's a great way for students to practice, and it gives parents a chance to hear their own child's stories.

would like to share their thirty-second or three-minute version with the group.

Close in prayer, but instead of having students close their eyes, encourage them to keep their eyes open and to look at the drawings they made earlier. Invite students to pray aloud that God would help them continue to process all their experiences, and that God would use this journey to impact those around them.

SHARING THE JOURNEY

1. What did you learn about yourself during your journey?

2. What new things did you learn about God?

3. What did you learn from people in the community?

4. Who/what do you specifically want to pray for after you return home?

5. How are you a different person now compared to when you signed up for this work?

6. How do you want our youth group to be involved in service at home? How do you want to be personally involved in serving or seeking justice?

BACK TO THE "REAL WORLD"

VETERAN

BIG IDEA

On cross-cultural trips, students often see the "real world" in ways they've never seen it before, including the *real* truth about poverty or glimpses of the *real* kingdom of God. This is the "real world" of following Jesus that they can continue to live out every day.

YOU'LL NEED

- Pencils
- Paper
- Optional: Copies of the *Sticky Faith Service Guide Student Journal*

Begin the discussion by asking:

Q: What have you missed about your life at home while you've been away?

Q: We often refer to life back home as the "real world." Why do we call it that?

Q: If life back home is the "real world," then what should we label the life we've experienced during our work here? What would the people who live here call it?

Q: If we asked Jesus which of these worlds (the world where we've been serving or the world back home) is the "real world," what do you think he would say?

Q: In what ways have we seen the "real" church as we've served, either among our team or among the local people?

Q: In what ways have we seen "real" relationships?

Q: In what ways have we seen "real" grace?

Continue:

Justice work can sometimes give us a different idea of what it really means to follow Jesus and be part of the kingdom community. If that happens, we have at least three potential responses:

>> **CONSUME.** You can go home with a couple of cheap souvenirs and say to yourself, "What happens in _____ [location] stays in _____ [location]." You can forget how God spoke to you in the midst of your time there and go back to your life as if nothing happened.

>> **CONDEMN.** You can get angry about the way your friends, family, and church all seem stuck in their old ways and just don't seem to "get it."

>> **CREATE.** You can go home and find ways to get involved in kingdom service in your own backyard. You can choose to create a community that's centered on mission and stay involved in righting wrongs so God's kingdom is made clearer.

Q: In the past, how have you felt the temptations to consume or condemn after returning from a mission trip or maybe even a camp experience?

Q: How have you participated in creating something new after a trip?

Q: How do you hear these three words — consume, condemn, create — used in our youth ministry or our church?

If the response is "not much," wonder aloud whether these would be helpful terms to shift the way you process experiences together.

Q: Based on your past experiences, what would it take for us as a youth ministry to create more of a missional community at home?

Distribute paper and pens and invite students to draw a line down the center of their paper. On the left side of their paper, ask students to draw a picture (or write words, phrases, or a poem) of how they have seen the "real" world of following Jesus this week. After students have finished that, ask them to draw (or write) something on the right side of the paper that captures how they'd like to live out the Jesus-focused "real world" when they get back home.

When students are finished, give them a chance to share their drawings. Notice any themes that emerge (e.g., sharing the gospel with our words, loving people who are poor, working hard to meet physical needs). For your time of closing prayer, invite students to gather in groups in different parts of the room around the theme that is most significant to them (e.g., "Anyone who wants to pray that we will be able to love those in our home community who are poor can meet by that back window").

HAVE MORE TIME?

In addition to praying along the themes that emerged from their drawings, invite students to get into working teams to tackle some of these issues at home. Give students time to brainstorm how they might be able to live out the "real world" they've seen in the midst of their service as they transition home. Invite each team to share some of their ideas and, if possible, schedule a time for those same teams to meet again within two or three weeks to check in and determine future action steps.

WHO'S MY NEIGHBOR?

ESSENTIAL   SCRIPTURE   ONE-DAY

BIG IDEA

We can share with people in our own schools and community the same love we lived out during our trip.

YOU'LL NEED

- Copies of your local newspaper from home
- Pens

- Paper or copies of the *Sticky Faith Service Guide Student Journal*
- Bibles

ⓘ If you are using this exercise to debrief a one-day local service project, simply adapt the opening exercise below accordingly by the language you use to describe your work and its location in proximity to home.

Greet your students and invite them to share a few brief stories about some of their favorite people they met during your trip. Then distribute local newspapers from your home community and ask them to share any initial thoughts or feelings as they thumb through images of home.

Acknowledge that flying overseas or driving away from home to serve in a different community can be exhilarating. It's easy to fall in love with people for a few days in the midst of the excitement of service and justice work.

Continue:

Coming back home to the people in our own neighborhoods isn't quite as glamorous. But we don't primarily live out the gospel in faraway places a couple of weeks a year. We live out the gospel 24/7 with the people at school, at home, and in the neighborhood.

Transition to one of Jesus' most popular stories—the parable of the good Samaritan—by giving students some background:

Jesus tells a fascinating story about what it means to love our neighbors in Luke 10.

The road from Jerusalem to Jericho was about seventeen miles long and curved through rugged terrain with plenty of large rocks for thieves to hide behind. As a result, traveling this road was very dangerous.

At this point, invite a few students to read Luke 10:25–37 aloud.

Q: **Luke 10:27 quotes the Old Testament's commands to love God and love our neighbor. How are those two love commands connected to each other?**

Q: **How does Jesus define a "neighbor"?**

Note that Jesus' definition includes people we might typically hate or exclude. In fact, the Samaritan who helped the hurt Jew represented the Jew's enemies. This is the very kind of person Jesus asks us to love "as ourselves."

Q: **Based on Jesus' definition, who are *your* "neighbors"?**

Q: **What would it mean for you to love them as yourself?**

Continue:

It's possible that our trip gave you new opportunities to interact with people whose racial or ethnic background is different from your own. It's worth considering how Jesus' story of the

HAVE MORE TIME?

Ask your students to get into small groups to come up with a modern-day version of this parable set in their own school(s) or your city. Once the small groups are finished developing their contemporary versions of Jesus' parable, have them act out these stories for the rest of the group.

good Samaritan speaks to issues of racism and racial stereotyping. Racism and stereotyping are not new problems. During Jesus' lifetime, both were widespread. For example, most first-century Jews couldn't stand Samaritans. So when Jesus used a Samaritan as the role model for living out the greatest commandments, instead of the priest or Levite, his Jewish audience must have been shocked!

Jesus not only called the Jews to watch out for the wounded and oppressed alongside the road, but he also invited the Jews to love the Samaritans and to realize that they as Jews had something to learn from the Samaritans.

Have students respond to the following on a piece of paper. Tell them no one else will read this:

Q: Who are the "Samaritans" in your life—the people who seem so different that you find it hard to relate to them? Are there certain groups or individuals who make you annoyed or anxious because they feel unfamiliar to you?

After your students have had some time to reflect on these questions, ask them to respond in writing to this question:

Q: What would it look like for you to love those neighbors as you love yourself this week?

After students have finished writing their answers to that question, invite them to write their answers to the following:

HAVE MORE TIME?

To help your students think about how they can love their neighbors all day long, during this exercise ask them to imagine a few of the places where they typically spend time (school, home, coffee shop, mall, workplace). At each place, imagine the people who are usually there. Ask questions like:

Q: With whom do you typically interact when you're there?

Q: Who is hardest for you to love there? Why?

Q: What if this were a mission trip destination instead? How might that cause you to change the way you view the people there?

Q: **What impact would loving those people as you love yourself have on the way you love God?**

After students have finished, invite them to form a circle to close in prayer. They will likely choose to face the center of the circle. Point out that our tendency is to face inward but that Jesus' words in Luke 10 invite us to face outward. So ask your students to turn around and face outward as a sign of their desire to be open to new relationships with people who feel different from ourselves. Invite a few students to close by praying aloud that God would help us love him with all our heart, soul, and strength, and also give us the strength to love our neighbors as ourselves.

AFTER: DEBRIEF—GOD AND ME
REVERSE CULTURE SHOCK

ESSENTIAL   SCRIPTURE   MIDDLE SCHOOL

BIG IDEA

Cross-cultural experiences can create a type of reverse culture shock when we reenter our home environment. We can process those experiences through the lens of God's kingdom-on-earth culture.

YOU'LL NEED

- Pictures from your trip. You may be able to display pictures for the entire group with a tablet or laptop, or you can ask participants to bring their cameras or cell phones and flip through pictures with teammates.

- Paper

- Pens

- Poster paper

- Optional: Copies of the *Sticky Faith Service Guide Student Journal*

- Optional: Copies of the Romans 12:1–2 passage from *The Message* included in this exercise

Just as you and your students may have experienced some level of culture shock when you began this trip, you may have even worse *reverse culture shock* as you reenter your home culture. As we return from intense cross-cultural immersion experiences, we can easily become overwhelmed by the differences between the two cultures, especially the abundant resources of Western culture. (Even the number of toilet paper options at the grocery store can be traumatic.) This debrief will help you and your students articulate your emotions and discover how God invites us to respond to different cultures.

Welcome participants and invite team members to get out cameras or other devices on which they captured photos of your trip. Explain:

> It's been said that a picture is worth a thousand words, and I'm guessing that will be true with some of our pictures. I want you to take several minutes to flip through each other's pictures. As you do, please pay attention to any feelings or thoughts that occur to you.

After participants have looked through pictures for a few moments, distribute paper and pens. Ask everyone to draw a line down the center of their paper to create two columns. The left column should be labeled ON THE TRIP, and the right column should be labeled

AT HOME. In the two columns, ask participants to write descriptive words or phrases about the different aspects of the two cultures. To jar students' thinking, you might want to write prompts on poster paper, such as:

- Airports
- Markets/grocery stores
- Schools
- Restaurants
- Homes
- Churches
- Methods of transportation
- Roads
- Landscaping
- Shopping areas or malls

After about five minutes, divide students into groups of three or four and have them discuss the following questions. (You can either print out copies of these questions in advance or read them one at a time, giving students a chance to discuss each question for a few minutes before you give the next question.)

Q: **In what ways do the two cultures differ?**

Q: **What are some things the two cultures have in common?**

Q: **What are your feelings toward each of the cultures?**

Explain:

People who travel and experience a new culture often experience "reverse culture shock" when they return home, as elements of their home culture suddenly seem unfamiliar and even strange.

Q: **What do you think you will struggle with the most in "reverse culture shock"?**

At this point, lead your students in the practice of *lectio divina* (pronounced LEK-tsee-oh dih-VEE-nuh), meaning "holy reading." *Lectio divina* is a method of prayerful reflection on a particular Scripture passage. In this case, we encourage you to ask students to reflect on Romans 12:1–2.

Begin by telling your students you are going to read a short passage from Scripture, and that you want to invite them to note any words or images that stand out to them. Then slowly read the passage aloud to your students, savoring each phrase. (If you'd like, you can make copies of the passage ahead of time so students can follow along.) Pause for a few moments, then read the passage aloud two more times, reminding them to listen for and then reflect on any particular words, phrases, images, or messages that emerge.

You might want to use this version of Romans 12:1–2 from *The Message*:

> So here's what I want you to do, God helping you: Take your everyday, ordinary life—your sleeping, eating, going-to-work, and walking-around life—and place it before God as an offering. Embracing what God does for you is the best thing you can do for him. Don't become so well-adjusted to your culture that you fit into it without even thinking. Instead, fix your attention on God. You'll be changed from the inside out. Readily recognize what he wants from you, and quickly respond to it. Unlike the culture around you, always dragging you down to its level of immaturity, God brings the best out of you, develops well-formed maturity in you.

After a few minutes, invite students to pray silently, expressing whatever emerges from the way the Lord and this Romans passage are speaking to them.

Finally, allow students to rest silently before the Lord, experiencing his presence, love, and peace.

When you're finished, ask students to discuss the following with their small groups:

Q: **What images or experiences came to mind during this reading?**

Q: **What, if anything, did God say to you?**

Q: **How can you apply any insight from Romans 12:1–2 to your experience of reverse culture shock?**

Note that while reverse culture shock can feel surprising and overwhelming, we don't have to stay stuck feeling that way. Through prayer and processing—especially with others from the team or adult mentors or prayer partners back home—we can offer these feelings to God and let them spur us to hopeful responses. You might find that the "consume-condemn-create" model on page 173 is also a helpful framework to teach your students, if you haven't done that exercise.

Close by reading Romans 12:1–2 one final time, asking God to help your students fix their attention on him as you return to your home culture.

THEN AND NOW

SCRIPTURE   ROOKIE   MIDDLE SCHOOL

BIG IDEA

The kingdom of God is bigger than we think.

YOU'LL NEED

- Copies of the "Then and Now" handout (p. 185) and/or copies of the *Sticky Faith Service Guide Student Journal*
- Poster board or a large piece of paper
- Bibles
- Mustard seeds (if possible — if not, use small pebbles or grains of sand instead)
- Bread, preferably freshly baked
- Paper
- Pens

Begin the discussion by asking:

Q: **What is your favorite reality TV makeover show, or what kinds of makeovers do you watch on YouTube?**

Q: **These days there are many television shows and posts that contrast what someone or something was like "then" (before some dramatic transformation) with what they or it is like "now." What makes these shows so popular?**

Explain:

In many ways, we're experiencing our own "then" and "now" during this work. I'm going to give you ten minutes to consider what you thought God and involvement in his kingdom were like

"then," prior to this trip. I'd like you to contrast that with what you think God and his kingdom are like "now" that you've been serving others.

Distribute the "Then and Now" handout and pens so students can write down specific views they had "then" and contrast that with their perspective "now" that they've been serving.

When students are finished, invite them to share some of their "then" kingdom perspectives, and write them on the poster board. Next invite students to share their "now" kingdom perspectives. Ask students to identify any themes they see among their "then" perspectives as well as their "now" perspectives.

Next invite a student to read aloud Jesus' description of the kingdom of God in Luke 13:18–21. Pass out to each student and leader a mustard seed (or some other tiny object that represents a mustard seed, such as a grain of sand or a small pebble) and a piece of bread.

Q: In what ways are mustard seeds and yeast helpful images for the kingdom of God?

Some possible answers include: "Our eyes may not show us the full potential of how God is working in and through someone"; "God uses the small or insignificant things of this world to make a difference"; "God's kingdom

You may want to use this last question about the kingdom of God as an ongoing theme for your group in the weeks and months to come. Keep a running list of the ways God is expanding your group's perspective of God's kingdom. Let it be a source of encouragement of how God is stretching your perspective and using your group to expand God's kingdom!

is unstoppable"; "A small act can have a huge impact."

Q: How have you experienced the kingdom of God on this trip? How has the kingdom of God become "greater" (expanded) for you during this trip?

Close in prayer, asking everyone to stand arm's-length apart. Invite the group to begin by placing their hands a few inches apart (palms up) in a time of confession of some of the ways we've minimized the power of the kingdom and its role in our lives. After a few minutes, ask everyone to open their arms broadly and invite God to continue to show us how great his kingdom is. Ask God to work through your team so his kingdom impact continues to expand wherever you serve.

HAVE MORE TIME?

If you are still in the community where you've been serving, give students a chance to take a short walk (in pairs or small groups for safety, ideally with an adult), noting things they see that sprouted up from something small. That might include flowers, bushes, trees, or a house that started as a pile of lumber or blocks of cement. After students have finished their short walks, bring them back together to debrief what they saw, and discuss how their observations relate to the power of the yeast and the mustard seed.

THEN AND NOW

I used to think God was like . . .	Now I realize God is . . .
I used to view myself as . . .	Now I view myself as . . .
I used to view my family as . . .	Now I view my family as . . .
I used to think of my friends as . . .	Now I realize my friends are . . .
I used to view my problems as . . .	Now I view my problems as . . .
I used to view my future as . . .	Now I view my future as . . .
I used to view people who don't know Jesus as . . .	Now I view people who don't know Jesus as . . .
I used to think of the world as . . .	Now I realize that the world is . . .

THE HOPE OF GLORY

SCRIPTURE   VETERAN

BIG IDEA

When we hear others' perceptions of how Christ has been working in our lives, we are encouraged to embrace that transformation for ourselves.

YOU'LL NEED

- Index cards
- Bibles
- Paper
- Pens

After your justice work, set a time to bring closure to your students' experience of praying for one another by leading this activity and discussion. Open by asking:

Q: **Over the past few months, each of us has been praying for another member of our team. What has that experience been like for you?**

Q: **Have you thought much about the fact that someone else is praying for you? What feelings has that sparked in you?**

This exercise will work better if you assigned prayer partners to your students during the trip as we suggested in our "Heads-up" note on page 61. But if you didn't, no worries — it can still be effective. Simply modify the discussion accordingly and then assign students into pairs when it's time to write letters.

Explain:

As we faithfully pray for one another, we are often changed in the process. Perhaps you've experienced that as you have been praying for your teammate. Would anyone like to share about an experience like that?

Next read Colossians 1:24 – 29 to the group, or invite a student to read it. Point out that Paul is writing this letter from prison to a church in Colossae. Then ask:

Q: **What is the "mystery" Paul is talking about?**

In verses 25–26 Paul describes it as "the word of God in its fullness," and in verse 27 he talks about the "glorious riches" of the mystery, "Christ in you, the hope of glory." Note also that Paul uses the word *mystery* in Colossians 2:2 and 4:3. Throughout Colossians it is Christ himself who is the mystery proclaimed.

Q: **What do you think Paul means by the "hope of glory"? What does it mean that we carry the hope of glory in us?**

Note that one way to think about this phrase is to think about the hope we have in the final resurrection when Christ returns to bring the fullness of his kingdom (see Colossians 3:4). Another way to think about it is the glory of God that lives in us because of Christ's presence with us as believers.

Q: **How does our work reflect the "hope of glory"? What actions, attitudes, and values reflect the "hope of glory" in our lives at home?**

Now think again about the person you've been praying for. Think about Christ in that person, the hope of glory. Remember back over the course of our work, and recall ways that person has impacted others—both within our team and outside it.

Today we are each going to write a letter to that teammate we have been praying for. In your letter, share about how you have seen that person grow and how that individual has contributed

These verses from the first chapter of Colossians are in one of the most important christological passages in the New Testament. Colossians 1:15–20 is often referred to as one of the earliest hymns about Christ. Paul follows that hymn with some powerful statements about Jesus' identity and the reconciliation brought by his sacrifice on the cross (vv. 21–23). He goes on to call Christ the revelation of a mystery, "the word of God in its fullness" (v. 25). This mystery is made known not only to Jews but also to Gentiles (and so to everyone everywhere), as "Christ in you, the hope of glory." By making this statement, Paul boldly proclaims the power of Christ to *transform* us by dwelling *in* us. As he does, our lives proclaim the gospel of hope to others.

to the team's growth and to the lives of the locals where we served.

We're going to focus our reflection through this one phrase from Scripture, which I'd like you to write at the top of the letter: "Christ in you, the hope of glory."

Allow students time to write their letters, perhaps playing music in the background or sending them out to reflect and write alone and then gather back together. Invite students to share their letters with each other and to pray for each other. If you have time, close this meeting with a meal or snacks to celebrate Christ in you (plural), the hope of glory!

CLASS SEPARATION: SEEING AND CARING

SCRIPTURE   VETERAN

BIG IDEA

As we identify the class separations in the community we served, as well as in the community where we live, we can seek justice more effectively.

YOU'LL NEED

- Bibles
- Paper
- Pens

Begin this discussion with the following questions:

Q: **How would you define** *social class*?

Q: **What have you observed about social class through the people you've met and the experiences you've had in the midst of our work?**

Q: **How visible were the social class differences during your service?**

Q: **In what ways could you sense class separation or tension?** (e.g., based on ethnicity, language, dress, geography)

Q: **What do you think might have caused those separations?** (e.g., religion, ethnic identity, different values, job status, prior conflicts, systemic oppression)

The next five questions invite your group to reflect on experiences of social division while taking a break from service to relax, sightsee, and/or shop. Skip these questions if you didn't take any time off.

Q: **What was the highlight of the recent break we took for some fun downtime?**

Q: **How were the locals we interacted with during our break similar to those we interacted with during our service? How were they different?**

This discussion will work best if your mission experience includes a "break" in which you spend a few hours, a half day, or a full day away from your service to enjoy time relaxing, sightseeing, or shopping. If you're planning to take that type of break anyway, you can use this exercise as a catalyst for a deeper understanding of social class and the contrast between those you interacted with when you were serving and those you interact with during your day of leisure and tourism. If you are not taking that sort of time away from your service work, skip the questions about the break.

Q: After spending most of our time working alongside the poor in this community, how did you feel about stepping into this other world? How did it feel to spend money on consumer products and for personal enjoyment?

Q: Some of you might have been troubled by the contrasts between our experiences, our surroundings, or the social class of the people we interacted with during our break as opposed to during our work. What are some of these differences, and why did you find them disturbing?

Q: Others of you might not have considered these contrasts, and perhaps that fact is troubling you now. Does anyone feel like that and want to share what you're feeling?

Transition to thinking about social class at home by explaining:

We may not have the same extremes of wealth and poverty at home that we've experienced here, but class structures exist at home too. In what ways do you see class divisions in our town?

Q: How about in your school?

If students don't mention this, ask whether social class affects who they do or don't talk to or hang out with.

Q: As followers of Jesus, how should we respond to the differences among the divisions in social class hierarchies? How can we work to create a world free of social hierarchies?

Invite a student to read Galatians 3:26–28 and then lead the following discussion:

Q: According to Paul, what happens to our social status after we become children of God through faith in Jesus Christ?

Q: And yet we still are male and female, and other social divisions still exist. So what do you think Paul means?

Q: What would a world, a community, or a church look like that lived out Galatians 3:26–28?

In Paul's day, there was enormous division between the Jews and the Gentiles—people who were not Jewish and therefore not "children of Abraham."

Q: **If you were to rewrite Galatians 3:26–28 so it spoke directly to the situation of the locals we served, what would you say?**

Distribute paper and pencils so students can actually write out the passage.

Q: **How would you rewrite that same passage of Scripture for your own school or community back home?**

Invite students to actually write out their version on paper.

At this point, ask students to get into small groups by either their school or by their grade (depending on how many schools and/or grades you have represented in your group), or simply pair up with another person if you are short on time.

After they are in small groups, invite students to read aloud to their group the versions of Galatians 3:26–28 they've written for kids in their school or community. Encourage them to talk about what's similar and what's different between the versions. Then give small groups a few minutes to pray that the Lord would break down social divisions in their schools and/or in their grades, just as Paul describes in Galatians. Ask that God would fill you with the grace and courage to move past social lines, even when to do so might be costly.

PART FIVE

AFTER: ONGOING TRANSFORMATION

These sessions for post-trip meetings will help you connect the dots between your work and daily life for the next several weeks and months.

Note that some of these sessions can be done with your entire youth group, not just the particular team who served on this trip.

AFTER:
ONGOING TRANSFORMATION—GOD AND ME
DEVOTION AND JOURNALING OPTIONS

ESSENTIAL   DEVOTION-FRIENDLY

BIG IDEA

Daily devotion times after the trip help us continue to process what God has been teaching us through the experience.

YOU'LL NEED

- Copies of the *Sticky Faith Service Guide Student Journal* for every participant
- Pens

Journaling options for post-trip reflection to help young people integrate their learning into life back home are included in the *Sticky Faith Service Guide Student Journal*. Specifically, here are the options that are ideal for participants' individual reflection times (though any of the Ongoing Transformation entries can be used as personal journaling exercises if you'd like to encourage students to work through them all):

AFTER: ONGOING TRANSFORMATION

AFTER:
ONGOING TRANSFORMATION—GOD AND ME
REENTRY

ESSENTIAL

BIG IDEA

Returning from a short-term mission trip can be difficult and disorienting, but it does not have to paralyze us. We can live differently as a result of our experience!

YOU'LL NEED

- Five sheets of poster paper, hung in different sections of your meeting space
- Markers
- Paper
- Pens or pencils
- Optional: Copies of the *Sticky Faith Service Guide Student Journal*

Note that ideally this exercise will be part of your first post-trip meeting within a week or two of your project.

Begin by greeting everyone:

Welcome back. It's great to be back together as a team again. Today we want to talk about what it feels like to be back home. Most of us probably have some mixed emotions about what we've experienced and how it relates to our life at home now. I want to reassure you this is normal. Let's begin by discussing two questions together.

Get into a circle (or break up into smaller groups if your group is large) and invite each student to answer the following two questions:

Q: What has been the best part about being back home?

Q: What has been the hardest part about being home?

Continue:

Reentry into life back home after a mission trip can sometimes leave us feeling torn. We come home excited about how God has changed us, and we want to live differently because of it. But it can be difficult to figure out how to do that as we enter back into our own culture and old habits.

Here are five common experiences of people returning from a cross-cultural mission experience:[31]

- Fun: We like returning to the comforts we enjoy back home.

- Flee: We miss our team and struggle to find people we can share our experience with, so we end up feeling lonely and isolated.

- Fight: We get frustrated with our own culture's selfishness or indifference and fight against conforming to it.

- Fit: We grow tired of fighting and just try to fit back into our own culture.

- Far: We experience God as seeming further away than on the trip and wonder whether we left God there in the other culture.

Take five sheets of poster paper, and write one of the five common reactions to returning home from cross-cultural mission experiences (FUN, FLEE, FIGHT, FIT, FAR) as a header at the top of each one. Under each header, write one related question that will prompt your group to deeper reflection. Some possible questions are:

- Fun: What was the most fun or best comfort to return home to?

- Flee: When have you felt lonely or isolated since you've been back? With whom has it been difficult for you to share your experience?

- Fight: What do you dislike about the culture you've come home to?

- Fit: What old habits have you returned to since you've been back? What new habits or commitments have been most difficult to follow since you've returned?

- Far: When have you felt distant from God? Why do you think that is?

Give every student a marker and invite all of them to walk around the room and write their own answers to the questions on each sheet. Once students have finished, gather the posters and share some of the responses with the group. With each poster, invite discussion by asking a few of the following questions:

Q: Would anyone like to share what you wrote about this response and explain why you wrote it?

Q: What are a few ways we could work through this response in a healthy manner?

Q: Why do you think it is important to pay attention to these responses and emotions?

195

Explain:

Again, I want to encourage you and let you know all of these reactions are normal and okay. The important thing is that we don't get stuck. We don't often change overnight; it usually takes hard work and a lot of dependence on the Lord to process what we've experienced and let it really transform how we think, relate, and live from now on.

Close by distributing paper to the students and inviting them to write a few words or images that describe how they would like to respond to their reentry to life at home. Then invite them to journal a prayer to God. Encourage students to write to God about ways their own lives have matched one or more of the responses (Fun, Flee, Fight, Fit, or Far) as well as how they feel about that. Prompt them to confess any sinfulness they see in themselves in the midst of the transition home, and encourage them to ask God to give them grace to be the kingdom people he wants them to be.

SUGGESTIONS FOR OVERCOMING A ROUGH REENTRY[32]

WRITE ABOUT IT! Journaling helps you sort through your thoughts and feelings and allows you to express them in a healthy way.

TALK ABOUT IT! Find two people you trust, and share your experience with them. Tell them your stories, your hopes, your frustrations—tell them everything—and ask them to pray for you as you translate your experience into your life back home. (For more hints on how to do that, see "Post-trip Prayer Partner Meeting" on pp. 197–199.)

DO SOMETHING ABOUT IT! Identify an issue or a need in your own community and do something to address it. If you are concerned with poverty, find out who is working to help impoverished people in your community and volunteer to serve with them.

EMBRACE IT! Incorporating what you have experienced on your mission trip into your everyday life and faith is an ongoing process. It's okay to have doubts, questions, and mixed emotions. Remember that every step of the journey is important, no matter how small.

POST-TRIP PRAYER PARTNER MEETING

ESSENTIAL

BIG IDEA

God shapes us in many ways, including through taking time to process with a trusted adult.

YOU'LL NEED

- Plan a sharing meeting that includes students' mentors or adult prayer partners. See the "Prayer Partner Guide" exercise on pages 82–84 for framing this relationship before the trip. Once you schedule the sharing meeting, it would be wise to design an invitation you can email to your students that they can forward to their prayer partners. If your students have been working through the *Sticky Faith Service Guide Student Journal*, encourage them to bring their journals with them as catalysts for their sharing. Also encourage students to bring photographs they can share as they talk about particular people and experiences. Five to ten printed photographs can be more helpful than skimming through hundreds of digital images. Ask adults to bring their Bibles. Make it clear in your invitation that students should attend the meeting even if they are unable to bring their prayer partners. Invite other adult volunteers to play the mentoring role in the meeting.

- If you'd like, you can combine this into one sharing meeting that includes both prayer partners and parents and use some elements of the post-service parent meeting on pages 40–42. You may want to focus less on the family goal-setting exercise and more on simply sharing stories.

- Set the tone for sharing by creating as warm and intimate an environment as possible. Adjust the lighting, light some candles, and serve drinks and treats.

- Copies of the "Sticky Faith Service Model" handout (p. 28)

- Copies of the "Prayer Partner Guide: Questions for Students and Prayer Partners after Our Work" handout (pp. 200-201) or copies of the *Sticky Faith Service Guide Student Journal*

- Any available trip video or digital photo slide show and a way to play it

- Clay or craft dough for each student

- Small plastic sandwich bags

- Bibles

To begin your sharing meeting, welcome students and their prayer partners (and parents, if you invited everyone). Set a friendly tone by sharing a few ways the trip and team impacted you personally.

Distribute the copies of the "Sticky Faith Service Model" handout to the group and give a brief explanation of all the stages. (You'll find some helpful talking points about the model in the "Initial Steps" chapter on pp. 15–28. The handout itself is at the end of that same chapter on p. 28). Point out that for many teenagers who serve, most of what impacted them fades

The same imagery of God's potter-ness and our clay-ness is also used by Paul in Romans 9:19–21.

away once they get home. Research indicates that having multiple adults support students as they connect the dots between their service and their lives at home bolsters students' long-term growth.

At this point, ask your students to introduce themselves as well as the adults who have come with them.

If you have a media presentation that captures your trip (video, digital slide show, etc.), this is a good time to play it.

Transition into a time of sharing by giving some clay or craft dough to each student. Invite them to squish the clay in their hands as you explain that our lives are like this clay and that God has been shaping us through our recent journey. Read aloud Isaiah 64:8, which teaches, "Yet you, LORD, are our Father. We are the clay, you are the potter; we are all the work of your hand."

Then give an opportunity for students to share with their prayer partners one or more *specific* ways the trip shaped them. You can either do this together as a large group, or ask students to gather with their partners to share individually. If students have brought their journals, encourage them to read aloud any excerpts that seem especially relevant or poignant.

After students have had time to share, explain:

> Now that the prayer partners have heard from their students, it's time for those wise adults to speak into our lives. My hope is that the adults will have insights or perhaps a Scripture verse that relates to what you've shared that can help you continue to be molded and shaped by the Lord.

Give plenty of time for adults to share with students, and for students and adults to ask one another questions. Make sure you're available to meet with students who were unable to have other adults with them.

During this time, distribute copies of the "Prayer Partner Guide: Questions for Students and Prayer Partners after Our Work" handout to help prompt additional processing questions now, as well as to start future conversations after this meeting.

When the sharing has concluded, ask students to divide the clay you've given them so every adult they've invited also gets a chunk of clay. Close in prayer together as every person in the room holds a piece of clay. Invite the adults to pray aloud that the Lord would continue the good work in these students as they face temptations and distractions now that they are back at home.

Before everyone leaves, distribute plastic bags to everyone so they can take the clay home with them. Also, ask students to talk with their prayer partners before they walk out the door about whether they'd like to meet again on their own or have a phone call in a few weeks to share more about how the Lord continues to shape them. Encourage adults to keep the question handout to use when they meet again.

QUESTIONS FOR STUDENTS AND PRAYER PARTNERS AFTER OUR WORK

1. What one word or phrase would you use to describe your experience?

2. If you could add a few more words or phrases to more fully describe your experience, what would they be?

3. What surprised you? How did that impact your work?

4. What disappointed you? What do you wish had been different about your experience? How did that impact your work?

5. When were you most overwhelmed? What did you do about that, or how did you respond to that feeling?

6. How was life in the place you visited different than you thought it would be? What discoveries did you make?

7. Where did you sense God at work in your life and in the lives of others during this experience?

8. What do you think other people saw in you during your time serving?

9. What has it been like to reenter life with your family and friends at home? What kinds of feelings are you experiencing?

10. How do you see life here differently now? How do you feel about that? Where do you sense God at work here?

11. What do you hope will change about your life as a result of this experience? Who can help you make those changes or hold you accountable for them?

12. How do you hope our church changes as a result of your team's experience?

13. How can you live out justice beyond this particular experience? What dreams do you have for justice both where you visited and here at home?

14. How are you going to talk with others about your work? If you were going to share a thirty-second version of your experience, what would you say?

LENSES FOR THE FUTURE

ROOKIE   MIDDLE
SCHOOL

BIG IDEA

After our work, it's important to spend some time dreaming for the future together, imagining what the "next chapter" might look like in our shared story of faith.

YOU'LL NEED

- Photos or video you've taken of five to ten everyday household objects (e.g., toothbrush, cell phone, screwdriver) or objects from around your youth room or church. Start with a very blurry (and perhaps too-close) shot, and then take a well-focused shot (or focus your video camera by slowly zooming out). Prepare a way to view these for the opening exercise.

- A piece of paper for each team to use in the opening exercise

- Pens, pencils, or markers for each student

- Three index cards for each student (it's a good idea to have extras too)

- Tape

- Four large sheets of poster paper on the walls, with one of the following labels on each one: TODAY, NEXT MONTH, NEXT YEAR, and ACTION STEPS. Ahead of time, hang the four pieces of poster paper on different walls in your meeting space. Make markers available by each paper.

This is an exercise you may want to do with the entire youth group, not just those who went on a particular trip or participated in a particular project. With minor tweaking of the questions below, you can adjust this so everyone feels equally included in the conversation. Ideally there would still be space for students who were part of the project to share with the entire group, and then the storyboarding activity would focus on an all-inclusive brainstorming session. If you're looking for a post-trip session that intentionally focuses on sharing with the entire group, also check out "Creating a Shared Rule of Life" on pages 207–210.

Open by saying:

> We're going to start by looking at some everyday items. In teams of three, please discuss and then write down what each object is as we go through the pictures.

Distribute paper and a pen or pencil to each group. Depending on how many objects you've photographed or videoed, have each team make a numbered list and write their guesses by each number as you first show them the blurry objects. Then show them the clear images, and see which team had the most right answers. (If you use video, you will want to pause it each time to let them write down their guesses before letting the camera refocus.) Give the winning team a special privilege, like going first in line at your next meal or getting some kind of treat.

Then debrief by asking:

Q: Was it easy for you to figure out what the items were at first? Why or why not?

Q: What kinds of feelings did you experience while we played this game?

Students might share that they felt frustrated, cheated, or helpless. Some might have given up, thought it was fun, or been too apathetic to try.

Q: Thinking back to our recent project, did you experience any of those same emotions?

Q: In what ways was our work similar to looking through a camera that's out of focus? In what ways was the experience like looking through a camera that's in focus?

Q: How many of you would say you have a clearer picture of life in our host community now than before our work? Why do you think that?

Q: How many would say you have a clearer picture of life back home now than before our trip? Why is that?

Q: Would anyone say the opposite? That you had a clearer picture of home or our host community before the trip—but now it seems fuzzier?

Continue by sharing:

Sometimes it can seem like life gets out of focus and we can't tell what we're looking at anymore. Doing service and justice work can lead to those kinds of feelings because over a short period of time we're given new lenses through which we must look at the world in a different way. Coming home can make those feelings even more confusing, because suddenly we look at our lives back home in a different way too.

Sometimes when we zoom out and refocus—or perhaps reframe the shot altogether—we see life more clearly. We might discover that we see God more clearly too.

Q: What are some ways you see life differently now than beforehand?

Q: When you think about the future of our youth ministry, how do you see things differently now? What do you like about what you see, and what concerns or disturbs you?

After students share some of these insights, continue by saying:

Next we're going to do some dreaming together about our future. In light of all we've seen and experienced, and in light of the new lenses we've been given, we are going to zoom out, reframe our shot, and focus in on where God might be leading us together.

Pause to take some time to pray about this before moving on, thanking God for giving us new ways to see and inviting God to speak into the vision you collectively develop for the future.

Next distribute three index cards and pens to each person and have students get back into their groups of three. Point to the three sheets of paper taped around the room labeled TODAY, NEXT MONTH, and NEXT YEAR and say:

Now we are going to write a story. It's our story—and while we know this story has been going on for a while, what I'd like us to do now is dream together about the next few chapters. I'd like for you to imagine this chapter in terms of three time periods: "today"—right now and the immediate future; "next month"—looking ahead a month or more; and "next year"—thinking at least a year out and further.

When authors write books, sometimes they use storyboards to help them brainstorm ideas and see their thoughts on paper—or maybe even on the walls. Today we are going to make these sheets our storyboard for writing our next chapters together.

With your small group, talk together for a few minutes about each of these three categories. The main question I'd like for you to think about is this: What dreams do you think God has for those time periods, in light of what we've just experienced through our work?

You might want to write that main question on a whiteboard or a different sheet of poster paper so students can remember it.

Brainstorm ideas and dreams for what God might want to do given all we've seen, experienced, and learned recently. Think locally as well as globally in your dreaming. On your index cards, I'd like for you to write down some of your ideas and dreams. You have three cards each, so as a group you can contribute three cards to each time frame on the wall. After you have written your ideas, tape them to the appropriate part of our story. Remember that there are no bad ideas when we're brainstorming—don't be afraid to write something even if it seems a bit wild.

You might need to give some examples of ideas here, such as tutoring at a local public school or raising money to help people who are homeless in your community.

Give students plenty of time to brainstorm and contribute to the storyboard. Then gather everyone back and read the ideas on each section of the storyboard, stopping after each category (today, next month, and next year) to ask:

Q: **What are your initial thoughts about these ideas and dreams? What themes did you hear as we read through them? What other ideas does that spark?**

Be sure to have someone write down those ideas on extra index cards and tape them to the storyboard.

After you've gone through all three storyboard sheets, ask:

Q: **What are some action steps we need to take based on what we've written together? Who will be involved in taking those steps?**

Have someone write your ideas on the "Action Steps" sheet, keeping them as clear and action-oriented as possible. (Hint: Each step should have an active verb and should be no more than one sentence. In the example of tutoring at a local elementary school, the action step might read something like, "Ellie will contact Madison Elementary and ask what we would need to do to become approved volunteers for their weekly after-school program.")

Close your discussion by saying:

One privilege of being part of God's kingdom ministry is that we get to participate in writing the story alongside God. This is a bit of a mystery; of course, God is in charge and knows the big picture, but at the same time he lets us all play a part along the way. Today we have written some God-sized dreams on the walls. Now let's pray that God will help us focus on and follow the ones that lead to God's will being done.

Conclude your time in prayer, perhaps having students break into groups of three again and inviting each person to pray for one of the three different areas on the storyboard. Or you might want to have students pray silently,

inviting them to come write their names by action steps to signal their commitment to help take that particular step forward. Pray that your dreams would be kingdom dreams, and that as a group you would pursue God's will. Close by saying the Lord's Prayer together.

This storyboard lends itself to a number of possibilities. You might invite student artists to paint images of your next chapter to display on the walls. Or you may have a creative writer in your group who can take down the cards and write a narrative using the ideas generated during your brainstorming. This narrative could be used to help your leadership think through the next steps your ministry may want to take toward seeing God's justice done on earth "as it is in heaven." You may also want to take this to a conversation with your mission committee or senior leadership.

Additionally, you may want to leave these storyboard sheets on your wall for the next month or so, then gather the team again to review your dreams and perhaps revise them based on how you have (or haven't) been living them out. Perhaps you'll want to create a new storyboard in another couple of months.

CREATING A SHARED RULE OF LIFE

ESSENTIAL

BIG IDEA

When our entire group gathers to celebrate a mission experience, those who participated in the trip as well as those who did not can join together to move the group in a kingdom direction.

YOU'LL NEED

- Food indigenous to the location in which you served. If possible, ask some of your students and/or their parents to provide the food so they feel ownership for the discussion (and so you can focus your time and energy on something else).

- Invite students to bring photos or videos to share with the larger group

- "Have More Time?" option: Supplies for a mural or collage

ⓘ Students who didn't get to participate in your trip for one reason or another are always in danger of feeling isolated from those who went. Inside jokes and stories only add to the frustration they sometimes feel. This exercise gets all your students involved in the bigger story of how God is moving you forward as a community. This exercise can help students remember that those who didn't participate in your recent work are just as important to the group as those who did. So please do this ongoing transformation exercise with your entire youth ministry.

Begin by sharing a story of a time when you felt left out. It's best if the story is from your own adolescence. (Most of us have a whole closet full of stories of teenage rejection!)

Q: I have a question for those of you who went on our trip: How do you think those who didn't go might be feeling? In what ways might they feel like they missed out?

Q: Will some of you who did not participate in the trip respond to that? What feelings do you have as you hear stories or highlights of the trip?

Continue:

The reality is that those who didn't go might have missed this particular trip, but they are an important part of God's ongoing work in our midst.

One reason we sent this group of students on a service trip was that we hoped they'd have an opportunity to serve God and see his kingdom in ways that would deepen their own faith. But it's also our hope that through them—their stories, their experiences, and the people they met and served—God will bring us all to a new place. We hope we'll all be compelled to change. We hope we will be a different youth group and a different church, not just because of this trip but because of our commitments every day throughout the year to live out our faith. As Micah 6:8 urges us, we're each called to "act justly and to love mercy and to walk humbly with [our] God."

But we can't make these changes alone, and we can't make them on our own strength. The only way we can succeed is together with the power of the Holy Spirit.

Today we're going to have a feast—literally—from the community that some of us just visited. We're going to share some food we ate there, and as we do, we'll share more about the experiences that gave us a glimpse of the kingdom

and the God who protects and guides us. As we eat, those of you who didn't go on the trip can dream with us about how God wants us all to move forward.

At this point, serve authentic food from the place you visited—whether it's Mexican, Chinese, soul food, or macaroni and cheese. If you have time, invite students who went on your trip to share stories, videos, or photos of what they experienced, as well as dreams they have for your ministry here at home.

Q: Those of you who didn't go on this trip, what themes did you hear from the stories and dreams?

Q: How do those themes relate to your own dreams for our ministry and community here?

Explain:

Today we are going to create a common "rule of life," which is an ancient practice among many Christian communities. Sometimes a group will commit together to a particular pattern of spiritual practices that helps them grow and serve together. Basically, adopting a common "rule of life" means that we choose together a few things we want to do regularly that help us become the kind of community God desires.

Thinking back to some of your dreams for this community, what might be a few things you'd like to see as part of our rule of life? Let's see how many ideas we can come up with.

It is much better for students to come up with these ideas on their own at a grassroots level rather than having them imposed from the top down (that is, by you). If they are having difficulty, help them recall how they saw the kingdom of God in the midst of their work and how they might begin to create similar opportunities to see God's kingdom back at home. Also encourage everyone to think about how your group's history of shared life together already includes common shared practices you want to keep doing. Here are some suggestions:

- Commit to gather for worship and prayer once each week (start with a basic commitment, but for many of your students, attending regularly might be a big step).

- When we share a conversation or a meal with each other, we won't constantly look at our phones.

- Develop a plan for Bible reading or morning and evening prayers for everyone in the youth group to practice a set number of times per week.

- Commit to fasting one day a week from "excessive" or self-focused purchases like candy, soft drinks, clothes, or music downloads.

- Spend one or two nights each week at home with our families, not watching television and not in our rooms.

- Once a week, sit with someone in the lunchroom who doesn't seem to have many other friends.

- Commit to encourage—rather than tear down or criticize—each other on social media throughout the week.

- Commit to be authentic in our interactions on social media and to hold one another accountable for that honesty.

- Commit together to the goal of giving a certain percentage of our income away to mission and justice efforts.

- Participate in a mission trip every other year and, in the years you don't take a trip, use the money you would have spent to help support ongoing, indigenous efforts at justice, development, and mission.

- If you traveled internationally, spend time once a month with local populations from that country. As a youth group, regularly go to church services, restaurants, or neighborhoods of that ethnic group.

After students are finished brainstorming, give each student four votes and ask them to vote for the practices they think will make the most difference in your ministry. After you've identified the four practices your group will adopt, have your students begin to make them specific rather than open-ended (e.g., What are we going to read together? How often? Whom are we going to serve? When will that happen? Who is going to lead us in doing that?). Once you have four specific practices, decide which two or three you will start immediately. The hope is that after your group becomes faithful with those two or three, you can begin to add other practices into your rhythm.

After you have come up with the few specific practices, ask how you can keep each other accountable to the rule and how you can share about what you've experienced together. Remind students that a rule of life is a way to grow in our experience of grace, not a legalistic set of absolutes.

Close in prayer in groups of three to five students, making sure each group includes students who went on your recent trip as well as those who didn't. Encourage students to pray for one another as well as for God's ongoing work in your youth ministry, your church, and your community.

HAVE MORE TIME?

Have your students make a collage or painting to put in the youth room as a visual reminder of what kind of community you'd like to be. If possible, highlight the two or three practices you've chosen as part of the collage.

A PICTURE IS WORTH A LOT OF WORDS

ROOKIE

MIDDLE SCHOOL

BIG IDEA

There are more connections between our service work and our lives at home than we might realize.

YOU'LL NEED

- Printed photos from your experience (make them at least 5 x 7 if not 8 x 10 inches). You want more pictures than students, so if you expect 12 students at your meeting, print 18 to 24 pictures.

- Similarly, print photos of various scenes that represent your students' lives at home. These might include a nearby shopping mall, a typical house in your town, a high school, a movie theater, or a coffee shop. You might even ask a few students to be the shutterbugs and take and/or print out these pictures.

- Optional: Copies of the *Sticky Faith Service Guide Student Journal*

Welcome students and then ask:

> Think back to our trip and imagine that your mind is a camera. What images and memories of the trip are most vivid?

Display along a table or a wall pictures of your time serving. Ask your students to come and look at the pictures without talking. After a few minutes, invite each student to choose a picture that triggers a significant thought or feeling. If more than one student wants the same picture, that's okay; they can both work from the same picture.

Divide your students into groups of three or four and explain:

> I'd like each group member to share about the picture he or she chose and why it's personally significant. After each person has shared, the rest of the group can add comments or insights about that picture or the person who shares it, based on what they remember from our work.

After the groups have finished, display the pictures of life at home in the same way. Again ask students to come and look at the pictures without talking and then choose one picture that's significant to them.

Invite the students to return to their small groups and share about the pictures they've chosen and why they are significant. The rest of the group should add comments or insights about that picture or what the person has just shared.

After the small groups have finished, explain:

> There's one more question I'd like us to discuss. You've talked about the picture from our trip, and you've talked about the home picture. But how do the two pictures relate to one another? Please talk about that in your small groups.

If students get stuck, encourage them to raise their hands so you or another adult can come and prod their thinking. In general, help them discuss what's similar, what's different, and how remembering the community you visited can help spark new visions of how to live in our own home community.

Ask students to return to one large group and invite anyone who wants to share about the relationship between the two pictures to do so. After a number of people have shared, ask:

Q: What themes stood out in either your small-group or our large-group discussions?

Q: What feelings emerged in you during this process?

Q: What does this say about us as a group?

Q: What does this say about our time serving and how that work relates to our lives now?

Q: How can today's exercise help us go deeper in our work to serve others and to seek justice for the poor and oppressed?

Close in prayer, but ask your students to keep their eyes open as you pray, looking at the two pictures they've chosen. If it feels appropriate, invite some of your students to pray aloud as well. Encourage students to take both pictures home and place them in a visible location as a reminder of how their justice work relates to home and vice versa.

REWIND AND FAST-FORWARD

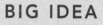

ROOKIE   MIDDLE SCHOOL

BIG IDEA

A month or two after the trip, it's a good idea to rewind time to remind ourselves of how we were impacted and then fast-forward to think about how we can better support one another in the future.

YOU'LL NEED

- Ahead of time, record some of your team's final debrief discussion(s) on audio or video. If you have time and/or a student who's into media, you might want to edit out some of the inevitable peripheral chatter. If you don't have time or a techie student, then make sure you have ample time to play the recording and then lead the discussion.

- A way to play that audio or video
- Whiteboard or poster paper
- Water bottles
- Rocks
- A large bowl
- Pens
- Optional: Copies of the *Sticky Faith Service Guide Student Journal*

Greet students and point out how long it's been since your trip. Distribute a rock and a water bottle to each student as you explain:

> I've learned that God's change process often resembles the way water shapes rock. Let's think for a moment about all the different ways water shapes rock:
>
> - God's transformation can seem slow at times, as if we're a stone that's being smoothed in a creek.
>
> - Sometimes it can even seem too slow, as if we're just a stone sitting in the middle of a pond and nothing much is happening.
>
> - Or sometimes it seems quick, like a rushing river flowing over stones in its path.
>
> - Other times it seems overwhelming, making us feel vulnerable, like a rock being pelted under a huge waterfall.

Q: In what other ways is God's transformation similar to the ways water shapes rock?

Q: Of all these water/rock images we've been discussing, which seems to resonate most with the way God has been changing you during and/or since our justice work?

After a few students have shared, continue:

> In the midst of God's work in our lives, I know it's sometimes hard to remember all we experienced and reflected on together, so today we're going to do a bit of rewinding. We're going to watch (or listen to) our debrief discussion, but as we're watching, I want us to stay alert for ways we were impacted—either as individuals or as a group.
>
> If you hear something that reflects a way our work affected us, I want you to come up and write it on the whiteboard even as the video continues to play. You can write emotions, attitudes, ways of thinking, behaviors/actions, or any other area of impact you think of as you reexperience our debrief conversation.

After the video has ended, lead the following discussion:

Q: What themes do you see in the ways we were impacted?

Q: How have these themes, or any of these individual ideas, made a difference in your life since our work?

Q: Let's be honest: What decisions or commitments did you make during or immediately after our service that haven't gone so well? Why do you think that is?

Q: Are there decisions or commitments you'd like to revise based either on the video we just saw or on what life is like now that you're back home?

Q: Let's fast-forward and think about the next month. What can we do to support one another in living up to these commitments for the next month?

Divide up into pairs or small groups, and ask students to exchange rocks so they are now holding their partner's rock. Give students plenty of time to pray that the Lord will empower them by his grace and continue to transform them into the people he wants them to be now that they are back home. Consider inviting your students to keep their prayer partner's rock as a reminder to pray for God's ongoing work in their partner's life.

AFTER:
ONGOING TRANSFORMATION—GOD AND ME
NET WORTH

SCRIPTURE   VETERAN

BIG IDEA

Serving in the kingdom of God reorients our ideas of personal value and net worth.

YOU'LL NEED

- Bibles
- Paper or copies of the *Sticky Faith Service Guide Student Journal*
- Pens
- Calculators
- A prize, if you choose to award one
- "Have More Time?" option: Copies of your church's annual budget

Welcome students and ask them to think back to your time serving together:

Q: **From what you could tell, how did the locals we served use their money? How is that similar to the way you and your family use it? How is it different?**

Give each student a piece of paper and pencil, and distribute as many calculators as possible to students. Explain:

Today each of us is going to total up his or her monetary value. I'd like you to calculate, to the best of your ability, how much money is represented at this moment on your person. In other words, what is your "net worth" right now? Make a guess at how much was spent (by you or someone else) on your shoes, jeans, jacket, purse, sunglasses, cell phone, jewelry, whatever is in your

This exercise involves students assessing the monetary worth of what they are wearing. Since you are the best gauge of your group, adapt this activity to fit your students' level of trust and vulnerability. Be especially aware of how differing income levels among the families of your students might make the exercise difficult for students whose "net worth" is lower than others in the group. And you may want to give parents a heads-up (or send a follow-up message) that you are discussing these important but sometimes-sensitive issues, including raising questions about the amount of money parents spend on clothing, etc., for their kids.

backpack or wallet, the braces you're wearing right now, the highlights in your hair ... anything you can put a monetary value on. List all this stuff, and add up the total dollar amount. Do not share your estimate of your "net worth" with anyone else.

Give students a few minutes to calculate their own total net worth. If you've not done so ahead of time, you should likewise calculate your own net worth based on what you are wearing and carrying today.

Lead the following discussion:

Q: What was the experience of calculating your own net worth like for you?

Q: What made it easy to calculate your own net worth? What made it challenging?

Q: What, if anything, about this exercise surprised or shocked you? Describe your response to that surprise—does it make you want to do anything, or does it raise any questions for you?

At this point, you might want to expand the conversation by highlighting an item most students have in common, like blue jeans or shoes, and pursue questions like:

Q: How much money would you say is appropriate to spend on a pair of jeans? Should that amount be any different for someone who follows Christ? Why or why not?

Q: How do you think the locals we served on our recent mission trip would answer the question about how much is appropriate to spend on a pair of jeans?

Q: How, if at all, is your own willingness to spend money on yourself different from what you would have said before our trip? Why do you think that is?

It's quite likely some students will say that their views about money were not significantly impacted by the time serving. If this is the case, consider carefully and lovingly, exploring why that might be. The main point is to help connect the dots between the justice issues they encountered on their trip and justice in everyday life.

Q: Whether it's jeans, shoes, or the number of albums you download from iTunes, how do you determine when you have crossed a line into what is "excessive"? As people who want to serve others, when—if ever—is it okay to spend extravagantly on ourselves?

Q: When we cross the line into what is "excessive," what is the impact on us? How about on others?

Q: Here's a startling reality: US citizens make up only 5 percent of the world's population, but we consume half the world's resources.[33] Given what we've seen in the midst of our service experience, how does that make you feel?

You may want to repeat this statistic to be sure students caught it.

At this point, ask a few students to read aloud the story of Jesus' encounter with the rich young ruler found in Mark 10:17–27.

Q: This young man clearly had tried to honor God in many ways, but Jesus said one thing was missing. How would you describe in your own words what the man was missing?

Note what the rich ruler asks Jesus: "Good teacher, what must I *do* to inherit eternal life?" (v. 17, emphasis added). Ironically, Jesus had just taught in Mark 10:15 that the kingdom is more about *receiving* than *doing*.

Q: If Jesus told you to do the same thing he told this young man to do, how do you think you would respond?

Q: In Mark 10:24, the disciples are "amazed" at Jesus' words. Perhaps that was because, like many religious people both past and present, they'd been told wealth was evidence a person was blessed by God. How is Jesus' teaching different from that common belief?

Q: So does Jesus intend for all his followers—including us—to sell all we have and give it to the poor? Why or why not?

Share that it may not have been this man's wealth itself that excluded him from following Jesus but, rather, his inability to be generous with it or free to live without it. Jesus repeats several times that it is hard—particularly for the rich but for everyone, really—to enter the kingdom of God. For some people, following Jesus may, in fact, require giving away everything they have. For everyone it requires a new way of viewing possessions and personal worth.

Q: How can we use what we've been given—our own net worth—in a spirit of extravagant generosity that offers good news to others, especially to the poor?

Close your time with a journaling exercise, asking students to reflect on what they value and why. On the same paper they used to calculate their net worth, have them create a "lowering my net worth" list—brainstorming ways they can reduce the costly material

stuff that clutters their lives and then possibly redistribute some of that money and stuff to others. Invite students to work in pairs or even in small groups. Make sure to give a few final minutes for students to prayerfully ask the Lord to show them which of the "lowering my net worth" ideas he might want them to implement.

HAVE MORE TIME?

Invite students to design their "ideal church budget." That is, if it were up to them, how and where would they spend the church's money? Instead of dealing with specific numbers, you might want to help students come up with the percentage of the budget they'd like to spend on each category.

When students are finished, distribute copies of your church's annual budget (maybe in percentage form or a pie chart), explain where the money goes, and discuss the similarities or contrasts between their "ideal" budget and your church's budget. (You may also want to give some framework for how the church budget is determined in your church.) What part, if any, does caring for those in poverty have in your budget? What would your church need to do in order to have a greater impact beyond its own walls? Consider inviting someone from your church's finance committee to be part of this conversation.

A DOLLAR A DAY

ESSENTIAL   MIDDLE
SCHOOL

BIG IDEA

More than one billion people around the world are forced to try to live on little more than one dollar a day, but it's barely possible. We have the ability to make a difference in their lives, and we can start by praying on their behalf.

YOU'LL NEED

- Enough dollar bills for (a) everyone in your group, (b) just a few, or (c) just you, depending on how you decide to carry this out

- "Have More Time?" option: Magazine pictures, pictures of various parents and children, pictures of leaders of various governments, a picture of your youth group, paper, pens, markers or crayons, a mirror, a jar

Welcome students and distribute a dollar bill to everyone in your group. If your budget doesn't allow for that, you could (a) ask everyone present who has a dollar with them to get it out, (b) bring up a few volunteers, give each of them a dollar, and then have them stand in front of the group holding their bills, or (c) hold up one dollar yourself, which you will later pass around. Then lead the following discussion:

Q: **With the dollar in your hand, what could you buy? What will a dollar purchase?**

This is another great exercise to lead with your entire youth group, not just the students who went on the trip or participated in a local service project.

We highly recommend that you incorporate the prayer journey described in the "Have More Time?" option for this exercise, so please try to schedule this activity when you have enough time for it.

Q: If you could spend this dollar any way you chose, what would you most likely do with it?

Q: Most of you probably weren't thinking of answers like, "Pay the rent," "Buy food for my family," or "Get my little brother's prescription filled," right? Why is that?

Q: Do you think it's possible to live on one dollar a day? What if you had to do it? Describe how you might look at that dollar differently.

Continue:

The truth is, people can barely live on one dollar a day. There is no economy in the world where all basic needs can be met for the equivalent of one dollar a day. Yet more than one billion people try to make it work. What's more, over two billion people—nearly a third of the world's population—live on just two dollars a day or less.[34]

Q: As you think about the poverty we observed or experienced during our service work, what do you think the people in that community have in common with those who live on one or two dollars per day? How do they differ?

Be as honest as you can about this. In many cases, you may not be serving in situations of the world's most extreme poverty, and yet you still may have seen people living in humble or even desperate circumstances.

Continue:

While extreme poverty has been reduced some in China and India over the last thirty years, in much of Africa and other parts of the developing world, the world's poorest are just as poor as those in extreme poverty thirty years ago. The average person living in extreme poverty tries to survive on 78 cents per day. What's more, half of those who are extremely poor are under age eighteen.[35]

Q: How many of you spent at least 78 cents to purchase something today?

Q: As you hear these statistics, what emotions do you feel? What is your honest response?

Do your best to help your students with this question. Check their postures and body language for cues, and perhaps push them a bit to share their responses. The point is not to shame each other about our available spending budget but to notice the disparity between what we see as pocket change and what someone else might see as basic survival.

Explain:

Whether we spent 78 cents or 78 dollars on ourselves today, how can we discern the ways God wants us to use whatever we have—meaning all that God has given us—for the greatest possible good?

One way to know how we can best use our money to help others is to pray. Today we're going to join with and pray for our brothers and sisters around the world who are forced to try to survive on less than a dollar a day.

As we pray, let's think about these dollar bills and start by repenting of our flippant use of money, our overspending on ourselves, or other ways we have not used our money wisely. I'm going to pass around this dollar and, if you want to, pray silently or out loud when the dollar passes through your hands.

After your time of repentance is over, transition to a different prayer emphasis:

Now I'd like us to pray that the Lord will take the resources we have as well as what those who are poor have and multiply them. I'm hoping several of you pray specifically for the locals we have recently served.

Let the prayer time last as long as feels appropriate, and consider closing with one or two worship songs.

HAVE MORE TIME?

Convert a room or hallway near your youth room into a prayer journey or labyrinth. You might use the prayer stations (see next page) along the way or create some of your own. Make sure you have paper, pens, and markers or crayons for Stations 2 and 3.

At the start of your prayer time, explain each station and invite students to proceed through the stations at their own pace. Depending on the size of your group, consider asking different students to start at different stations to avoid any bottlenecks. Make sure students remain silent as they pray through the stations:

- **STATION 1: CONFESSION.** (Post a few advertisements for things we don't need from both guys' and girls' magazines.) Confess our flippant use of money, our overspending, or other ways our use of money has not honored God.

- **STATION 2: PARENTS.** (Post pictures of dads and moms from developing nations, or pictures of parents you met in your own recent work.) Dads and moms (and/or perhaps grandparents, aunts, or uncles who take on the role of parents) carry most of the burden of feeding and caring for their families' needs. In countries where an individual makes less than one dollar a day, imagine how that causes parents to feel. Pray for parents who can't afford to care for their families. Write down words that describe how you would feel if you were responsible for taking care of someone and knew you could not. Give those words to Jesus.

- **STATION 3: CHILDREN.** (Post pictures of children of various ethnicities engaged in different activities; if possible, include pictures of kids your youth ministry recently served.) Pray for children whose parents are dying of disease, whose parents can't afford to care for or feed them, who are unable to go to school, who are forced to work or beg, or who are sold as slaves. Write out prayers for those children using crayons, pens, and paper. (If your youth ministry sponsors a child through an organization like World Vision or Compassion International, have that child's picture present and give students an opportunity to write a prayer for that specific child.)

- **STATION 4: GOVERNMENTS.** (Post pictures of leaders of various governments, including your own local, state, and national leaders.) Pray for wisdom for those who govern. Pray that their eyes would be opened to the needs around the world and that they would have wise responses to poverty. Pray for nations to help other nations.

- **STATION 5: ME, US.** (Have a mirror at this station and a picture of your youth group.) Pray that God will open your eyes to the needs around you. Pray for your youth ministry, that together you will be able to impact your community, nation, and world, and that the resources you give will be multiplied. Have a jar there for students to place their dollar bills in.

At the end of their time in the prayer journey, bring the jar of bills in front of the whole group. Note that while a single dollar bill looks insignificant, when you put a bunch of bills together, you can begin to offer creative justice. Hand out the dollars to the students again, this time with the invitation to go and find a way to multiply this dollar. Ask students:

> **How could you invest this dollar—as well as other money you have— to make a difference in the lives of the poor, whether it be the poor you recently served or others around the world? What you do with this dollar is ultimately up to you, but imagine the possibilities ... and pray about expanding this dollar.**

AFTER:
ONGOING TRANSFORMATION—GOD AND US
WHAT NOW?

BIG IDEA

When young people want to change the world, we can help them identify practical next steps to make a difference.

YOU'LL NEED

- Copies of the "What Now?" handout (pp. 227–228) and/or copies of the *Sticky Faith Service Guide Student Journal*.

As we mentioned in the "Initial Steps" chapter at the start of this book, we collaborated early on with Drs. David Livermore and Terry Linhart to develop the Sticky Faith Service Model. As we close this journey, we want to point you to another resource they developed together: *What Can We Do? Practical Ways Your Youth Ministry Can Have a Global Conscience.*

Dave and Terry point out how complex it can be to help young people respond justly to our world's problems, ranging from AIDS to water shortage to global warming. Near the end of the book, they speak a truth that you might be feeling at this point in your journey with young people: "This is the tension: Students will be motivated to make a difference when you expose them to the needs of the world. What will you do when they approach you with those dreams?"[36]

You don't need us to tell you that this can be overwhelming. We often get overwhelmed by the needs of the world. We can get equally overwhelmed by the ways young people want to respond.

Dave and Terry encourage us to help our students "view wide and engage deep." When it comes to world justice issues, we think believers should be some of the savviest, best-informed people on the planet. What issues most resonate with your students? Do the teen girls you know seem especially touched by sex trafficking? Do the kids in your community who have had either stellar or subpar experiences with public education have a consequent

burden to tutor younger kids? How can you help them take next steps?

Here are a few practical suggestions for how to help students view wide and engage deep:

- Expose them to needs as well as to existing efforts to meet those needs.

- Listen well to their ideas, and encourage them to continue thinking outside of themselves and their own preferences.

- Help them channel their excitement toward the hard work of actual response, including research and action.

- Pick an issue, and pick a place. The only way we can engage deep is by focusing our efforts carefully. This doesn't mean abandoning all of the world's other needs. Students may need your help to see this.

- Let students organize the work as much as possible, and guide them in ways that promote awareness without overglamorizing the cause in a way that exploits the people impacted.

If you'd like, you can use the handout on pages 227–228 or the *Sticky Faith Service Guide Student Journal* to work with some of these eager students individually, or to encourage all of your students to explore possibilities.

Whether your students want to educate the world or bring clean water to Malawi, chances are you are hearing bits and pieces of big dreams in the aftermath of your service work. As we live amid the tensions, let's help young people steward those dreams well.

WHAT NOW?

Now you're all stirred up. You know more than you did at the start of this journey—maybe a lot more. You've seen needs you hadn't seen before—maybe a lot of needs. You want to do something.

But it can be overwhelming. The needs of the world are big.

How do you take the next step?

Here are a few suggestions and questions to get you started:

1. *View wide, engage deep.* When it comes to world justice issues, we think Christ-followers should be some of the savviest, best-informed people on the planet. But you can't tackle *every* problem. Start with a wide view, then begin to engage deep into something you care about deeply.

   Q: What justice issues most resonate with you or stir you up?

   Q: What do you know already about what's being done to meet those needs? How can you find out more?

   Q: What are some big ideas and dreams you have for serving in response to one or two of those needs?

2. *Pick an issue, pick a place.* The only way we can engage deep is by focusing our efforts carefully. This doesn't mean abandoning all of the world's other needs. It just means choosing to zero in on one issue and one place *for now*.

   Q: What one issue and/or one place (a city, neighborhood, country, or people group) are closest to your heart? If you had to pick somewhere to start, where would that be for now?

   Q: What ideas do you have to make a difference in that one place focused on that one issue?

Q: Who else can you invite into your planning? What friends might be interested? What adult can you talk to? What family members might want to join you in your efforts?

Q: What do you think is your very next step in this process? Is it more research? A conversation with a leader? Making time to pray?

Q: When can you get started? Pick a date and set up a time to take your next step!

As you move forward in your journey, may our Lord continue to guide you on your path. As you keep in step with God's kingdom work, the best is yet to be!

ENDNOTES

1. Robert Wuthnow, *Boundless Faith: The Global Outreach of American Churches* (Oakland: University of California Press, 2009). See also L. Probasco, "Giving Time, Not Money: Long-Term Impacts of Short-Term Mission Trips," *Missiology: An International Review* 41, no. 2 (2013): 202–24.

2. Robert J. Priest, Terry Dischinger, Steve Rasmussen, and C. M. Brown, "Researching the Short-Term Mission Movement," *Missiology* 34, no. 4 (October 2006): 431–50.

3. One study found that missions-based giving is losing ground to giving earmarked for congregational needs. John L. Ronsvalle and Sylvia Ronsvalle, "The State of Church Giving through 2005: Abolition of the Institutional Enslavement of Overseas Missions," 17th ed. (Champaign, IL: Empty Tomb, 2007), 11.

4. According to the National Congregations Study, data trend from 2006 to 2012. See thearda.com/ncs/explorencsfreq.asp?V=249.

5. Pedro Olinto, Kathleen Beegle, Carlos Sobrado, and Hiroki Uematsu, "The State of the Poor: Where Are the Poor, Where Is Extreme Poverty Harder to End, and What Is the Current Profile of the World's Poor?" *Poverty Reduction and Economic Management (PREM) Network Economic Premise*, no. 125 (October 2013), siteresources.worldbank.org/EXTPREMNET/Resources/EP125.pdf.

6. See the recent ethnographic study by Brian Howell. Howell also notes that resources and labor may be less valuable contributions than the potential social capital we might share with our hosts. Brian M. Howell, *Short-Term Mission: An Ethnography of Christian Travel Narrative and Experience* (Downers Grove, IL: IVP Academic, 2012).

7. See Steve Corbett and Brian Fikkert, *When Helping Hurts: How to Alleviate Poverty without Hurting the Poor . . . and Yourself* (Chicago: Moody, 2012), 99–116.

8. Robert D. Lupton, *Toxic Charity: How Churches and Charities Hurt Those They Help, and How to Reverse It* (New York: HarperOne, 2011), 6.

9. Ibid., 14.

10. We are deeply indebted to our coresearchers Dave Livermore and Terry Linhart for the design and facilitation of these summits, in addition to all the participants who sacrificially gave their time and deep insights: Jared Ayers, George Bache, Noel Becchetti, Terry Bley, Todd Bratulich, Tom Carpenter, Sean Cooper, April Diaz, Brian Dietz, Joel Fay, Hal Hamilton, Brian Heerwagen, Eric Iverson, Tom Ives, Cari Jenkins, Johnny Johnston, Kent

Koteskey, Sandy Liu, Mark Maines, Mark Matlock, Daryl Nuss, Derry Prenkert, Rich Van Pelt, Kurt Rietema, David Russell, David Schultz, Bob Whittet, and Kimberly Williams. We are also grateful to Matt Laidlaw and Laura Addis, who gave critical input to the updated version of this curriculum.

11. See Chap Clark and Kara Powell, *Deep Justice in a Broken World: Helping Your Kids Serve Others and Right the Wrongs around Them* (Grand Rapids: Zondervan, 2008).

12. These insights are adapted from chapter 5, "Justice That Sticks," in Kara Powell, Brad M. Griffin, and Cheryl Crawford, *Sticky Faith, Youth Worker Edition* (Grand Rapids: Zondervan, 2011).

13. Gregory Boyle, *Tattoos on the Heart: The Power of Boundless Compassion* (New York: Free Press, 2010), 188.

14. The following section is adapted from an article coauthored by Kara Powell, David Livermore, Terry Linhart, and Brad Griffin titled "If We Send Them, They Will Grow ... Maybe," available at fulleryouthinstitute.org.

15. Laura Joplin, "On Defining Experiential Education," in K. Warren, M. Sakofs, and J. S. Hunt Jr., eds., *The Theory of Experiential Education* (Dubuque, IA: Kendall/Hunt, 1995), 15–22.

16. Terrence D. Linhart, "Planting Seeds: The Curricular Hope of Short-Term Mission Experiences in Youth Ministry" *Christian Education Journal* 3 (2005): 256–72. For the purposes of this curriculum, some of the terminology in the model has been modified.

17. See David A. Livermore, *Serving with Eyes Wide Open* (Grand Rapids: Baker, 2006, rev. 2014). CQ was initially developed by P. Christopher Earley and Soon Ang in *Cultural Intelligence: Individual Interactions across Cultures* (Palo Alto, CA: Stanford Univ. Press, 2003). Soon and Earley built on Howard Gardner's research on multiple intelligences. Livermore has been one of the key developers of CQ and its many applications for ministry and business. See culturalq.com for a host of resources. For a quick tutorial on CQ, see Brad Griffin's article at fulleryouthinstitute.org titled "No Longer an Option: The Essential Role of Cultural Intelligence in Youth Ministry."

18. See Diana Garland, *Inside-Out Families: Living the Faith Together* (Waco, TX: Baylor University Press, 2010).

19. Ibid., 125–36.

20. Joplin, "On Defining Experiential Education," 15–22.

21. Linhart, "Planting Seeds," 256–72. For the purposes of this curriculum, some of the terminology in the model has been modified.

22. Vygotsky's work is well described and illustrated by Jack O. Balswick, Pamela E. King, and Kevin S. Reimer in *The Reciprocating Self: Human Development in Theological Perspective* (Downers Grove, IL: InterVarsity, 2005), 90–97.

23. See Kara Powell, *The Sticky Faith Guide for Your Family* (Grand Rapids: Zondervan, 2014).

24. See chapter 4, "Sticky Churches," in Kara Powell, Brad M. Griffin, and Cheryl Crawford, *Sticky Faith: Youth Worker Edition* (Grand Rapids: Zondervan, 2011).

25. This prayer of review was adapted from pray-as-you-go.org, a website of Jesuit Media Initiatives.

26. Werner Elert, *Eucharist and Church Fellowship in the First Four Centuries* (St. Louis: Concordia, 1966), 1.

27. Nicholas Wolterstorff, "The Contours of Justice: An Ancient Call for Shalom," in *God and the Victim: Theological Reflections on Evil, Victimization, Justice, and Forgiveness*, ed. Lisa Barnes Lampman and Michelle D. Shattuck (Grand Rapids: Eerdmans, 1999), 113.

28. See Stanley Grenz, *Theology for the Community of God* (Grand Rapids: Eerdmans, 2000), 511–20, for more on the theology of sacramental practices in the church. To read more reflections on worship, ritual, and identity formation in light of faith practices within youth ministry, see "Singing Ourselves Nowhere: The Like-It-or-Not Impact of Worship on Identity Formation" and "Through the Zone: Creating Rites of Passage in Your Church" at fulleryouthinstitute.org.

29. Henri Nouwen, *Life of the Beloved: Spiritual Living in a Secular World* (New York: Crossroads, 1994), 48–49.

30. Ralph P. Martin, *Worship in the Early Church* (Grand Rapids: Eerdmans, 1964), 122.

31. The first four experiences are adapted from Tim Dearborn, *Short-Term Missions Workbook: From Mission Tourist to Global Citizen* (Downers Grove, IL: InterVarsity, 2003), 94–96.

32. Ibid.

33. *The World Factbook*, last updated August 2014; see cia.gov/library/publications/the-world-factbook/ and the International Database for the U.S. Census Bureau: census.gov/population/international/data/idb/informationGateway.php.

34. See the World Bank's "Poverty Overview," worldbank.org/en/topic/poverty/overview.

35. See Pedro Olinto, Kathleen Beegle, Carlos Sobrado, and Hiroki Uematsu, "The State of the Poor: Where Are the Poor, Where Is Extreme Poverty Harder to End, and What Is the Current Profile of the World's Poor?" *Poverty Reduction and Economic Management (PREM) Network Economic Premise*, no. 125 (October 2013), siteresources.worldbank.org/EXTPREMNET/Resources/EP125.pdf.

36. David Livermore and Terry Linhart, *What Can We Do? Practical Ways Your Youth Ministry Can Have a Global Conscience* (Grand Rapids: Zondervan, 2011), 149.

Sticky Faith

Everyday Ideas to Build Lasting Faith in Your Kids

Dr. Kara E. Powell and Dr. Chap Clark

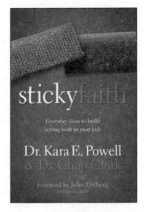

Nearly every Christian parent in America would give anything to find a viable resource for developing within their kids a deep, dynamic faith that "sticks" long term. *Sticky Faith* delivers. Research shows that almost half of graduating high school seniors struggle deeply with their faith. Recognizing the ramifications of that statistic, the Fuller Youth Institute (FYI) conducted the "College Transition Project" in an effort to identify the relationships and best practices that can set young people on a trajectory of lifelong faith and service. Based on FYI findings, this easy-to-read guide presents both a compelling rationale and a powerful strategy to show parents how to actively encourage their children's spiritual growth so that it will stick to them into adulthood and empower them to develop a living, lasting faith. Written by authors known for the integrity of their research and the intensity of their passion for young people, *Sticky Faith* is geared to spark a movement that empowers adults to develop robust and long-term faith in kids of all ages.

Sticky Faith, Youth Worker Edition

Practical Ideas to Nurture Long-Term Faith in Teenagers

Kara E. Powell, Brad M. Griffin, and Cheryl A. Crawford

Many of the statistics you read about teenagers and faith can be alarming. Recent studies show that 40-50 percent of kids who are connected to a youth group throughout their senior year will fail to stick with their faith in college. As youth workers are pouring their time and energy into the students in their ministries, they are often left wondering if they've done enough to equip their students to carry their faith into adulthood. Fuller Youth Institute has done extensive research in the area of youth ministry and teenage development. In *Sticky Faith Youth, Worker Edition*, the team at FYI presents youth workers with both a theological/philosophical framework and practical programming ideas that develop long-term faith in teenagers. Each chapter presents a summary of FYI's quantitative and qualitative research, along with the implications of this research, including program ideas suggested and tested by youth ministries nationwide. This resource will give youth pastors what they need to help foster a faith that sticks with all the teenagers in their group long after they've left the youth room.

Sticky Faith Teen Curriculum with DVD

10 Lessons to Nurture Faith Beyond High School

Kara E. Powell and Brad M. Griffin

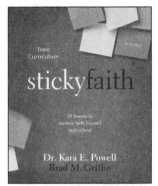

Churches are waking up to the reality that almost half of their high school students struggle deeply with their faith in college. Offering special high school "Senior Seminars" or giving seniors a graduation Bible and hoping for the best are too little, too late. In response to this problem, the Fuller Youth Institute conducted a national study to answer the question: What can youth workers do to help students develop a lasting faith in God? By following high school seniors into their first three years of college to gain an understanding of the transition from high school to college, they found their answers. And *Sticky Faith Teen Curriculum* enables youth leaders to impact to their students with a faith that sticks. This 10-session book and DVD study gives youth workers a theological and philosophical framework alongside real-world, road-tested programming ideas. The study is designed to help high school students develop a solid foundation that endures through the faith struggles they will face in college.

Available in stores and online!

Sticky Faith Guide for Your Family

Over 100 Practical and Tested Ideas to Build Lasting Faith in Kids

Dr. Kara E. Powell

The *Sticky Faith Guide for Your Family* addresses one of the top current concerns about youth and the church: the reality that nearly half of all young people raised in Christian families walk away from their faith when they graduate from high school. That's the bad news. But here's the good news: research also shows that parents are one of the primary influences on their child's faith.

This book arises from the innovative, research-based, and extensively field-tested project known as "Sticky Faith," designed to equip parents with insights and ideas for nurturing long-term faith in children and young people. Because of the Fuller Youth Institute's six years of research with more than 500 young people, 100 churches, and 50 families, four of this guidebook's unique qualities make it a "must have" for families eager to point their young people toward long-term faith:

First, it's grounded in sophisticated, academically verified data. While Dr. Powell is a parent of three children who authentically weaves her own experiences throughout the book, the chapter topics correlate with parenting principles proven in national research.

Second, it is positive. Amid gloomy and theoretical resources, this book leaves parents empowered and hopeful that even little tweaks to their family rhythms can make a big difference.

Third, it is practical. Readers get what they want most: more than 100 ideas from other parents they can try today, this week, or this month.

Fourth, its "guidebook" format is accessible. For busy parents who don't have time and inclination to read, this format is a welcome resource that they can return to time and time again for fresh ideas and inspiration.

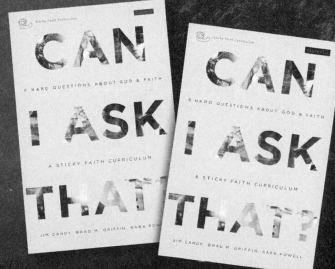